KAMAL HAASAN

KAMAL HAASAN

A CINEMATIC JOURNEY

K. HARIHARAN

HarperCollins *Publishers* India

First published in India by
HarperCollins *Publishers* 2024
4th Floor, Tower A, Building No. 10, DLF Cyber City,
DLF Phase II, Gurugram, Haryana—122002
www.harpercollins.co.in

2 4 6 8 10 9 7 5 3 1

P-ISBN: 978-93-5489-962-1
E-ISBN: 978-93-5489-922-5

Typeset in 12/16 Arno Pro at
Manipal Technologies Limited, Manipal

Printed and bound at
Thomson Press (India) Ltd.

To the Indian film industry and to my father, whom the members
fondly remember as Kodak Krishnan

CONTENTS

1

A STAR IS BORN

Few children could have been as precocious as young Kamal Haasan. Born almost twenty-five years after his parents' marriage, much after his other siblings, he was everybody's darling; not only his relatives but also the people in the small town of Paramakudi, where the family was well known.

The days leading to Kamal's birth were fraught with tension, almost as dramatic as some of his films. When his mother, Rajalakshmi, went into labour, his father, D. Srinivasan, a reputed lawyer, realized that his wife could face complications due to her diabetic condition. She was overweight and short of breath. She was rushed to the local hospital for delivery where the rather inexperienced doctor looked at her sceptically and declared that a normal birth would be impossible, as both the baby's and the mother's lives would be at risk. But there was no alternative. After many long hours of labour, Kamal was born, a big baby with a fat umbilical cord. The doctor gave Kamal's elder sister Nalini the task of monitoring the baby's condition, while his mother was taken away for an emergency post-delivery operative procedure. Nalini was just over eight years old and had no clue how to take care of a newborn.

Charuhasan, Kamal's older brother, and his wife, Komala, were waiting in the corridor of the small maternity clinic when they saw a big bundled-up baby being carried to another room by the nurse. He recalls, 'Kamal

1

was huge, pink and a bit scary. My mother, fearing that she might not survive the delivery, had recently got me married to this highly educated girl from Madras. On seeing this baby, my newly wedded wife did not know how to react. She was probably wondering what kind of family she had married into!'

It is said that newborns start responding to sounds first and after that, they open their eyes slowly and start watching the world around. It is also supposed to take about three to six weeks for a baby to recognize people and its surroundings. But Kamal responded to the sounds around him and even started noticing Nalini's moving fingers when he was only three days old. It was spooky. The nurses told Nalini that since her mother had had high sugar levels during her pregnancy, the baby had developed levels of sensibility comparable to a three-month-old in the womb itself. Although this may be debatable from a scientific point of view, Nalini recalls that Kamal was quite alert for an infant.

Rajalakshmi was a fighter and somehow survived the post-delivery complications. She lived till the age of sixty-eight. For everybody else in Paramakudi, this birth in the Srinivasan household was a miracle. Nalini has an interesting story to narrate about the post-birth days: 'Although Kamal does not believe in God, I believe that his survival was due to divine intervention. Having escaped the jaws of death, my mother was seen as someone intimately blessed by the Almighty. Soon, several pregnant women in the neighbourhood started coming by to seek my mother's blessings!'

Kamal's father Srinivasan's childhood was disrupted when his own father died very young. When Kamal's grandfather was on his deathbed, he requested his father-in-law, Srinivasan's maternal grandfather, to bring up all his six children and teach them to become good citizens. Being a lawyer himself, the grandfather wanted young Srinivasan and his brother to study law after completing their schooling. Srinivasan, however, was not interested. He was inspired by his grandfather's client, the prince of Pandanallur, who was a dance aficionado. After watching stellar performances in the prince's reputed durbar, Srinivasan became interested in studying vocal music and even attended several classes without anybody's knowledge. It was not long before the news of his clandestine music tuitions reached his grandfather's chambers. The family was aghast to find out that Srinivasan had neglected his studies to pursue something which had no hopes of any monetary returns whatsoever. They summoned him and ransacked his small cupboard to discover the music notebook that he had so carefully preserved. While they didn't beat the boy, they tore the notebook to shreds and flung it onto the street outside. Srinivasan, just ten years old at that time, picked up the torn pieces and shouted, 'I will obey you now, but let me assure you of one thing. I won't let this happen in my house. One day I too will have kids and I will see to it that all my children grow up to become musicians and artistes. Wait and watch!'

Almost everybody in Srinivasan's family did turn out to be artistes. Nalini learnt dancing, partially to fulfil her father's dream. When young Kamal expressed his complete disgust for routine academics, his father was the happiest and encouraged him to pursue performing arts. This was way back in 1966, when it was compulsory for every middle-class Indian child to at least complete their graduation. Even Kamal's elder brothers, who had taken up law, were excited rather than unhappy to see how this maverick would turn out as an 'artiste' with no formal education.

As a child, Kamal met some highly inspiring personalities. Visitors to the Paramakudi home included senior Congress stalwarts such as C. Rajagopalachari and K. Kamaraj. Srinivasan would insist that the women of the house come out of the inner chambers to the front room to meet and talk with these prominent figures. There was no resistance from Rajalakshmi either when these freedom fighters would freely move around the interiors of the main house, unlike the norm where outsiders were not allowed into inner rooms. She used to cook huge quantities of food for them, to be served as 'samapandhi bhojanam' (lunch for a crowd).

One day Srinivasan invited P. Kakkan, another freedom activist and Dalit leader, into the kitchen area. His orthodox Brahmin aunts did not seem to be affected by this ingression. After Kakkan left, curious neighbours asked them how they could admit a low-caste man into the kitchen. An old aunt replied quite casually, 'Hey, these kinds of people have no caste at all, they are freedom fighters and therefore belong to the nation.' Srinivasan's spirit of nationalism was indeed infectious, affecting even the seventy-year-old grandaunt!

There was not a single family in Paramakudi who did not know Kamal. He would take the liberty of walking into any house at any time, receiving mixed reactions! He was capable of enthralling people with his antics, but would also leave behind a trail of damaged windowpanes and broken pots. One day, their neighbourhood doctor brought Kamal home with his right palm all bandaged up. Before the child could be admonished, the doctor said that the little boy was the bravest patient he had ever seen. He was the first patient to sit through six stitches without emitting even a whimper! The real story—that Kamal had gone to the doctor's house and experimented with his brand-new shaving razor, which had led to the cut—was told much later.

Kamal's curiosity regarding films was satiated by a member of his house staff, with surreptitious visits to the old thatched cinema talkies. Under the pretext of taking care of him, the worker would get him to watch all of M.G. Ramachandran's and Sivaji Ganesan's movies. An enthralled Kamal would come home quoting the films' dialogues and earnestly mimicking all the actions. He would then create his own stories about a princess fleeing from enemy soldiers and how he, the hero, would come swinging down the vines of the tropical forest, jump into a well and rescue the damsel in distress. And then Kamal would add his special touch—the hero would promptly clean her wounds, dip into his satchel to pull out an injection and inject her with an antibiotic called Streptomycin to prevent any further damage. Obviously, his connection with the neighbouring doctor had gone beyond a few stitches!

The family later moved to Chennai, where Kamal pursued his higher studies. One day, when Nalini was out on a domestic errand, she saw a motley crowd assembled at a roadside teashop near their house on CP Ramaswamy Road. They seemed to be in splits. When she went closer and looked through a small gap in the crowd, she saw Kamal regaling them with a swashbuckling scene from some movie. She knew that the news about the famous lawyer's kid entertaining the 'masses' would surely reach home by sundown, somehow or the other. Suddenly Kamal noticed Nalini, shock written all over his face. He stopped the show, much to the crowd's dismay, and walked over to her, begging her not to tell his mother anything about this. She ordered him to sit on the cycle carrier behind her and assured him that she would report the incident, but without adding any spice to it. Kamal kept pleading and trying to shake the cycle to throw her off-balance all the way. Nalini did not report the event, nor did the news reach home.

Kamal got his first chance to act when his mother was taken to a doctor, Sarah Ramachandran. The doctor noticed his charismatic personality and suggested that he should meet another patient of hers for a screen test. This was renowned producer A.V. Meiyappan, who saw Kamal and immediately cast him as the main child artiste in *Kalathur Kannamma* (1960). The legendary producer's son, A.V.M. Saravanan, fondly recalls, 'My father was reading a book on his sofa with a table lamp switched on next to him when Kamal was escorted in. When my father was told that the child would be willing to act in his film, he looked up and sized him up. After a few moments he turned the table lamp on him to see his reaction. Kamal remained unflustered under the light. My father smiled and I knew that he had approved casting him.'

In a conversation later, Kamal remarked, 'I truly consider myself fortunate that a stalwart like A.V. Meiyappan turned the spotlight on me, literally!'

When I met director S.P. Muthuraman, he reminisced, 'This film about an orphanage was also my first film with the AVM banner as the seventh assistant director. Though I was supposed to be representing the editing department, I was also put in charge of the child artistes. Undoubtedly, Kamal stood out as a kid who was alert and inquisitive.'

One of the first things young Kamal did was to touch the background screen in the big studio on which the compound wall was painted. 'This is not a wall at all!' he exclaimed. He then looked around the artificial orchard in the studio and wanted to pluck the mangoes on a tree. SPM had to tell him that the tree and the mangoes were all fake, but would look real on screen. There was a look of dismay on the boy's face when he realized that he was working in a fake environment.

On the second day, elaborate preparations had been made to create an orphanage set inside the studio for a scene in which benefactors come to see the unfortunate ones and help them. In one scene, the legendary actress Savitri was supposed to feed Kamal, who was playing an orphan. The shot was all set and on hearing 'Action', she smilingly offered him some food. Kamal froze and refused to eat. Director A. Bhimsingh had to cut the shot and was about to reprimand him when SPM broke protocol and entered the shooting area. Quietly, SPM asked him why he refused to eat. Looking quite distraught, Kamal said, 'This food can't be real, right? It will get stuck in my throat!' Savitri laughed out loud but Kamal was not amused. SPM had to eat some of the food just to prove that some things in the movie business were real too! Soon enough, Kamal later did the shot with the full emotion required of a starving orphan.

Whenever there was a break for resetting the shot, almost all the kids would run out to play in the garden outside the set, except Kamal. And SPM knew where to find him. Kamal would be seated in the projection cabin of the theatre next door, where actors would come to dub, or producers would come to inspect their rushes and edited songs. Since he was so small, he had charmed the projectionist into picking him up, and from this vantage point he enjoyed watching the screen on which he would later become an icon.

Kalathur Kannamma was a big success and little Kamal became a star at the age of six. He even won the National Award in 1961 for the Best Child Actor, presented by President S. Radhakrishnan. The women in Paramakudi, who believed that he was gifted because of the miraculous circumstances of his birth, were now doubly sure. There were posters and banners on the streets in those days to celebrate the success of *Kalathur Kannamma*. And Kamal would look at them with a certain pride. Since he was unable to read what was written on them, he would ask Nalini to read them out to him, and she would take full advantage of the situation. She would tell him that they were quite critical of his performance and in fact were suggesting various ways to improve his acting. Nalini recalls, 'I even pretended to read out a line which said that he pissed his pants while facing the camera! Kamal was obviously not too happy with all these opinions being publicly displayed and said that those people were very mean to say such nasty things about him! As the older sibling, I just had a good laugh secretly on seeing his sad and droopy face!'

Nalini was close to her mother and was often given the responsibility of babysitting her little brother even when she was only eight years old. Kamal and she developed a certain bond, which cannot really be explained in words. Although he was a silent admirer of Charuhasan and Chandrahasan, his highly talented older brothers, there was too large an age gap between them for them to really get close.

A few people think that Kamal learnt Bharatanatyam from Nalini. She clarifies, 'He may have watched me, but I never taught him anything. It is unimaginable! As was the standard practice in most middle-class Brahmin homes of the 1950s, I did learn elementary classical dancing. He would see me practise but was not going to be content with mere practice. There was a strong impresario in him, which somehow drove him to believe that whatever he did had to be appreciated by others at a popular level. So he would accompany me to my dance performances and do his bits during the breaks that I would need to change costumes. The kind of stuff he was doing and my classical items were obviously poles apart, but his short performances would get all the applauses and cheers.'

Nalini later graduated in mathematics from Queen Mary's College. Most of the classes were conducted in Tamil and so, to improve her grasp of the English language, she would go to the library and read a lot of fiction. She would also go to the British Library with some Anglo-Indian friends and listen to their library of English music. And in due course, when she was singing Elvis Presley and Nancy Sinatra songs at home with an English songbook, Kamal could not conceal his envy. These were songs he could not sing at all, because his English wasn't good! He was just about twelve years old and she remembers him sobbing away one day, saying that this was an unfair advantage for her. However, he went on to learn the English language and its songs on his own almost with a vengeance. Many years later, Nalini saw a film of his where he mimicked Elvis Presley. He actually sang an Indian classical song mixed with Elvis's style of music in *Nala Damayanthi* (2003). Was it a way of acknowledging his dear sister?

Unlike most married women of the pre-Independence period, Rajalakshmi was not content with just bringing up kids or cooking and cleaning. Srinivasan got her to wear a six-yard khadi sari and encouraged her to read. Despite studying only till the fifth grade in school, she would borrow a lot of literature and journals from the nearby library, after which she would love to sit and narrate the stories to her children. Kamal grew up listening to all these tales and since Nalini would also be around, nodding away, he had to at least pretend that it was all comprehensible. 'Thinking back, I feel that as a one-year-old, he was actually grasping everything and followed up on all those tales while making his 250-odd films over the next fifty-five years. Along with the stories, he also soaked in the atmosphere and all the people who lived around him. The old lady in *Dasavathaaram* (2008) looked like one of our old aunts, while the beautiful *Avvai Shanmughi* (1996) was a replica of our mother,' Nalini says.

Rajalakshmi would often get tired with all the domestic chores and managing Kamal was a task she loved to delegate. Combing his hair became one of Nalini's onerous tasks, as she had to always appeal to his flamboyant side. If he was in the mood to appreciate Kalaignar Karunanidhi, then she would do a centre parting; when he was in a slightly wicked mood, she would oil his hair completely and flatten it out like Hitler's hairdo. His favourite style was that of Pandit Nehru! For him, the white cap was part of the look. So she would gel his hair well and shape it like a Nehru cap. How proud he would feel when he looked into the mirror! And one can imagine how he would have reacted when he saw a photograph of Pandit Nehru without his cap, completely bald!

Academics at the Hindu High School was burdensome and boring. Every class was a punishment for Kamal, other than the lectures by his history and geography teacher Mr Govindarajan, which were awe-inspiring. That's probably why he began *Hey Ram* (2000) at the Mohenjo Daro archaeological site. Along with two other equally impatient classmates, he would run away from school almost every day. The principal and all the teachers, except Govindarajan and the PT instructor, would keep complaining to his parents and were hell-bent on having him expelled. However, knowing that these kids came from reputed families, the school kept promoting them. But by the end of the eighth grade, even his favourite teachers had given up on him. One day, when Kamal came back home late in the evening after playing cricket on the streets, he was shocked to see one of his schoolteachers seated in the drawing room and his mother standing in apologetic silence. He knew something was wrong by the way his mother was staring daggers at him. After an interminable pause the teacher got up, bid goodbye and walked out. 'I cannot believe that you are such an evil boy,' his mother then said. 'The teacher told me that instead of books, you actually carry a box of paper arrows to throw at him and other teachers in class. Poor man! He does not seem to mind your arrows, but he came all the way here to request you not to place those sharp pins in front of them. Can't you be a bit gentle on them?'

An incident that occurred while he was studying in the eighth grade at Hindu High School perhaps foreshadows his talent to do his own daring stunts later. School had ended for the day and Kamal was rushing down the spiral staircase. He was next to the railing and started climbing over it to overtake someone in front when another student jostled him from behind. The impact threw him into the stairwell and after crashing down a few banisters, he landed on the floor, only to be caught in a stampede of running kids. Writhing in pain, he screamed over the din. Some attendants rushed to pick him up. At a nearby clinic, his broken bones were cast in plaster and then he was brought home. His parents comforted him but were unable to figure out what could be the best solution for him. As if in answer to their dilemma, the following day a classmate came home to deliver Kamal's textbooks and note sheets that he had found scattered everywhere. His name was Manivannan and his father was T.K. Bhagavathi, the founder of the famous Tamil theatre group, the TKS Brothers. When the legendary theatre actor came to know about this boy who had survived such a fall, he expressed a desire to meet him. Kamal visited him in the hallowed rehearsal hall of the theatre and the rest is history. The lights, sets, costumes and the hallowed aroma of incense wafting in that space was going to be his future.

Fortunately, Kamal's parents were extremely understanding and chose not to take the overbearing path most parents would have. In fact, when Kamal finally told his father that he was not interested in school anymore, Srinivasan was probably delighted. He may have recollected that fateful night when his music notebook was thrown into the street and he'd vowed that all his children would be artistes! 'Do what you want and be a true artiste,' he told Kamal. With this encouragement and assurance Kamal went to apprentice under T.K. Shanmugam, the legendary stage producer, a decision that would change his life completely.

Kamal recalls with moist eyes, 'I was so lucky to have such parents. Over the next few years, as an apprentice, I learnt so much from a theatre actor-director like T.K. Shanmugam. He would take me to temples where he would make me recite the Thevaram and Thiruvasagam, the holy scriptures of the Shaivite path. Being born into an Iyengar family, I did not have the opportunity to hear and chant the Thevarams. Not only did I listen to Hindu religious poems, but I also had an opportunity to study other religious works, like the Thembavani of the Christian liturgy. When I read those works, I felt that I was floating in an ocean of books, and the secular wisdom ensconced in it expanded to accommodate larger spectrums. Many years later I would dedicate an entire film to Shanmugam called *Avvai Shanmughi*.'

Tossed between the emotional tugs of his family background and the reckless thrills of the film world, Kamal developed his persona in ways that few filmmakers in the world could have imagined.

Kamal's first film as an adult actor came about in circumstances as strange as his birth and his first role as a child actor. By 1969, his tryst with T.K. Shanmugam's theatre came to an end when the troupe folded up, as all the actors wanted to try their luck in the world of movies. Kamal was just about fifteen, with all the awkwardness of an adolescent, yet saddled with the reputation of being a famous child actor who had won the National Award at the age of six. After joining a touring dance troupe, he ended up with a fractured ankle. Not one to give up hope easily, he then joined Thangappan as one of his several assistant choreographers, thus quenching his thirst to enter film sets and be amidst the iconic stars who populated the cosmology of his mindscape. Long hours of rehearsal, poor living conditions, odd working hours and little money did not deter him from the vow that he had taken when he had left home and abandoned the typical privileges a formal education would bring to a Brahmin boy in post-Independence India.

S.P. Muthuraman recollects that although Kamal had given up formal school education, he was not one to give up his goal of learning something new. About ten years after *Kalathur Kannamma,* SPM spotted him arranging dancers while working under Thangappan in one of the director's early ventures. For a moment, SPM had to pause and admire the determination of that boy; he was willing to do anything to achieve his goal! The heroine on set was none other than a young Jayalalithaa and it was an epic dance being performed on stage where she was supposed to entice the meditative Buddha. Immediately, SPM told the dance master to relieve Kamal of his assistantship and made him dress up as the serene Buddha. And that's how destiny made SPM relaunch the adolescent Kamal on screen, though in a bit role. SPM would do a lot more in later years to keep the popular side of Kamal's journey alive and kicking!

In the same kind of situation as Kamal was another young man from Paramakudi, Kamal's hometown, waiting for a golden opportunity to become a filmmaker. His name was R.C. Shakti. After making a name for himself as a Dravida Munnetra Kazhagam (DMK) playwright and theatre director, he chose to enter the film industry like everybody else in his ilk to fulfil his dreams of making progressive Tamilian dreams. Shakti's first big chance came around 1971, when he was chosen to be the first assistant director for Thangappan's debut directorial venture, *Annai Velankanni* (1971). Tagging behind Thangappan was his assistant, Kamal. Two atheists, Shakti and Kamal, thus met each other on the sets of an ultra-religious movie extolling the virtues and miracles of Mother Mary on the shores of Velankanni! When Thangappan introduced Kamal to Shakti asking, 'Have you guys met before?', Shakti replied, 'Of course I know him from the illustrious family of my hometown, but he wouldn't know me!'

Befriending Shakti changed Kamal's life. In him, Kamal found the perfect partner. Kamal had the emotional intelligence required to grasp the complexities of film language and Shakti had the managerial abilities to survive the brutal Tamil film industry. Whenever there was a break, Kamal would pour out to Shakti all the stories and ideas from the various films that he had seen or heard of. Thangappan would shout at Shakti for being inattentive, but he was also reconciled to the fact that only the latter knew the art of breaking down scenes and shots. Shakti would encourage Kamal to perform some directorial duties, such as striking the clapboard and maintaining continuity routines. One day, there was a scene in which a rich landlord fulfils a devotee's needs. When the actor who was supposed to play the landlord's role did not turn up, Shakti suggested that Kamal play that role. The lean and hungry-looking Kamal was far removed from the portly image of a landlord, but at that moment, they had no choice. As expected, Kamal, despite his looks, excelled in the role of the landlord and in this way his first shot as an actor, however insignificant, was filmed.

But when the first cut was ready and viewed by financier Sadayappa Chettiar, his reaction was, 'Who is that guy playing the landlord? Have you all gone nuts? That one scene will kill the whole film. Throw it out or I am out.' The landlord scene went into the dustbin and the journey started all over again for Shakti and Kamal.

When I asked him about it, Shakti recollected, 'Walking the streets of Madras's tinsel town and discussing film stories was an obsession for both of us. I certainly had more contacts among producers and financiers than Kamal, and he would egg me on to make all the proposals while I would urge him to put all his wonderful ideas into words. One night, we decided on a story and headed to catch the last bus at 11 p.m. to go back home. As we reached the main road, we saw the bus leaving! So we just parked ourselves on the steps of a teashop, hoping that another bus would come by. There was no bus, but the story went through several drafts over the next seven hours and with a big smile of achievement on our faces, we boarded the first bus at 6 the next morning to catch up with some sleep.'

The film was aptly titled *Unarchigal,* meaning 'heartfelt expectations'.

'We found a producer in the well-known Azhagappa Chettiar, who was willing to invest about Rs 5 lakh in the film, provided I could raise Rs 50,000 as seed money,' Shakti continued. 'With this budget, we could get a reasonably well-known cast of actors and technicians. Luckily, we also found an angel investor in Mr Kalayanasundaram, a typical landlord aspiring to become a producer, who invested the seed money. We rented an office space in the Venkateshwara Lodge near the newly opened Kodambakkam bridge in 1972. As expected, aspiring assistants and actors started making a beeline to get their chance to star in our venture. Sharada Studios was booked and the opening date, with a somewhat famous actor, finalized.'

A day before shooting, disaster struck. 'We went to Mr Kalyanasundaram's room to pick up some cash and to our shock, we found him crying away. His elder brother-in-law had come earlier that day and taken away all the money. He told us, "That money actually belongs to my mother-in-law who is living in a village. Suddenly she has changed her mind and sent my brother-in-law to bring it all back. Now I can't show my face to anyone in my village. If the movie is not made, I am going to jump down that new bridge and kill myself on the railway tracks!"' Recollecting this, Shakti started rolling in laughter.

'Not only did we lose a film, but this idiot was threatening to kill himself. I could only imagine my career, and probably Kamal's too, ending in a stinking jail. I had to come up with a solution. So I asked him how much cash he had on him. He said he had Rs 5,000! So with deep resolve I announced that I would start with this "princely sum" as per the plan and Kamal would play the main role! Almost everyone, including Kamal, jumped up in shock. How could a writer play the main role? But everyone knew I had a bad temper and they all decided to follow the leader. Sharada Studios was dropped, and I told a shocked Kamal that the film would now be shot in his house at Alwarpet. Kamal was flummoxed and with great hesitation asked his mother for permission. She thought we were all crazy but finally let us shoot. My cameraman said he would need plenty of light. So we shifted a lot of scenes to the terrace and managed to do the indoor scenes with a few extra lights.

'On the very first day, around lunchtime, we saw three cops coming in. They asked us to pack up and report to the police station. We had no clue what crime we had committed. But I did see the electrician run away from the spot. The cops informed us that we had actually tapped the electrical mainline directly, which was a crime. I had no clue about this and the main culprit had fled. That's when one of my friends from the stunt artistes' union took the cops into a separate room and threatened them that he would kill himself if this already screwed-up shoot was going to be stopped. Now we were faced with one more death threat, as if we had not had enough. Seeing our desperation, the cops relented and walked away after eating our frugal meal and giving us a small warning.

'Despite this small respite, our shooting again stopped after five days when we ran out of money. Kamal was heartbroken, but news of his acting skills spread like wildfire and K. Balachander offered him a good role in another aptly titled film, *Arangetram* (1973), meaning "the opening performance". That brought him more offers and before long, he got calls from Malayalam producers who felt that Kamal's acting style was eminently suitable for their realistic films.'

Meanwhile, Shakti kept looking for financiers. And then one day, after four months, Kamal came to him and said that a Malayali producer wanted to buy the story rights for *Unarchigal*. Shakti was shocked and amazed at the same time. The money was attractive, so Shakti relented and before long the Malayalam version of the film called *Rasaleela* (1975) was completed and released. A few months later Shakti managed raise some money and the 'original' Tamil film was completed and released in 1976. Unfortunately, the reviewers who watched *Unarchigal* on the opening day praised the film as an excellent copy of the Malayalam original!

Shakti concluded, 'By this time, Kamal had moved many miles forward and I stayed back as a passive observer, seeing my young friend taste the kind of success few actors had ever seen on the Tamil screen. While savouring his success, it never struck me that I should use my friendship with him for my own commercial progress. Producers would ask me to get his dates if I wanted money for my next film but I could not bring myself to do this. We would meet each other briefly but drift away for longer periods. And then one day Kamal produced and released a successful film called *Kadamai Kanniyam Kattupaadu* (1987) with Sathyaraj as the main hero. He invited me for the hundredth-day celebration. I was embarrassed to go for the function since I had not seen the film, but I went anyway. At the function, he invited Sivaji Ganesan as the chief guest onstage and then he invited another filmmaker called Manivannan. I was shocked when he called me over to the dais as well and made me sit next to Sivaji sir. The audience was visibly puzzled about my presence. Kamal explained that Manivannan was on the stage because he was responsible for bringing out the actor in Sathyaraj. Then, looking at me, Kamal announced that I was the person solely responsible for whatever he was that day. Listening to his fond remarks, I wept almost uncontrollably onstage. Who else would recollect and acknowledge an old friendship like ours with such warmth and love?'

When I went for the interview, R.C. Shakti was convalescing from a serious illness which required him to undergo dialysis on a weekly basis. I wished him all the best and left with a rather heavy heart, feeling sorry about the condition of one of the doyens of the avant-garde in Tamil cinema, yet amazed that he was still dreaming of making another breakthrough film! His *Unarchigal* was still not complete.

R.C. Shakti passed away on 23 February 2015. A heartbroken Kamal said, 'If I am able to direct films today, it is largely because of the confidence Shakti bestowed in me. I would have been a nobody if he had not entered my life and motivated me to open my heart and mind to the world of cinema.'

2

WORKING WITH K. BALACHANDER

What made K. Balachander the angriest young filmmaker of 1970s mainstream Indian cinema? To launch five films with no big production house to back him, and only the support of a crew of admirers, speaks highly of his confidence. Few independent filmmakers could achieve the kind of prolificacy he did, completing twenty-two feature films in about eight years. The only parallel to this one can recollect is the German enfant terrible Rainer Werner Fassbinder, who packed in twenty-two films between 1969 and 1982 along with scores of short films, TV episodes and even staged plays. But post this, Balachander chose a new avatar. From his first collaboration with Kamal in *Arangetram* (1973) onwards, he radically exploded into a true modernist capable of exploring the nuances of a technology-driven art form while navigating the choppy waves of a Tamil socio-political milieu gone berserk.

According to Kamal, around 1973 Balachander, aged forty-three, had a minor stroke. While he was convalescing, he worked out an entirely new strategy. And quite like Fassbinder, whose work reflected the serious issues that emerged in the fallout of the Cold War, Balachander was also struggling with the dilemma of Tamil identity politics.

One could also compare Balachander with another maverick, equally maligned and revered—Ritwick Ghatak—as he unravels other layers of

17

cinema while working on narratives of young Indian women joining the large urban workforce to help their families survive. Unfortunately, like Ghatak, Balachander was also not given his due at international forums, a factor so crucial for a filmmaker to be recognized in the modern era. Fortunately, Balachander did not choose to drown his sorrows in alcohol. And this optimism came largely from the youthfulness of his protégés like Kamal and Rajinikanth, along with the self-taught cineaste/screenwriter Ananthu.

The question that arises is how a storyteller contains and channelizes his anger both at the suffocating sociopolitical system and the ridiculous formula-driven mainstream film industry through the medium of commercial cinema. How does this filmmaker find a balance between expressing his wrath and appeasing the audience? While exploring this set of five films by Balachander, I have attempted to navigate the various contexts that surrounded the making and screening of his films.

Let's begin with *Arangetram*. This is the movie with which Kamal positioned himself as an actor whom the nation would revere soon after.

Arangetram

In this film, Kamal plays a character named Thyagu who aspires to be a doctor, even though his father, a Brahmin priest in a small town, cannot make ends meet. However, the father had been quite productive when it came to children, with Thyagu being one among six kids. As time goes by, the responsibility of fulfilling Thyagu's ambitions falls on the eldest sister, Lalitha, who decides to earn more money by seeking employment in the evil metropolis of Madras. There, she realizes that the fastest way of making money for Thyagu's tuition fees is through prostitution. Thyagu gets to study medicine and the family receives a sudden inflow of wealth. Nobody in the small-town family suspects that anything is amiss with Lalitha. Balachander and Ananthu divert the audience's attention through an unending series of rhetorical punchlines in the dialogues and songs that symbolize the family's move from deprivation to a middle-class status. But all hell breaks loose one day when a neighbouring non-Brahmin landlord's son lands up in Lalitha's brothel and discovers her there. The narration goes through a series of twists and turns, which climaxes in the ungrateful family driving Lalitha out of the house for bringing 'disrepute' to their high-class status, with Dr Thyagu at the forefront.

From a popularity point of view, playing such a heartless villain could have been a most inauspicious start for seventeen-year-old Kamal. But under Balachander's tutelage, this film became his trial by fire. After this, he would go on to do twenty-six more films with the director. Kamal learnt that his mentor's masterly control over melodrama, along with his production strategy of working with the same group of players repeatedly, would position him as an actor who prefers roles with specific character traits. Some of the unusual tropes introduced in this mainstream film were: the usage of voiceover narration to introduce characters, exaggerated behaviour such as Lalitha laughing out loud with a trumpeting sound, a blind boy wearing dark glasses who is a movie buff, a madwoman who plays the drums on the seashore, the mother who gets pregnant for the sixth time despite the ubiquitous 'family planning' campaign, and all of this happening within the context of an orthodox Brahmin family.

Arangetram marked the inauguration of a new discourse, which had been streaming as an undercurrent within the elite Tamil cultural scenario—the opening up of the Brahmin–non-Brahmin imbroglio, which dominated the political discourse of Dravidian leaders such as Periyar E.V. Ramasamy Naicker and Karunanidhi.

The concept of the Dravidian ecosphere was uncovered in its system of languages and ethnicity in the corridors of the Madras Presidency around 1813. Renowned historian Thomas Trautmann states in his book *Languages and Nations*, 'The collector of Madras, F.W. Ellis, publishes proof that the languages of South India, while they contained many words from Sanskrit, were nevertheless not descended from it, but were related to one another as another distinct family.'[1]

The North–South divide was thus developed and spelt out in no uncertain terms and by the late 1800s, when the Congress movement was seen as largely driven by North Indian leaders, the southern states started rumbling. While the southern linguistic groups of Malayalam, Kannada/Tulu and Telugu rallied around their powerful monarchs of Travancore, Mysore and Hyderabad respectively, the Tamil people had no one to look up to. And the few Tamilians who dominated the bureaucracy of Madras Presidency and participated in the 'northern' Congress movement were all high-caste Tamil Brahmins who constituted a mere 4 per cent of the Tamil-speaking populace.

This lopsided power structure enraged the wealthy landlords and traders, the 'non-Brahmin' majority, in the Tamil hinterlands as they rushed to establish their presence in the city of Madras. Writing about the pioneer Pitti Theagaraya Chetty, who published the first 'Non-Brahmin Manifesto', A.R. Venkatachalapathy states, 'Anti-national was not the only abuse hurled at him. His party, the South Indian Liberal Foundation, was later called the Justice Party after its flagship newspaper was debunked as collaborationist, serving British colonial interests.' Such accusations by the Congress party leaders only strengthened the resolve of the wealthy non-Brahmin Tamil leaders to take progressive steps in the field of public education, secularization of temple lands management and reservations for the marginalized in the public service sectors. Venkatachalapathy continues, 'The non-Brahmin movement took a vernacular turn with the rise of E.V. Ramasamy Naicker, later to be venerated as "Periyar" (The Senior). Periyar challenged the roots of inequality by attacking caste, religion and patriarchy.'[2]

Kamal said determinedly, 'For youngsters like me at that time, Periyar was like a rockstar, so ahead of his time and yet so down to earth. If so many of us placed social welfare and atheism on top of our agendas, he was the primary mover.'

Periyar's oratory skills united the Tamil people under one banner, which would announce itself later as the DMK, led by C.N. Annadurai with the powerful support of Karunanidhi and M.G. Ramachandran. These three cult figures of the Tamil spirit had one factor in common— they were well-known icons in the world of Tamil cinema. For the people of the state at least, their films benchmarked some of the crucial ideological issues that would dominate electoral political discourse for decades to come. In this manner, the entire Madras film industry had to reckon with the politics of being a Tamilian in some way or the other.

With this in mind, Balachander deliberately placed this dystopian story in a Brahmin family, with Kamal playing the insensitive Brahmin male. It should be kept in mind that even the literary avante-garde in Tamil Nadu and Karnataka were leading an unforgiving yet popular Brahmin-bashing campaign. Most of the writers involved, such as Jayakantan or U.R. Ananthamurthy, came from Brahmin/upper-caste backgrounds and took this opportunity to chastise their own community for the years of apathy towards the lower castes and downtrodden. In my last conversation with him, Balachander was swift to add, 'That did not mean that I was simply taking advantage of the popular anti-Brahmin feeling among most of my middle-class audiences. I was actually commenting on the responsibility of each citizen to value modern life, in an urban, "alienated" situation, with a conscious and empathetic perspective; to see the struggles of an older sister as possibly happening within even non-Brahmin families. The city has brought us all to work together, irrespective of our castes and creeds. And as citizens, do we not owe this working class, especially women, a definite sense of decency?'

Undoubtedly, Balachander was attempting to focus the angry discourse onto a new 'rationalist' platform. Around the time that he was entering this new cinematic phase in his career, a powerful critique by Periyar was published on the authoritarianism of Brahminic hegemony where he wrote:

They have made us, 97% of the people, illegitimate children and invented religion, gods, commandments, and Dharma (duty), in order to keep us where we are. They have fortified their positions with 'God', Religion and Scriptures. Foreign rulers and the Brahmins sit on us and uphold caste and the disgraceful position that we are in with the words 'according to laws'.[3]

Periyar's rationalism at this juncture was to pinpoint that the root of Brahminic indolence, located in the community's ownership of such gods and icons, was hypocritical and only used to subjugate the gullible lower castes to Brahminical authority. For Balachander, rationality and patriarchy were opposed to each other, and he took Periyar's outburst into larger domains, attacking the hegemony of film financiers, hypocritical writers and conservative distributors by assembling a bunch of newcomers to 'storm the Bastille'.

Playing a character that his idol Periyar would have condemned made Kamal understand the true meaning of role-playing. But he faced another dilemma: is role-playing the unquestioned domain of the actor alone? How about the spectators? Aren't they also indulging in some sort of voyeuristic roleplay when they assess the quality of the actor's performance? For example, Periyar berated these very audiences, seated in large crowds, about their superstitions, fraudulent religious beliefs and their abominable temple-going cultures. Did they go back as 'transformed' citizens after listening to him? Did they stop believing in caste systems and seasonal temple-oriented rituals? No. But they did enjoy a well-articulated speech, some fiery rhetoric and cuss words that would have 'turned' respectable faces red in anger. Sadly, Periyar believed that the people were going to be with him at all costs. How was Kamal going to navigate this ideological ocean left behind by Periyar?

In this was Kamal's greatest lesson. The performance and conviction that builds the story's characters are many times more important than the personal story and beliefs of the actors essaying the roles. How else could a Malayalam-speaking MGR and a Telugu-speaking Karunanidhi attract so much adoration from their Tamil-speaking fans? The two of them were great artistes who could make their audiences aspire for a better world when the audiences knew well the trials and tribulations they had to undergo as individuals. Thus, the audiences were there not to listen to perspectives on real political problems but to see the way a story could be built around such a discourse, which could, in turn, provide greater insights. When asked about the ambition that stands on the top of his list,

Kamal would repeatedly say, 'I want to be the best "rasika", the best fan, that cinema could ever have!'

Aval Oru Thodar Kathai

Aval Oru Thodar Kathai (Her Story Is a Serial) takes off loosely from Ritwick Ghatak's *Meghe Dhaka Tara* (The Cloud-Capped Star) to narrate the story of a young working-class girl who has to sacrifice her aspirations to become the sole breadwinner for her family.

Kamal's second outing with Balachander must be seen in the context of a very turbulent period in Tamil Nadu's history. The early 1970s witnessed the virtual collapse of the major pillars that upheld the DMK party's 'exclusionary' philosophy, thanks to the desperate attempts to stay in power by then Chief Minister M. Karunanidhi. Added to that were some serious cracks in the central government machinery too. This collapse in Delhi was being steered by another renowned Tamil leader, a Congressman named 'Kingmaker' Kamaraj who was also the DMK's arch rival in Tamil Nadu. After having serious differences with Prime Minister Indira Gandhi in Delhi and sensing the Congress party to be in disarray, Kamaraj pulled the rug from under her and formed a new party called the IN Congress (Organization). Seizing this strange opportunity, the DMK felt that their enemy's enemy should be their friend. So, in 1971, Karunanidhi signed an alliance with the party's arch enemy, the Congress party under Mrs Gandhi, before the general elections. From her point of view, she wanted to wreak revenge on Kamaraj who headed what he claimed was the original Congress party. So, she chose not to contest in Tamil Nadu, instead letting the DMK contest all the parliamentary seats. With an unprecedented victory, garnering all twenty-three seats, the DMK became the largest regional party in Parliament. Soon after, a heady Karunanidhi appointed himself as president of the party, a post that had always been kept reserved for Periyar, the founder of the movement. To quote A.R. Venkatachalapathy, 'The decimation of the original DMK's leadership is indexed by how many journals, run by its leaders, all folded

up, leaving *Murasoli* [a newspaper started by Karunanidhi] alone tall.'
Karunanidhi's nephew Murasoli Maran, a member of Parliament who
was running this newspaper, set the ball of family dynastic politics rolling
in a party which had been wedded only to leadership of the meritorious
so far. Karunanidhi's sons, M.K. Stalin and M.K. Alagiri, also went on to
become party heads later.

The politics of patriarchal manipulation became the central theme of
Aval Oru Thodar Kathai. Kavitha, a young working-class girl, becomes
the sole breadwinner for her family, while the family, like greedy, mute
witnesses, takes advantage of her charitable disposition. To play this
complex character, Balachander entrusted the renowned actor Sujatha.
Kavitha has all the aspirations of a modern working-class woman, but she
is trapped in a family where her father has abdicated his responsibilities
to become a mendicant and her unemployed older brother drowns his
sorrows in alcohol. So, while she toils to provide for them, she is not
going to keep quiet and give up her critical perspective of the injustice
meted out to her. Is she forced into this position or is it her choice to be
the 'unquestioned' leader? Did the Tamil Nadu leadership become so
desperate that they had no other choice but to take complete control?

Kamal makes his appearance as Gopal, a mimicry artist, half an hour
into the film, a neighbour singing a Hindi film song *'Na koi umang hai'*
from *Kati Patang* (1971) to express his sympathy for Kavitha's widowed
sister Bharati, played by Sripriya, who would also go on to become a
successful actor. As an outsider, he does not know the family background
or Kavitha's situation. He does not know that Kavitha is very possessive of
her family and the tight control she has on each of her siblings. Although
he adds humour, Gopal is just a structural device to counterpoint Kavitha.

For Kamal, this was his first lesson in scriptwriting: 'Take your
characters seriously but not your actors.' Lesson 2: 'In such films, populate
your narration with as many characters as possible. Not only do they
become minor windows into society but also give the major characters a
lot of thinking time.'

Gopal appears another thirty minutes later, still incapable of understanding the complex emotional tangles of his neighbouring family. Obviously, the significance of that Hindi song is beyond a simple expression. Does it contain allusions to the rapid changes in Tamil Nadu's Dravidian politics?

Participating as a minor character was also a great opportunity for Kamal to see his mentor navigate a typical family drama with a sacrificing elder sister wading into the choppy waters of sexuality and the varying levels of freedom that problematize the identity of women, who are citizens of a state gone berserk. Balachander studied the fluctuating ways in which six very diverse female characters reveal or conceal their sexual desires—from widows to married and unmarried women, from poor to rich, from traditional to modern, all seem to face the need to exercise their sexual preference. Nobody is spared when it comes to such a choice. Do we see a metaphor here about the idea of 'boundless democracy', which we are supposed to enjoy simply because we hold an electoral card? Is it antithetical to all previous notions of duty, honour and discipline? Gopal gets some prominence in the last thirty minutes when the neighbouring women come to him for counsel on their problems and dilemmas. These were not just fictional scenes, Kamal realized; his mentor was using the character of Gopal like his own alter ego watching the Madras urban class go berserk in search of sexual fulfilment, jobs, wealth, education and that elusive term called 'identity'. Was Balachander sacrificing his successful career at the altar of social criticism or was he critiquing his audience for partaking in an absurd drama of betrayal? This question would haunt Kamal throughout the rest of his career as he too had to manoeuvre the harsh pathways between celebrating his stardom and playing an impartial watchdog at the box-office gates.

For Kamal, walking onto Balachander's sets was like going to a modern high school. Everything and anything under the sun was up for discussion and dissection. He observed Balachander examine the notion and practice of patriarchy by positioning Kavitha as a metaphorical character who indirectly represents the disintegrating Tamil political situation. The unusual methods deployed in this film ranged from jump cuts, freeze frames, ultra-tight close-ups, overlapping commentaries, symbolism, discontinuous editing and constant references to other films.

Balachander's social criticism was not a typical journalistic exercise, an attempt to portray or chronicle the cracks and failures in the socio-political conditions as 'content', something we witness in the typical mainstream works of MGR, Sivaji Ganesan and other popular Indian filmmakers. While their films address the problems of unemployment, corruption and hunger, Balachander's movies addressed primarily the 'form' of a failing system, the so-called 'orderliness' which has failed to support the growing problems of modernity and democratic aspirations. His films called for a 'linguistic' solution that could correctly articulate the problem first before finding solutions. From my point of view, Balachander seems to have found the answer in the culture of 'Pattimandram' or oratory, when orators at a public-speaking arena would give speeches steeped in rhetoric and 'pure' flowery Tamil. When politicians adopt this technique, they call it 'Medai-Pechu' or platform speeches, quite similar to the televised American presidential debates. In either democracy, this form unfortunately overtakes the content and often subverts the politician's intention to create political ruptures and disruptions in the guise of luring citizens and winning at the ballot booth. Somehow, crowds also relish the nature of this so-called debate from the standpoint of 'performance art', rather than recognizing the 'actual' seriousness of the socio-political issues highlighted in it. They end up appreciating the sheer beauty of such verbiage and often forget which political side is actually delivering it.

Balachander and Ananthu were masters at this art of rhetoric. Quite often, many of the scenes in these films were not born from the intrinsic nature of plot delineation as much as from the sheer joy of writing such lines. Balachander once remarked to me, 'The world of allusion is always more interesting than direct reference. Some might call this "artistic tactfulness", which allows a critic like me to escape direct confrontation, but I personally see allusion as the essence of Tamil poetry, allowing the audience to go beyond the direct meaning and even become self-critical. The protagonist Kavitha's problem could actually happen in the realms of many a middle-class home watching the film, or it could be seen by experts like you as a political analogy!'

Renowned modernist writer S. Ramachandran, who worked with Balachander as an advisor in those early five films, said, 'Balachander understood the middle-class/upper-caste urban psyche very well. He understood that young, college-going girls were not going to listen to a Shankaracharya who would advise them to be morally conservative. So, just to provoke the sanguine upper classes, Balachander portrayed all his women characters as potential rebels by their overt capacity to express their sexual desires. While my mother was aghast at the arrogance of Kavitha, my sisters, in turn, were diehard fans of the actress Sujatha. The older menfolk seriously felt that grave injustice was being done to the [characters of the] alcoholic older brother and the ascetic father. And of course, all the young men swore by Kamal as the greatest actor ever!'

Kamal was also struck by the ways in which Balachander interjected English into the larger context of Tamil poetry. Was it his way of announcing English as an 'unfortunate' benchmark of modern urban progress or was it to inform Tamil viewers of the semantic differences of expressiveness in the two languages? In an office scene in *Aval Oru Thodar Kathai*, we see Kavitha's manager sending her a love letter enclosed in an office file. An offended Kavitha promptly hands the letter over to his superior, who in turn asks her whether he should take any disciplinary action, or will she accept the manager's amorous entreaty. Kavitha replies, 'Please take stern action against him for his poor English-writing skills!'

After his inaugural film, *Arangetram*, Kamal had acted in five more films as lead actor. Yet, he took up this almost insignificant role in a film about the dilemmas of modern women in post-Independence Tamil India.

One reason was to work with Ananthu and understand the complex ways in which he interpreted Ingmar Bergman, another master from Sweden working on similar subjects. While admiring Bergman's austere formalism, Kamal could see how Balachander deftly adapted Bergman's dramatic intensity into his films without diluting the tenets of mainstream entertainment. But how and why did this film become such a blockbuster that it was later remade into five more languages? I would undoubtedly give first claim to the amazing last ten minutes of the film, where Balachander gives up all rhetoric and does a Hitchcockian climax with just action, sound effects and background score. 'Audiences were just speechless when they left the theatres, with tears of combined joy and sorrow,' recalls Kamal.

Apart from the fact that the film alluded to modern Tamil conundrums, it also had a rising star like Kamal who provided the redemption to a rather depressing tale. For viewers, he was the consummate modern Tamilian: handsome, scholarly and so delightfully sexy. The Chaplinesque song he sings at the pre-climax sequence where the widowed sister gets married is both funny and poignant at the same time. In retrospect, one realizes that he was an actor who greatly outshone the rest of his contemporaries with his guts to take on unconventional roles at an early age and a fearless on-stage persona. For him, the ability to playback or sing a song well onscreen and the confidence to dance with or romance his love interest, creating a good chemistry with her, was as simple as a crafty locksmith opening the front door. Lastly, his flawless 'British' English in Tamil films used to be the cause of much admiration. As he says, 'I somehow gathered a huge fan following among slightly older women. Thanks to the kind of roles I played, I was seen as the guy that middle-aged women could trust their daughters with.' For the new-age young woman, the ultimate eligible bachelor had arrived, handsome, capable of speaking his mind, armed with reason and a truly universal outlook. And his next film in the Balachander pentalogy only reinforced that.

Apoorva Raagangal

Kamal's tryst with K. Balachander spelled out several interesting discourses. Thanks to *Apoorva Raagangal* (Strange Melodies; 1975), he announced himself as one of the first icons to represent the dilemmas of the post-Independence generation in Tamil Nadu. Though it was appropriate that a youngster should have taken on such a mantle, Kamal had, in fact, entered Balachander's film sets to learn the craft of directing, not acting. Thus, it happened that a reluctant adolescent seeking a new and free identity was asked to portray uncomfortable negotiations with moralistic, overbearing parental authorities. Using an operatic form, the film locates itself in the Brahminical upper-class corridors of classical music concert halls only to challenge the arrogance of this upper caste and their hypocritical ethico-moral positions. Why was this so popular, with millions of Tamilians, especially the young ones, coming back repeatedly to watch this film?

We need to return to the Dravidian issues of those times, as explained in the beginning of this chapter. Sadly, the ideals espoused by Periyar, Karunanidhi and MGR deteriorated rapidly during post-Independence electoral politics, and the utopian dream of a casteless, godless, egalitarian Tamil society burst like a bubble with the 1971 elections. The Congress, which had once dubbed the Dravidian movement as anti-national, unconditionally supported the DMK, which romped home with 184 seats out of 234. With M.G. Ramachandran walking out of the DMK to form the All India Anna Dravida Munnetra Kazhagam (AIADMK) in October 1972, the Dravidian leadership and cadre split manifold by the mid-1970s and vied with each other to court the 'upper-class' Congress leaders, once their sworn enemies, for alliances.

Posing this horrendous conflict or greed as a cinematic question were two Brahmins, angry director Balachander and his equally livid protégé, Kamal.

For a twenty-year-old, Kamal demonstrated enormous maturity as he enunciated the various shades of sexuality that his character's journey required. *Apoorva Raagangal* starts off with him playing Prasanna, walking out of his father Mahendran's (Sundarrajan) comfortable home. Elsewhere Ranjani (Jayasudha) walks out on her mother Bhairavi (Srividya), a renowned classical music singer. Prasanna is a political extremist, devoid of any interest in the world of desire. He does, however, start to feel the lack of maternal affection in his life when, thanks to an accident, he meets Bhairavi. While recovering in her house from an accident, he slowly enters the world of sexual desire by exhibiting his talent at playing the mridangam (which could be interpreted as a phallic symbol) to impress her. Symbolically, he provides the rhythm to her life, which is dedicated to classical music. Once he is able to court her, he feels empowered to demand her body. Her confession of having given birth to an illegitimate girl child when young does not deter him—this clearly portrays him as one who has bid goodbye to the idea of a virginal, sacred 'nation-state'. A bastard can and shall be legitimized through sheer love and acceptance.

Meanwhile, in another city, Ranjani has chosen to live with her benefactor Mahendran (Prasanna's father) who wants to be a father figure and get her to settle down with a young, suitable partner. But she wants to stay with him and, if possible, even marry him. Mahendran and Bhairavi are both clueless as to how they should handle their respective suitors, while the viewers are left even more scandalized. The film, in this way, questions what kind of legitimacy is required to declare oneself a truly moral Tamilian. What kind of access can the people of the Tamil nation-state give themselves in order to claim some kind of identity? Twenty-five years after Independence, where and to whom does the Tamilian belong when the parental figures have become so totally compromised in the name of 'political' survival? The Tamilian identity is further problematized by an equally important Tamil political figure who was once Mrs Gandhi's right hand as the president of the Congress party in Delhi—K. Kamaraj. Kamaraj was revered by the Tamil masses and his presence must have provided the voice for young filmmakers to oppose the popularity of Karunanidhi's DMK and MGR's AIADMK. In his biography of Kamaraj, K.V. Narayanan writes, 'Kamaraj refused to see anything positive or helpful in the birth of the new DMK party. In a forceful statement he described the two parties as "Orey kuttayil, ooriya mattai" which can be translated as "two bits of foliage soaked in the same cesspool".'

At the time, Indira Gandhi was playing another game. 'She had three choices before her. She could dangle offers of alliance to either of the two parties, playing one against the other, or she could work for the merger of her Congress into the more popular and visible party led by Kamaraj.' Was Balachander deconstructing these three choices as the three knots that signify a typical Tamilian marriage, an idea explored in his next film *Moondru Mudichu* as well? One can well imagine the dilemma of the Tamil people who saw their legitimate Tamil dreams being completely drowned in such a quagmire.

Apoorva Raagangal cannot be simply contained into the Freudian tropes of Oedipal and Electra complexes where Prasanna, the awkward boy, starts desiring his mother-like benefactor Bhairavi while in parallel, Ranjini seeks a relationship with her father figure/employer Mahendran. Balachander's parallel melodramas are indeed voices of protest to critique the archetype of post-Independence authorities, trying to set the rules of the game for two fiercely independent juveniles. Representing the modern generation, Ranjini sells soap while Kamal, as a self-styled revolutionary, wants to overthrow the establishment. Neither of them wants to be tamed; they willingly choose to befriend or antagonize the two parents, who in turn are struggling in their disastrous marriages.

Special mention must be made of Ananthu. At first, he decided that the main issue to be addressed in the film was gender bias. Kamal's character chooses to stay on in Bhairavi's house after recovering from his injuries, not because of lust for her but admiration of her strength. The script plays it straight by getting him to engage in an arm-wrestling match with her, which he loses. Slightly humiliated, he decides to prove his mettle later by competing with her talent. If she is a good vocalist, he is going to prove his talent as an equally 'good' percussionist. And Balachander does something amazing to play this out. Bhairavi is taking a shower and humming a classical melody. Prasanna responds by playing it back on the mridangam and she pauses to wonder who is performing. An entire scene takes place, intercutting between the shower and Prasanna on the mridangam. Unable to resist, she runs out in her wet towel to discover that the musician is Prasanna himself. After rapid-fire intercuts of them staring at each other, it culminates in another arm-wrestling match, where

Prasanna wins, but as the prize, he wants her recognition. The audience waits. Will this young man sleep with Ranjini's mother, now his benefactor, a woman old enough to be his mother? Will Ranjini lure the elderly man into a marital alliance? What happens when the two youngsters get to sleep with each other's parents?

At this point, a trump card is thrown on the table—Ranjini's father, played by debutante actor Rajinikanth, arrives in the third act. Like Kamal, Ranjini also chose to enter cinema with a grey role. Playing Pandiyan, a character suffering from terminal cancer, he reaches the scene to seek forgiveness from the woman he had once deserted. When Prasanna comes to know about him, he wants to kill Pandiyan. But when he sees the latter's helpless condition, he chooses to go out of his way to arrange for the man's medical treatment. Prasanna understands that the deserter has realized his mistake and that his ex-lover, now his mother figure, is all that the other man has, and he must live with her at any cost. Rajini recalled this career-defining moment during a talk he gave:

When I walked into this film, Kamal was already a well-known star, the cynosure of all eyes. And I was a nobody, at most an ordinary actor. All that was needed was a nod of disapproval from Kamal and my career would have ended. But symbolically, he breathed life into this terminally ill character and gave me a new path to walk upon. From that moment, I realized that if I needed to march further into the minefield of cinema, I needed to keep a role model, a mentor in constant observation. And how fortunate I was to have an actor like Kamal in my sight all the time.

In a climactic musical concert, mother and daughter come together; father and son reconcile with each other and their haunted memories vapourize with Pandiyan's death at the end of the concert. But Balachander was still an angry young filmmaker. He would not allow his women characters, the victims of such patriarchal flagrancy, to live happily with their 'spouses'.

The film ends with the mother and daughter bidding goodbye to the two men who had come to believe that their women would capitulate to them.

This dystopia had a strange background when the film was released. The year was 1975, when the nation was shocked by an Emergency clamped by Prime Minister Indira Gandhi. The constitutional sanctity of a young twenty-five-year-old republic and its fundamental rights had come under question. Whose nation was it and what would constitute the reality of a national identity, of a nation which had hitherto lived together like a family under 'patriarchs' like Gandhi and Nehru? Was the gender of the new prime minister, claiming so much power for herself, a thorn in the side of the male-dominated national political scene of India? When I asked whether the political turmoil leading to the Emergency and its consequences in Tamil Nadu motivated him to do this film, Balachander replied, 'It was not as simple as that. I have always been disturbed by social injustices, especially among the middle-class people who are both victims and perpetrators. But sadly, notions of justice among these people were always about convenience, about who would benefit how much. And I chose to play the interlocutor, perhaps of the inconvenient type. That anger had to be externalized and cinema was my voice.'

For Kamal, this third association with Balachander was even more significant as it brought him face-to-face with his idol, actor Nagesh. Nagesh plays a Jekyll-and-Hyde character in *Apoorva Raagangal*—Dr Suri by day and his twin brother, the drunkard Hari, by night. Towards the end of the film, the audience realizes that they are not twins but the same doctor who takes out his frustration by becoming an alcoholic, dressing up and talking differently. Kamal recalls, 'Nagesh could play such a variety of characters and lace them all with different intonations and exquisite gags. Balachander sir had to only give him a hint of the character and Nagesh could expand on it in a hundred different directions. His enactments in slow motion as a drunken man were just out of this world. I used to watch him dumbstruck because if he had had his way, he could have turned the whole film into his story. I knew I was competent but in front of this man, I was just a budding apprentice. There have been occasions in later films with Balachander sir when there were no roles for Nagesh, and we would all miss him so much. Sometimes I would take a while trying to understand some of the nuances being explained by him on the sets and he would mumble, a bit frustrated, "I think I had Nagesh in mind when I wrote this scene." It was humbling at that moment but then I could not fault him, for he was truly trying to extract the kind of work only Nagesh could accomplish. In *Aalavandhan* (2001; known as *Abhay* in Hindi) there is a song which says, "I am half-god and half-animal." That animal in me is Nagesh, ever hungry for new ideas, forever alert and once it gets a bite on something, it will chew it apart into shreds.'

Kamal understood that the character of Dr Suri and his alter ego probably represented Balachander's own mindset—a man who wanted to treat the malaise that plagued the whole world but, when faced with hardcore reality, had to destroy himself and numb his sensitivities, only to wake up the next day and start treating the sick world all over again.

From a formal point of view, the melodrama in the film is organically enhanced with Balachander's origin in theatre and Kamal's schooling in choreography. This coming together of theatre and dance provides the perfect backdrop for enacting this opera of modern Indian sexuality. It is my belief that Kamal's understanding of this sexual predicament goes beyond the male–female polarization to enter the androgynous zone where he interiorizes the two 'opposite' magnetic drives. Kamal's performance is as masculine as feminine, and this helps him move out of the conventional orgasmic catharsis in order to make viewers see the moral problems at a larger societal level. This is better understood if we look at the problems faced by male Bharatanatyam dancers, a tradition that has been largely the preserve of women artistes. Unsurprisingly, Kamal is also well known for his Bharatanatyam dancing skills. A certain visual assertion of the 'male' body rhetoric, such as body-building exercises or playing 'strong-forearm' pushovers on a table with a woman, is required as a counterpart to enter the androgynous discourse. In many ways this idea moves beyond the 'Ardhanariswara' (half-man–half-woman) concept to establish a unisexual portrayal where viewers of both genders can feel equally attracted and comfortable in such a presence.

All the young aspirants in the Tamil film world were fans of Balachander's screenwriter Ananthu, who spent most of his time foraging through the cans of world cinema at film festivals and other screenings. Through him, Kamal discovered the world of French New Wave cinema and Italian neorealism. He realized how great filmmakers constantly made references to their mentors in their own works, such as Akira Kurosawa formulating the structure of *Rashomon* (1950) after being influenced by Orson Welles's *Citizen Kane* (1941) or Jean-Luc Godard paying homage to Humphrey Bogart and B-grade Hollywood filmmakers in *Breathless* (1960). And finally, Kamal realized that filmmaking was a unique synergy driven by a team of creative thinkers, their influences and talented performers. The actor was as much a filmmaker as any of the directors.

These were the influences on Kamal as *Apoorva Raagangal* paid homage to the roving wide angles in Mikhail Kalatozov's *The Cranes are Flying* (1957), the intense deep-focus compositions seen in Welles's *The Magnificent Ambersons* (1942) or the moralistic dilemmas enacted in Éric Rohmer's *Claire's Knee* (1970). For an almost illiterate Kamal, these were his best schooling years under the self-effacing Ananthu, whose love for pure cinema was as intense as the juveniles' desire for sexual liaison in the film. Ananthu had no children, and he loved reading. Though he normally never lent his books to anyone, Kamal was the exception—he was allowed to borrow books on the strict condition of returning them as soon as possible. Kamal recalls, 'After his death, his relatives sent me two trunks full of his books. I really cried inconsolably that day. Those books symbolized the love and great relationship I had with Ananthu sir!'

Kamal not only had to translate Balachander's rhetoric but also live up to all the informal education he was getting. But unlike most of their new-wave counterparts in the erstwhile Bombay cinema, all this experimenting was done by the trio without an eye on the National Awards or getting selected for prestigious screenings at European film festivals. This was their cinema, their journey, for the sheer joy of existence. This was what occupied them twenty-four hours a day. In the blink of an eye, Kamal ended up doing over 150 films in the fifteen years between 1972 and 1987.

Moondru Mudichu

In this movie, in his unique self-reflexive style, Balachander introduces Sridevi watching his film *Aval Oru Thodar Kathai* in a cinema hall, weeping away. Right at the start, the character seems to be virtually doomed to sacrifice herself at the altar of the male ego. But no, Balachander would neither allow this to happen, nor would he let his prodigy Kamal get besmirched by the stamp of a heartless male aching to become a patriarch. At the same time, Kamal too is watching the same movie. Later, in their respective homes, troubled discussions about the reality of the movie's events intercut with each other. In this trade-off between sexual desire and the erotic intention, Balachander lets the mantle of the predator fall on his other prodigy, Rajinikanth. With this decision, he virtually set up a new dialectic that would challenge the hitherto-dominant rhetoric of the two icons, Sivaji Ganesan and M.G. Ramachandran. Sivaji's characters were known for their sacrificing humaneness while MGR was the man in pursuit of justice, punishing the errant while extolling the virtues of the victim. This film depicted the transition of the earlier two icons into the two new heroes of the Tamil modern era.

Moondru Mudichu (Three Knots of a Wedding, 1976) has Kamal playing Balaji, whose only identity is his friendship with Prasad (Rajinikanth) with whom he shares a room on a terrace. Sridevi plays Selvi, a college student living with a sister who plays bit roles or acts as a body double in movies. Despite being treated badly on movie sets, the sister fends for the two, surviving in a poor tenement below Balaji's terrace apartment. Balachander thus departs yet again from the convention of a normal melodrama in which the narration always locates primary characters within the boundaries or hierarchies of a family. In this film, all characters exist in a so-called 'independent' zone, where the only troubled precinct is the conundrum of an Indian marriage. With this institution, the woman's identity seems to get completely sacrificed; she is transferred as a 'piece of property' to another patriarchal space where the challenge lies in negotiating her legitimacy to articulate her sexual preferences and desire. The modern industrial era has for long seen sex and desire within the Freudian discourse of psychological complexes and the realm of 'upper-class' decency; namely, the less people talk about it, the better. In his typical symbolic manner, Balachander treats the three knots of the sacred thread around the woman's neck as a hangman's noose, forcing a decent woman to abrogate all notions of desire to serve the male-dominated family—an analogy for the state. And in the words of George Bernard Shaw, 'One cannot talk about decency without being indecent.' Can Sridevi playing Selvi subvert this discourse of sexual desire and bring the patriarchal institution to its knees?

Balachander questions whose fundamental right is exercised in the institution of marriage and whether exercising such a right comes with full freedom of choice for both partners. How does the agency of desire at both the private and public level play up in such a conflict?

Coming back to the film, Balaji is a shop assistant in a store selling film-music records where Sridevi comes to spend some time to listen to music. From here onwards, in the true nouvelle vague tradition, Balachander chooses to develop their relationship through orchestrating sound effects, using sound beyond mere dialogues, songs and illustrative background scores. What happens when the diegesis of a movie employs sound effects at par with spoken words? Sridevi and Kamal's first introduction is interrupted by the incessant chiming of wall clocks in the shop. The second time they communicate, it's through the playful washing of wet clothes on a stone, like drummers jamming in a jazz band. Next, they fold up thick green leaves and play the trumpet to each other.

Kamal recalls, 'I still cannot forget the lessons of that day. Imagine a young man and woman trying to convey their love for each other by beating wet clothes on a stone! At an appropriate moment, Rajini (playing

Prasad) interjects himself into the middle of the panning shot between these two innocent lovers and lights a cigarette. At another instant, I play a melody on the mouth organ for her and Rajini watches this with the sound of a hand pump in the background. What a way to define characters! Balachander somehow understood the true meaning of cinematic diegesis where the entire emotion of a scene can be epitomized in the minimal and precise staging of an action. And under the vision of cameraman Lokanath we wrapped up that scene in fifteen minutes.'

Kamal went on to do many such experiments with sound in other films, from playing a ventriloquist in *Avargal* (1977) to a dialogue-less film like *Pushpak* (1987) to a song played entirely in reverse in *Manmadhan Ambu* (2010).

The first faltering step towards marriage in *Moondru Mudichu* is taken by a young Malayali maidservant working in another part of the same building. She tells Selvi that she can make all the wedding arrangements easily if she can get enough money. And to achieve that, she is willing to sacrifice anything. In the lure of a better life, the maid is pressured to have sex with Prasad. Selvi is not so convinced about her immature plan but does not feel competent to advise her. Balancing the character of this young girl is her antithesis: a character of a ragged, bearded man called 'social conscience' who appears out of nowhere as a surreal apparition to warn Prasad.

Feeling jealous of Balaji's proximity with Selvi, Prasad brings about a misunderstanding between the two by burning holes in a dress that Balaji had given Selvi as a gift. Balaji cannot believe that Prasad could have done this. Prasad enjoys overhearing the conflict between the lovers and as Selvi walks away teary-eyed, the same surreal character of 'social conscience' appears, who again warns Prasad of dire consequences if he betrays the values of true friendship. The 'social conscience' ties a knot on a piece of cloth and gives it to Prasad, saying that this knot is his first chance to turn back and lead a proper life. Such a character seems right out of a film by Luis Buñuel or Robert Wiene's *The Cabinet of Dr. Caligari* (1920), all thanks to Ananthu's love for world cinema.

But the ignited Prasad will not rest till he gets what his best friend has—Selvi. Through Prasad, the film shows the fundamental weakness of patriarchy in its forced and desperate need to desire. Desire appears menacing when something one wants becomes difficult to acquire through one's right or power. Desire also reveals a weakness in every system, a certain vulnerability. In front of Selvi, Prasad is a weak man, and in the presence of his best friend Balaji, he can only feel envious. Balachander once remarked to me, 'I learnt this writing cue from Hitchcock's films. In all his films, there is an element of desire which drives the protagonist mad. It could come from within people who long for their mother's warmth, their lover's attention and for the politically powerful, their subjects' affection. This "lack of" leads to extreme forms of desire, resulting in equally extreme actions, from betrayal to murder.'

Balaji's love for Selvi goes beyond the realm of desire. One of the most sensuous scenes I have seen is where Kamal and Sridevi exchange and play a mouth organ in front of a gushing waterfall. At first, they keep wiping the mouth organ clean before passing it on, but slowly the wiping stops and both of them play, or rather kiss the mouth organ alternately in a lingering single take with the orgiastic white cascade in the background. From their playful meet on the terrace to this scene, Balaji and Selvi have come a long way. This 'kiss' further fans the flames of jealousy in Prasad as he invites them to enjoy a ride on his boat on the lake. As expected, Balaji sings a song along with Selvi while Prasad rows the boat. At an unexpected moment, Balaji slips backwards and falls into the lake. He screams for help. He does not know how to swim and despite Selvi's pleas to rescue him, Prasad continues to row away. Now the scene suddenly has Prasad continuing Balaji's song in his deep baritone. Desire has finally reached the realm of the macabre. Balachander narrated, 'I think Hitchcock's spirit really helped me and the film. You see, out of nowhere, hundreds of birds, as if from his famous film *The Birds* started hovering over the boat [during that scene], enhancing the demonic quality of a man who has become completely possessed by desire. And strangely, such a man cannot think of himself as "evil". That is the beauty of desire immersed in power!' The

social conscience character appears yet again to warn Prasad that he is
not taking the ethical path and this will soon ruin him. But Prasad is too
brash—like Mrs Gandhi during the Emergency—to heed such warnings.

The story of Balaji ends with his death by drowning, but the spirit
of the character resurfaces in an unexpected manner. Selvi is obviously
distraught and when she returns home from the disastrous picnic, she sees
that her sister has been injured in a fire that has left her face completely
scarred. With her sister out of work, Selvi must find a way to survive. This
is where the subversion begins. Balachander strategizes a series of events
and coincidences. Selvi responds to an advertisement seeking a bride for
a widower with four children. The widower is, in many ways, a reflection
of Balaji—decent, respectful and bereft of sexual 'desire'. Selvi requests for
some time to take the decision to enter a marital relationship but chooses
to engage in a quotidian world of survival, bringing up the four children as
if they were hers; a nanny who doubles up as a mother, just like her sister
who played a body double in movies. The twist in the story comes when
the widower asks whether she would be willing to marry his son who
has gone away on work. And the second mind-numbing twist is when it
is revealed that the son is none other than Prasad. Seeing this as the best
moment to take her revenge, Selvi demands that her employer fulfil the
terms of the advertisement by getting married to her.

Selvi now becomes the stepmother of the man who had been lusting
after her. And she gets to live on her own terms with the idea of love
that Balaji represented for her. Finally, as a married woman, she never
consummates her relationship. Kamal recalls, 'Even though my character
was not required in the entire second half of the film, I hung around,
learning the unconventional ways in which Balachander would set up
his scenes. Most memorable is the way he reintroduces Rajini's character
to Sridevi's, who has taken up the nanny's job in his own house. Rajini
arrives wearing a tiger mask and distributes similar masks to all the kids
and servants at home. Suddenly the atmosphere is one of a "carnivorous"
carnival set to music and dance. Somewhere the audience comes to
know the identity of the man behind the mask and waits for Sridevi to

be surprised. The story changes sharply when she comes to know that Rajini has come back to haunt her; yet she has chosen to challenge the story! The usage of masks as a folk form to communicate multiple layers of interpretations here also fascinated me. I have used this idea in several of my films and it is only with *Uttama Villain* [2015] that I could finally do justice and partially pay back some of my dues to this giant [Balachander].'

Back in the film, the young maidservant who had been abandoned earlier by Prasad lands up with a baby. But Prasad is not the type to give up so easily. He insists that his 'desire', his Selvi, must belong to him alone and even his own father cannot stop that. A possessed Prasad tries to get his father drowned in the same lake as his friend Balaji but the father saves himself, comes back home and challenges Prasad to pull the trigger on him. A repentant Prasad now decides to drive away to kill himself. Yet again, fate intervenes, this time in the form of his little 'illegitimate' child who has somehow got into the car. Balachander did not believe in deliverance by death but through reconciliation and compromise. Prasad comes back to his dysfunctional family and accepts the maidservant as his wife.

Avargal

Avargal (They; 1977) could be the perfect antithesis to Ghatak's classic *Meghe Dhaka Tara*, profiling the complex domain of man–woman relationships in the most post-modernist terms. If *Meghe Dhaka Tara* is about family/feudal exploitation of women as labour, *Avargal* explores the area of sexual politics. It is about contesting feudal morality, but the terms of reference are, from the protagonist point of view. The plot of *Avargal* revolves yet again around a modern urban woman, Anu, played by the dynamic Sujatha. Anu is in love with Bharani (Ravi Kumar), a flautist whom she rejects as he is meek, old-world and unable to match her emotional demands. Circumstances shift her to Bombay with her father and she loses touch with Bharani because his demented sister tears up all her letters. Anu then meets Ramanathan (Rajinikanth) a helpful man who gives her a job. He proposes, they marry and after their marriage she discovers the sadistic side of her husband. Ramanathan suspects that their child is illegitimate and does not want her to go anywhere.

The film narrates how none of the men can meet Anu's demands in a post-Independence urban middle-class society. It acts like a clinical case study of how certain kinds of characters or categories of existence perform within prescribed parameters and standard deviations. This results in characters functioning like caricatures from an essay or frozen tableaus in a didactic play on modern sociopsychology and its impact on women's liberation. Every scene in the film is treated like a category of an action, which is expected to elicit a certain reaction. And when the scene ends, it has no apparent impact on the next one in terms of a continuation of that changed emotional status. The antagonistic husband and wife, Ramanathan and Anu, always seem to begin from square one. For instance, in the beginning, there are a series of scenes that show how cruel Ramanathan can be. We see Anu come lovingly to serve him coffee as he is ready to go to work. He insults her and Anu reacts with a suppressed look of anger. In the following scene, Anu is seen ironing clothes when Ramanathan enters. She smiles at him and after a few sentences, he insults her. Anu reacts again with the same look. Both are relentless in their demonstration of harassed emotions and after a few such altercations she walks out on him, leaving Bombay to come to Madras with the intention of finding her original lover, Bharani.

In the process, she gets a job in an office where she meets Janardan, an accountant, played by Kamal, a silent lover who expresses his feelings through a ventriloquist's puppet called Junior, symbolically suspended in an eternal time zone. From his introduction to his last scene, he remains the same in terms of 'life and career growth'; in fact, the office and all its employees look the same. All emotional, conflict or story progress is charted only through the rhetoric employed in the conversations. While so-called 'realistic' filmmakers would rule this out as a piece of radio-play, *Avargal* is a lesson in the crafting of a new-age fable which uses the typical devices of one-liners and incredible metaphors and coincidences to push the narrative forward.

Janardan lets Anu stay in his house while withdrawing to his outhouse. Three coincidences happen here—the discovery of Bharani, the old lover, as Janardan's neighbour; Ramanathan arriving in Madras as Anu's new boss; and Ramanathan's mother, Leela, discovering that Anu's past with her son was a disaster. Bharani again proposes to Anu, although he is about to get engaged to Padmini, a fellow musician and admirer; Ramanathan is deeply apologetic and wants her to reconsider their divorce; Leela works incognito in Anu's house as her maid to repent for her son's brutality. And on top of this, Janardan communicates his love for Anu through his dummy, much to her amusement. When Anu agrees to get back together with Ramanathan, she discovers that he has already remarried and has a child. An enraged Anu walks out on all of them accompanied by her mother-in-law Leela to meet an unknown person called Madhavan in Trivandrum.

The question that comes up in several forums is whether a film analyst has the right to 'impose' his or her paradigms on a work without knowing whether they were the original intention of the filmmaker. My stand on this is that while it would be good to know what the various professional contributors had in mind, it is perfectly valid to make assumptions based on the material realities the film has to offer in terms of images, actions and sounds. Secondly, it is quite often the case that the 'listed' contributors may have done their work intuitively with no 'pronounced' intentions at all. Therefore, looking at this structure, I notice that in order to balance the scale in terms of character graph, the story keeps balancing man–woman positions. Within the logic of melodrama, Balachander treats his characters like a set of archetypes who have to interact with a woman in order to keep the discourse alive on what could be the practice of women's liberation in South India. How do we map this discourse?

When I asked Balachander about the complex layering of his stories he had a simple reply, 'But this is the very essence of our folk tales and the puzzles that they weave to offer a mirror to ourselves. I am merely a new folk-tale narrator!'

In a typical post-modernist manner, Balachander refuses to give details of the background or lineage of any of the characters. Each one of them could be endowed to react with certain basic responses, a sort of 'sthayi bhava' or a miasma. Ramanathan is aggressive, always on the offensive; Bharani lacks enthusiasm and is in self-destructive mode; the chivalrous Janardan is always about correctness, despite getting hurt. He is also so timid that he uses a puppet to express himself. Anu is the raw energetic force, unstoppable, instinctive and even erratic. She is the representation of modern times, forever moving, dynamic and incapable of being foisted into one logical position. None of them really change their temperaments, despite all their trials and tribulations. And yet the film is not about destiny or fate governing these characters. It is all about mirroring our social environment and individual psychologies. If Anu is kept at the top of the pedestal, the pyramid drawn by Balachander would look somewhat like this:

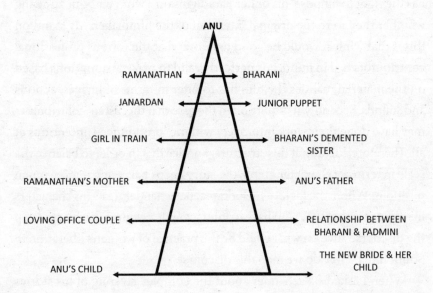

Somewhere, the text also locates the three primary male characters in the three 'gunas' or innate emotional characteristics, namely 'Rajasik', the hyperactive; 'Tamasik', existing in a constant mode of sleep and ignorance; and 'Satvik', who is knowledgeable yet remains withdrawn. Therefore, in his line of success as a 'Rajasik' character, the aggressive Ramanathan succeeds in stopping Anu from getting married to Bharani. But at the end, in an almost playful gesture by Balachander, like one would see in Luis Buñuel's *Los Olvidados* (1950), Ramanathan is wounded in his eye (or punished) by some children playing on the street.

The withdrawn 'Tamasik' character Bharani gropes in the dark, gives up the pursuit of the woman he loved so much and accepts the proposal made by a bohemian Padmini, who enjoys his singing. And when Anu arrives at their engagement he, like a loser, runs after Anu seeking forgiveness. But it is too late.

The 'Satvik' Janardhan is too bothered about ethics and appropriateness to propose without doing any basic 'lifestyle' groundwork. His ego is just too constricted and so he would rather let his id (in Freudian terms) take the form of a puppet. Yet, he is not a coward like Bharani, for he is adequately compensated with the strength of compassion, tolerance and patience. If Ramanathan would be the epitome of male narcissism, then Janardhan could be termed as unabashedly 'androgynous' in nature.

Balachander recollected how he arrived at the idea of using such a Western trope as the ventriloquist and his toy spokesperson, 'The usual and clichéd way of describing one's inner turmoil would be to use a voiceover with a slight reverberating effect. That was just too facile, and I had to find something different. On one occasion I saw Murugan, the son of the famous producer A.V. Meiyappan, demonstrate this ventriloquist's toy gadget he had got from abroad. And then, with a week to spare for the shooting date, I decided to place the entire responsibility on the amazingly versatile Kamal. I just put Murugan and Kamal together and made it work. Not only did Kamal master the art of speaking with lips closed within one week, but he also learned to operate the facial gestures of the Westernized toy with amazing precision. He would show all the antics to me with childish delight and in the process the film got enriched manifold.' This novel idea of a toy talking thrilled the audience immensely at a simple level of novelty, but at the same time, it enhanced the anguish of Janardan, a character who is too self-conscious to reveal his true feelings for a woman who was simply far ahead of his times. The well-dressed, suited, Western puppet also contrasted with the very Indian-looking dhoti-clad Janardan and thus made his contradictions more apparent.

Anu is time incarnate, a 'Nirguni', bereft of all sentimental attributes, like the adventurous Sinbad from *The Arabian Nights* who is capable of walking out on her husband, living in the same house as an unmarried Janardan and then going over to cook food for Bharani. Balachander's masterstroke is a scene in which the three men assemble in the same apartment to take care of Anu, who is down with fever. This is the maximum danger that an incorruptible, unsentimental Anu can encounter. Each man hovers around doing a different duty to cater to her comfort while the camera connects them all in single shots panning from one to another. Like the narrative, Anu is not concerned with what the world around would think about her.

An equally strong counterpart would be Leela who works for Anu, her estranged daughter-in-law, as a servant, at the risk of being identified. The narrative could not be bothered about how such a rich woman manages to escape the prying eyes of society. The synthesis of these two women would be Padmini, who lives life completely on her terms. She is rich, flirtatious, patronizing and could also not be bothered about the consequences of being identified or a loss of identity at the same time.

This last line could be the sum and substance of Balachander's position on women's liberation. Who is the elusive Madhavan Nair that Anu runs off to meet in Trivandrum at the end of the film? Is this also Balachander's attempt to subvert melodrama and deny the film a redeeming conclusion? Yes, we can hear Anu's protest, but why are all three men abandoned, unredeemed? Janardan is left behind hopelessly at the railway station.

Bharani is denied any form of closure as Anu walks out of his 'ridiculous' engagement with Padmini. And how does Ramanathan handle the Hindi-speaking wife and child waiting at his doorstep when he gets back home?

If melodrama is all about the triumph of virtue over evil, then Balachander leaves the film open-ended, like a tale from the *Arabian Nights*. Truly a Sinbadian story! This last part of the pentalogy is so unique and epic that the closest connection I can find for this is the Rainer Fassbinder classic *Effie Briest* (1974) whose structure defies all realistic logic to make apparent a kind of Brechtian world without the fourth wall. Balachander simply wants to offer a mirror to the viewers to have a look at themselves and the society they live in. The stories of Anu and her suitors at different times were only functions to keep the audiences engaged. One woman, four different men, or three different minor women characters and one invisible final protagonist somewhere at the end of the rail journey.

Kamal recalls, 'This film is the most complex among the pentalogy, where the story's form is so transparent that viewers almost experience a sense of vertigo, as if the storyboard or floor has become a sheet of glass, leaving the viewers in a constant state of tension about when the form and the story would actually meet. It is this inverted form of storytelling that I wanted to work with in *Uttama Villain* and thus pay my tribute to Balachander sir.'

More about that film later.

3

MANMADHA LEELAI:
AN EXPLORATION OF SEXUALITY

In a crowded press conference, K. Balachander once remarked, 'In our first few films, I can take the credit for propelling Kamal to become a true artiste. But for the rest of them, I cruised on his success.' At a crucial and formative age, Balachander influenced several of Kamal's perspectives on cinema and the way his audiences would view him. Perhaps it was the order of the day at the time for directors to have an alter ego on the screen. François Truffaut and Jean-Luc Godard shared an amazing actor called Jean Pierre Léaud, Akira Kurosawa had Toshiro Mifune, Ingrid Bergman had Liv Ullman while Satyajit Ray cast Soumitra Chatterjee over and over again.

Kamal was introduced, quite appropriately, by Balachander in *Arangetram* in 1973, after a two-film internship with him, when he did smaller roles in *Nootrukku Nooru* (Cent Per Cent; 1971) and *Sollathan Ninaikiren* (Wanting to Tell; 1973). In both those films, Kamal saw the rather strange and unique ways in which Balachander handled modernist themes of sexual dysfunctionality and marital and familial aberrations in India's new southern metros. Located inside such adult dilemmas, a pubescent Kamal at the age of seventeen not only understood

Balachander's multi-layered approach to psychological intrigues but also experienced his new, indigenous treatment.

By 1973, both Kamal and Balachander had moved away from metaphors about Brahminical patriarchy and started working on scripts which were more caste-agnostic. Perhaps they realized that social inequality did not always arise from prevalent caste systems and all their earlier attempts at mitigating caste-based problems had mostly ended up being counter-productive.

What is more interesting is to see Kamal in the context of the unique feminist discourse that was at the core of Balachander's films. What happens when a young man lands in films that are situated in the narrative of women's struggles? How are the audiences expected to view the male protagonist in such films? As Patricia White, a strong proponent of feminist cinema, says in her book *Feminism and Film*, 'The woman's film could be seen as performing "cultural work"—speaking to, if displacing, genuine social conflicts—between women's economic dependence and [their] desire for autonomy, between heterosexual or maternal ideology and sexual self-definitions.'[1] The traditional Indian woman, as depicted in most mainstream movies, was seen as a category who struggles through the world of patriarchal orientation only to become the ideal mother with the hope of producing an offspring who would have the courage of freeing 'his mother' from the tensions of an oppressive male-dominated society. Balachander hoped to redeem the female protagonist and establish her as a rogue element, disrupting the conventional mores of the emotional slave to emerge as an 'independent' person. In Kamal, he found the ideal antithesis—the youthful vulnerable male who must accept this change as the only realistic way out of a controlling patriarchal narrative.

To provide a more universal context to these rather intimate problems, Balachander chose to look at them through the lens of the folk tale. Thrown out of the window were the so-called 'authentic or realistic' portrayals of man–woman conflict, as seen in Bergman or even Satyajit Ray's films, pure archetypal depictions of urban men and women as office executives, independent music teachers, lawyers, disco dancers or even student leaders. Balachander instead used songs, on-camera statements, mythical references, random freeze frames and jump-cuts to disorient and provoke the mainstream cinemagoers.

In *Arangetram*, Balachander had provided Kamal the centre-stage and placed him in a relationship with a much older woman who has been denied her sexuality. But it was four films and four years later that Kamal got the most complicated dramatic arena in *Manmadha Leelai* (1976), meaning 'The Legend of Manmadha', based on Giacomo Casanova, the eighteenth-century Italian who famously bedded 116 women over a forty-year span. Around the same time, Federico Fellini was also working on this subject, while Godard was doing similar experiments in films like *Two or Three Things I Know About Her* (1967). Balachander created stars out of talented women actors such as Sridevi, Sripriya, Srividya, Jayaprada and Pramila, and tossed Kamal into that burning cauldron, only to discover the possibility of the new-age male who could appeal equally well to feminine sensibilities without demonstrating any form of machoism.

The year 1976 also saw Tamil women in the thick of the Emergency imposed by Indira Gandhi, a woman who, by default, was out to punish the bloated Dravidian male ego in the most severe political battle the state had ever witnessed. Were Tamil women going to rejoice or recoil in horror?

In *Manmadha Leelai* Kamal plays Madhu, an archetypical male who sees the possibility of a sexual encounter with every woman he sets his eyes upon. To ensure that the audience wouldn't think of this as a 'pornographic' film, Kamal and the actors distanced themselves from their characters with peculiar gestures, props, loud dialogues and songs playing intermittently. In one song, as part of the exercise in distancing audiences from Madhu's errant two-timing world, Kamal sings a song to a married woman, which starts like a typical song sequence but breaks up after the opening melodic lines to suddenly announce names, like a typical RJ in a daily radio broadcast, of listeners expressing their choice to play that very song. This action gets the viewer to reflect whether this is being really sung by the hero or being played back through a medium. Later in the same song, which is originally sung by Yesudas, Kamal breaks it again to make a phone call to his wife and speaks in his own voice to say he will be late coming back home and then comes back to lip-sync the Yesudas song to this new woman.

At a surface level, one can see that Kamal's empowerment to become such a 'Casanova' comes from the authoritarian patriarchal society that seems to have been caught in the sudden and concurrent transition that India encountered, from a feudal atmosphere to a modern pseudo-corporate and state-governed urban regime. This created a strange jungle-like space where males were 'naturally' programmed to seek out as many partners as possible in order to increase their chances of sustaining familial legacies, at the same time also partaking in corporate affairs and democratic state governance. Part of the definition of upward mobility among affluent Indian males in the early 1970s was, in fact, openly having more than one spouse, and several practitioners in the film industry seemed to be practising this.

Balachander recollected, 'When I cast Kamal in this role, he was just twenty-two but was essaying the role of a man much older than him; [the film was] about married men in their early forties who desired to have illicit affairs and exposed themselves to the inherent dangers of such adventurism. Could this young man pull it off? I took the decision to cast him because I knew he was an enormously talented actor and secondly, he could listen and digest the knowledge I would impart to him about such wild adventures, of which some were personal experiences while others were hearsay!'

By taking up this role, Kamal was also paying homage to another major Tamil film icon, M.K. Thyagaraja Bhagavathar, who had done a similar film called *Ambikapathy* (1957) in which the song which lent its name to Balachander's film, '*Manmadha Leelai*', was sung by him and became an important landmark. Kamal was not just connecting the story to the dilemmas of a modern Casanova but also synthesizing it with a similar mythical tale of Ambikapathy within the narratives of the feudal South Asian affluent class.

Such a narrative is also legitimized, at another level, by the mythical positioning of primary male deities such as Shiva, Vishnu and Muruga having two or more consorts and being worshipped and celebrated in their other divine forms. While modernists would find it misogynistic, Krishna is valourized as someone who is forever teasing women on the streets and in celestial spaces. Balachander used Kamal as the vehicle to seriously critique these hypocrisies and perceptions of sexuality in South Indian society and make daring statements which would make his middle-class viewers, aspiring to be super-affluent, squirm in their seats. On the other hand, these outspoken declarations could also be seen, or cheered, as sheer grandiloquence. Quite often, they were not meant to be understood in common parlance. Kamal remarked about this concept in a recent speech, 'Sometimes, all I am looking forward to is the applause from my fans. It is another matter if they understood the importance of the statement or not.'

Kamal plays out the folk tale of a modernized Krishna as Casanova only to be constantly obstructed and even abused for his indiscreet attitude towards women. As Madhu, he keeps lamenting that his manic obsession for women is undoubtedly a serious psychological problem, but unfortunately it is also the source of his emotional sustenance, which in turn is part of his 'urban' personality as an upwardly mobile new Indian. The women in the film, on the other hand, are not stereotypes. Balachander had the courage to unleash a variety of 'modern women' archetypes encountering, seducing and admonishing Kamal's character. Such characters had never been seen before on the Tamil screen.

Madhu is married to a woman who is the epitome of domestic subservience. She cooks, washes clothes and waits on him unquestioningly until a lawyer friend intervenes to reveal her husband's escapades and cajoles her to divorce him. But her unsuspecting nature does not allow her to take such a drastic step. This gives the incorrigible Madhu the time and space to gaze at a pretty secretary in his office who has a problem of winking constantly. The second woman uses Madhu to make her two-timing boyfriend jealous. He connects with a third one over a wrong telephone call and courts her too. And then there are other women like his Brahmin accountant's film-crazy daughter or his psychoanalyst's wife. Kamal executed these encounters with a hilarity that has a dual purpose. On the one hand, he wanted the audience to hate him for what he was doing but on the other, he wanted to show the character as caught within certain socio-historical circumstances enveloping modern Indian urban aspirations of growth and affluence.

Trapped amidst these multiple attractions, Madhu comes to know that his wife has finally realized the condemnable nature of his behaviour. In an amazing psychic revelation, Balachander shows her to be a super-powerful woman as Madhu envisions her as a giant apparition, like Krishna revealing himself on the battlefield, known commonly in India as the 'Viswaroopam' or universal image. It is indeed amazing to see the similarity between Balachander's approach and the contribution to psychoanalysis by Erich Fromm, an expert in decoding post-Freudian discourses. Fromm surmised that the reason why a patriarchal bourgeois system has not been able to entirely dominate the discourse of sexuality is the residual power of a pre-existent matriarchal society, which was the dominant socioeconomic mode a thousand years ago and continues to exist in several minor mythical/religious discourses across the world. Without visiting India, Fromm seemed to have understood aspects of the country's complex social psychology where female goddesses continue to dominate the religious landscape. Fromm's matrilineal analysis of a Marxist worldview would later blossom into a variety of powerful feminist discourses that emerged in the 1940s and '50s.

In some unique ways, Balachander and Kamal could be the primary heralds or chroniclers of a modern feminist argument in Indian cinema. Of course, it is not so simply stated in their cinematic interpretations and I am sure such a claim would elicit protests from several feminist critics in South India. Balachander and Kamal were not part of the realistic narratives of the so-called women-oriented films of Shyam Benegal and Satyajit Ray in the 1970s. But apart from Balachander's disruptive scripting style, I feel that Kamal's presence on the screen could be capable of being seen in multiple dimensions. Firstly, Kamal was not about machismo. In fact, quite contrarily, he comes through as almost sexless, androgynous. Secondly, his ambivalence towards the sexual act is depicted very strongly. He really does not know what to do with the women he has lured. The Casanova in him is just the manifestation of an incurable pervert and yet, morality has nothing to do with it. Lastly, the way Kamal negotiates his prevarication in the individual song sequences with each one of his women can be seen as a depiction of the underlying complex themes of sexuality in the film. These songs distance the viewers and, at the same time, provide enormous pleasure. The film bridges the contemporary narratives as depicted in the bizarre worlds of Fellini, the dystopic visions of Fassbinder and the eccentric scriptwriting of Jean-Claude Carrière (a good friend of Kamal) in the films of Luis Buñuel. *Manmadha Leelai* is undoubtedly Kamal and Balachander's diagnosis of the discreet charms of the Tamilian bourgeoisie.

The climactic song is a coup of sorts. Madhu's wife has filed for divorce and sneaks into his room to find evidence of adultery when he confronts her. Instead of an argument, he sings a song clamouring for sincere love and affection, like a motherless child. In a flash, they embrace each other. Cut to a few months later when the appeal for divorce comes up and she realizes that she is pregnant. Madhu, meanwhile, is on the verge of a nervous breakdown and in typical folk-tale style, repents for all the trauma that he has inflicted upon her. When he gets no response, he runs away in a panic through busy traffic. At the same time, a similar frenzy envelops her and she too starts running towards him. The film ends with the two hugging each other passionately in the middle of a main road, much to the dismay of hundreds of vehicles which have been brought to an abrupt halt.

The superego of patriarchal/societal authority crumbles along with Madhu's libidinal impulses, allowing for a proper restoration of the ego in the typical melodramatic sign-off in a folk tale: 'All's well that ends well.'

4

16 VAYATHINILE: THE END OF A UTOPIAN DREAM

If K. Balachander positioned Kamal as the thinking actor for the Madras middle class, then the credit for catapulting him into the so-called new rural Dravidian ethos goes to Bharathiraja's debut film, *16 Vayathinile* (At Age 16; 1977). Unlike Balachander, Bharatiraja had very little film experience—just a brief stint assisting the Kannada maverick filmmaker Puttana Kanagal. Like many of Kamal's earlier films, this was also centred on resilient family-centric Tamil women. And, as a counterpoint, the key male characters were all orphaned in their own ways.

In *16 Vayathinile*, Kamal plays Gopalakrishnan, a mentally challenged orphan being brought up by a widowed aunt. Rajinikanth as Parattai is a wastrel with no familial locus, who hangs around with two sidekicks. Shabbir Ahmed plays veterinarian Dr Satyajith, the educated outsider who comes to the village, allured by the atypical Mayil, played by Sridevi, a young girl pursuing the dream of becoming an 'educated' teacher who functions as a 'national' metaphor as she 'comes of age'. The narrative thus develops around the three males whose eyes are focused on the sixteen-year-old Mayil.

At the re-release event of this film, Rajinikanth said,

I cannot stop admiring the guts of Rajakannu, this extraordinary producer who convinced us with his belief in this unconventional story of underdogs in a Tamil village. The Rs 5 lakh he invested was all he had. And when the distributors rejected the film, he released it all by himself, borrowing heavily from the market. The film was a big hit, but Rajakannu did not cash in on its popularity and exploit the crew members for his next venture. He went on to do his next film with another set of newcomers. That requires enormous guts![1]

For a typical melodrama released in 1977, this film makes a unique departure by discarding the mandatory family roots required as the emotional basis for all characters in such a film. The venerated rural family system is also not spared, depicted as dysfunctional and heartless. The portrayal of the mother—usually shown in Indian melodramas as perennially compassionate, sacrificing and ever-suffering because of the deprivations caused by a 'post-colonial/independent' arrogant patriarchal system—is different here as well. Placed within the subtext of the Indian Emergency (1975–77), Mayil's mother is a brash, outspoken woman with no sense of decorum, causing serious embarrassment to her educated daughter and the community.

The archetypes of 16 Vayathinile thus give birth to a variety of representations, which are both political and cinematic at the same time. In this, his very first film, Bharathiraja joined hands with some of the finest iconic talents who would go on to dominate Tamil cinema for quite some time to come. The veteran Kamal, Rajinikanth, Sridevi, music composer Ilaiyaraaja and screenplay writer Bhagyaraj chose to work under a debutante's direction for the first time and the film catapulted them to a celebrity status hitherto unseen in Indian cinema. For this reason alone, this film must be celebrated. However, its production was a saga of deprivation.

Bharathiraja took everybody to a remote village, where the only accomodation was a small old government guest house. Since Kamal was the best-known personality—and had been paid a princely sum of

₹27,000—he got the main bedroom. Rajinikanth, who was being paid ₹3,000, got to sleep in the adjoining veranda along with Bharathiraja. At lunch, the director could afford tender coconut water only for his hero and heroine; the rest just had to make do with normal water. Matters came to a head in the most unlikely way. Sridevi was giving a take for a scene where she had to get angry and spit on Rajini's face. While shooting the close-up they tried to splash soap suds, cream, oil, etc. on Rajini. Nothing worked and precious raw stock was being used up. Rajini, unable to tolerate the waste of stock, told them not to fake it, let Sridevi actually spit on his face with force and be done with it. Everybody around was shocked. This was a travesty, but raw stock and time were priceless. And thus it was done!

Recalls Bharathiraja, 'Finances were so tight that even the cheap ORWO colour-film raw stock was bought in small quantities from nearby Bangalore. One day we ran out of film. I could not reveal this to Kamal and Sridevi who were ready for the take, so cameraman Nivas and I decided to playact. But a few moments after I had shouted "Action", Kamal paused during the take and said, "Hey! There seems to be something wrong with the camera. It sounds different", and began walking towards me. I told him the truth. Kamal placed his hands on my shoulders and said, "You should not suffer so much to make a film. I will give you money for this raw stock. Let's do the film well." Tears came to my eyes, for I had promised my producer I would complete the film within the budget. However meagre, Rs 5 lakh was all that he had. And through Kamal I had to tell the film's heart-rending story.'

In the film, Kamal's real name is Gopalakrishnan, but he's called Chapaani (the lame one), the name his aunt bestows on him. Why and how did the term 'Chapaani' come about? Was this name supposed to resonate with the name and persona of Charlie Chaplin or to recall the tragic ways that the Machine Age had dumped the innocent working class as cattle for slaughter in an assembly line? In the Tamil political situation, it seemed to represent the predicament of the gullible Tamilian who had by then realized that the heady utopia of the Dravidian Land, compromised by Tamil leaders during the Emergency, was a promise gone awry.

Chapaani can be seen as being orphaned by an imaginary Tamil father, leaving him to fend for himself under a dysfunctional nation-state in the form of the cantankerous aunt whose daughter, Mayil, also treats him with utter disdain. All factors weigh against Chapaani. He is treated with disrespect everywhere he goes and the only thing that sustains him is the food that his widowed aunt dishes out in return for all the odd jobs he does. In fact, he equates himself with a dog, an animal that the aunt never actually has, although she owns goats and some poultry. Why would a budding star like Kamal take such a big risk and make himself look so depraved instead of pushing the audience to have sympathy for his character?

Kamal recalls, 'In a very intuitive way, I was actually echoing the distraught feelings of my audience. The more I pushed my character to the brink of misery, the more powerfully could I take him to the angry climax when Chapaani would stone the rapist to death and thus seek the complete support of the audience. The limping walk that I had to do continuously was another risky issue, for it had to be consistent. I remembered seeing David Lean's *Ryan's Daughter* in 1971 in which one of the primary characters walked with a limp. I just played back his images and followed that exactly. That way, I knew I would not fail!'

Despite appearing to be the complete country bumpkin, Kamal's portrayal shows the audience that Chapaani is not an imbecile. He is sensitive enough to register the barbs flung at him but is incapable of dealing with such forces. A certain monotony drives both his inner energy and outer expressions in a persistent way. It is this insensitive persistence—which also functions as a metaphor for the Tamil people 'betrayed' by their leadership in the mid-1970s—that actually keeps Chapaani alive.

The educated vet Dr Satyajith is scripted in sharp contrast. Mayil aspires to be urban and educated and hopes that this doctor will fulfil her dreams. At the same time, she is also afraid that he might ditch her and head back. The vet, who is not interested in a relationship with Mayil but wants to seduce her, decides to approach Chapaani for a favour and make him look urban, decent, hopefully sending the right message to lure Mayil. So, when Satyajith gifts him some formal Western wear, Chapaani grabs it at once, changing from a dishevelled country bumpkin to a slightly kiddish-looking man with a neat haircut. To top off the transformation, he insists on being called only by his official name, Gopalakrishnan. He is unperturbed by the fact that everybody in the village will make fun of his new haircut and attire. The new 'proper' name suggests that he is now in a position to compete for Mayil's hand. But when he sees that this 'outsider' Westernized doctor is actually using him as a go-between to curry favour with a gullible Mayil, he rips up the Western clothes in rage and goes back to wearing just a loincloth. And when he realizes that Mayil is, in fact, enamoured by the 'North Indian' archetype, he decides to give up hope. Ironically, the vet's plot fails too.

Recalling the scene in which Chapaani bids goodbye to Mayil, Bhagyaraj says, 'Kamal sir tells her with his typical innocence that her late mother reared goats, cows and poultry, but instead of having a trusted dog, she nurtured him. As he finished saying his lines, the entire unit was in tears. They had never seen such a performance.' Bhagyaraj was possibly the most influential changemaker at that time, thanks to his screenplays and dialogues. If Balachander's rhetorical style hinted at Tamil Nadu's leap into modernity, Bhagyaraj gave up on all Tamil flourishes and chose to address the illiterate world.

In one of our conversations he said, 'I wanted to focus more on the accent, the inner rhythms that the poor folk had evolved in the districts of Madurai. It had to be rooted. In fact, I used to find the lines spoken in most Tamil films those days patently absurd ... so unrealistic! But the real problem on location was how to tell Kamal sir the authentic tone in which I wanted him to deliver these lines. Bharathiraja, the director, was equally apprehensive about expressing his views. It was Kamal sir who broke the ice and asked us to come out of our shells and speak out. I summoned some courage and spoke in a certain accent and rhythm. Within seconds he had grasped it and taken it to a higher level.'

This film gave Kamal sufficient screen time to display the complex emotional shifts between loyalty to his aunt, his slavish attitude towards Parattai, his unrequited love for Mayil, his childish behaviour with the rest of the villagers and his somewhat ambivalent attitude towards the veterinarian. Kamal recalls, 'Something made me feel that I was about to be part of an epoch-making film event. From director Bharathiraja to maestro Ilaiyaraaja, everybody was a debutant, but they all had some amazing self-esteem. I met them for the first time and chipped in with my experience of twenty-five-odd films to partake in this adventure.'

Kamal's gradual transformation from Chapaani to Gopalakrishnan served to somewhat offset the rather abrupt manner in which the veterinarian gave up interest in Mayil and the equally abrupt (and unanticipated) decision in the last minutes of the film by Parattai to attempt to rape Mayil. This sudden closure could also be due to budgetary constraints, which may not have allowed the director to expand the scope of the narrative or attain higher production values. The climax, in fact, had to be worked out with the same handful of actors that the film had begun with. It was Bharathiraja's ingenuity to mix documentary footage of temple festivals to give the impression of a larger, well-populated village in such scenes.

Coming back to the idea of Kamal as the 'orphan', there is an interesting Janus-faced duality here. Why should these males be 'orphaned' in the first place? Who is this Gopalakrishnan and what does he represent, other than a country bumpkin with a changed demeanour? In many ways, such narratives of orphans and of being orphaned in multiple ways reflect a renaissance of the Dravidian ethos, although bound in tragedy. The tragedy in films such as *16 Vayathinile* is a reflection of the predetermined, almost fatalistic attitude of the rebellious Tamil filmmakers of the mid-1970s, reeling under the disillusionment of being let down by their leaders, but unable to state it in clear terms. The only way they could 'convey' a certain kind of protest was by not allowing the protagonist to enjoy the fruits of his labour.

Coming back to the film, Chapaani, who is almost a step away from consummation, comes home to see Parattai trying to rape Mayil. Seeing this barbaric sexual harassment, he decides to do something which he has never done. He takes a giant stone and cracks Parattai's head in one stroke and that leads to his arrest by the police and being carted out of the village. This act not only leaves Chapaani an orphan but also leaves Mayil in the lurch to face the wrath of an unpredictable future.

The lure of Mayil is the central metaphor in this entire dramatic struggle. She is everything that the utopian Tamil Nadu aspired for. A young, angelic girl who finishes school against all odds, nursing ambitions to become a qualified teacher, suddenly falls prey to the hypnotic ways of a Westernized, non-Tamil doctor. The Westernized look of the 'suspect' is obviously a hangover from the colonial past; his being a non-Tamilian is a reference to the Delhi-centric hegemony that is always alluring to the educated rich; and the doctor being a qualified veterinarian enables Mayil to engage in amorous liaisons under the guise of bringing the animals in her backyard for him to examine. The audience realizes at some point that this character was never ever going to be steady in this relationship but was not so desperate as to force himself upon her.

From Parattai's point of view, played with enormous gusto by Rajinikanth, Mayil is always the subject of the larger lecherous male gaze. In fact, in the opening scene, when she announces that she has passed her class 10 examination, a bystander tells her that she is now fit to join the film industry crowd as another 'masala' actor, another icon. So, when Parattai keeps wooing her in his highly arrogant way, only to be rebuked by her, do we see an extension of the travails of the modern Tamil woman as projected in the films by K. Balachander?

It is with Chapaani that Mayil encounters a variety of fears, frustrations, anger and desires. She befriends him when necessary, dumps him at opportune moments and abuses him at will. Chapaani does react, but since he is not able to make any informed judgements due to his mental imbalance, she is able to get away with anything. Despite the aunt's cantankerous nature, Chapaani is able to put up with her as the past world of the Tamilian. But he is not able to deal with Mayil, the future of the Tamil state.

16 Vayathinile ran for several months, won several national, state and Filmfare awards, became a cult classic and established Kamal as a saleable actor even in the so-called B and C centres. It was remade in Hindi in 1979 as *Solva Sawan* (The Sixteenth Monsoon), with the same crew members, but could not evoke the sense of political angst it did in Tamil Nadu.

5

VARUMAYIN NIRAM SIVAPPU: AN EXERCISE IN NON-NARRATIVE CINEMA

'Even the great poet Bharati's books are finally sold to wastepaper merchants for vendors to pack peanuts. In the country that I live in, my ideals cannot bring lunch to the table. I am afraid that this hunger will weaken and disarm me. But I will not let this hunger consume me as a sacrificial rite. I will give up my life but not my ideologies. So please go away and do not depend on me. And when time permits, just remember a madman like me had crossed your path,' says a devastated Rangan to Devi, who hopes to settle down with him, in this film by Kamal Haasan's mentor Balachander. Through his intense gaze, one can visualize Kamal reminiscing about his early days in the industry when he wandered the streets of Kollywood with compatriot R.C. Shakti, hunger gnawing at their bellies, trying to find a producer for their film, *Unarchigal*.

After several collaborations, Balachander and Kamal got together once again in 1980 to make another film – *Varumayin Niram Sivappu* (Red Is the Colour of Poverty), a film that they would have given up as impossible just five years earlier. Kamal recalls, 'I would pester him with all kinds of stories and experimental ways of exposing social and political problems.

And Balachander sir would reject them as European art film concepts
which were perfect recipes for disaster. He would warn me of the cruel
and unforgiving film industry, which had no space for a second chance.
If I had to make myself a success, it could only be in front of the camera.
And that's how I ended up as a reluctant actor!'

With this new film, Balachander and Kamal chose to experiment with
serious subjects like unemployment, corruption of social values and
gender dignity. It was a strong reaction to (or a correction of) a scatter-
brained musical called *Ninaithale Innikum* (Sweet Thoughts) which they
had finished in 1979. A new coalition, called the Janata Government, had
come to power at the centre after the tyrannical Emergency imposed by
Indira Gandhi between 1975 and 1977. *Varumayin Niram Sivappu* flows
more like an editorial on the plethora of issues that plagued India at that
time. Every scene in the film is devised as a snippet on some issue, from
corrupt contractors who trade flesh for securing deals to employment
interviews which are a farce. In addition, you have some pet obsessions
which Balachander and Kamal shared—the orthodox Brahmin father
who believes in nothing other than the upper-caste sanctity of Carnatic
classical music; submissive wives who keep pleading for some sympathy;
rich businessmen who jog in plush gardens with no care for the poverty
around them, and so on.

The film's theme revolves around the thought: 'What would have
happened if a C. Subramania Bharati were to be born again in a milieu
where people have given up on simple family values, citizens live with
no social security and politicians and businessmen are bereft of national
ideals?' Balachander showed three young Tamil lads who choose to try and
eke out a living in the capital city of Delhi. In the true spirit of this film,
Kamal, with about sixty-plus movies already to his credit, blended into an
ensemble cast with new actors like S.V. Shekar, Dilip, Pratap Pothen, and
Sridevi, with whom he had already done a dozen films by then.

Another typical director's touch is Bharani the painter (played by
a practising painter by the same name) who has a speech impairment.
Around him evolves an entire discourse about communicating, the cordial

versus the dissonant in languages and, of course, the larger synaesthetic and linguistic issues that govern the transcreation between words and images. The abstract ambience of the painter's studio becomes a refuge for Sridevi to come and pour out her woes, to which Bharani can only give a patient hearing. At another level, one can see him as the alter ego of the film director who can only make interpretations while leaving interventions to more active players. However, the ruthlessness of the world does not spare such mute witnesses, and the painter is run over by a speeding car and dies still holding paintbrushes tipped with red paint in his hand. The storyteller chooses death, leaving the climax open to the triangle in which Devi (Sridevi) must choose between a crazy theatre director (Pratap, played by Pratap Pothen) and an idealistic unemployed poet (Rangan, played by Kamal).

Five years earlier, Balachander probably would have said, 'Is this any kind of a choice for a climax? Who is the good guy? The theatre artist who is well off but brutally possessive of his lover, or the angry jobless MA in philosophy who has only respect and gentle love for her?'

To locate this emotional dilemma, there is an interesting though clichéd snippet earlier from Sridevi's point of view. It is a scene where Devi is taking a bath when the doorbell rings. When she comes out, she sees that Rangan has opened the unlocked door and is staring at her body. After the mandatory intercutting between come-hither close-ups, Rangan comes over and kisses every part above her neck. And suddenly the viewer realizes that this is her imagination. She is back to bathing and the doorbell rings yet again. Devi comes out to see a cold Rangan standing, unmoved. She runs over and hugs him, but he pushes her back, calling her shameless. Yet again, a shocked Devi comes out of her reverie and continues her bath when the 'real' doorbell rings. Rangan walks in and when he sees her in a towel, he apologizes and agrees to leave. And despite Devi telling him to wait, he gently goes out and shuts the door. Devi stands there with mixed feelings of being left behind and a bit of admiration for his 'proper' behaviour.

To be 'proper' simply means being honest with one's conscience. But
what happens when that conscience speaks another language? Seen within
the Tamil people's context, it assumes rather complex proportions. The
Tamilians in the film are struggling to make their presence felt in the capital
city in which powerful articulations of the Hindi language are entrenched.
Devi acts in Hindi plays, while the three jobless men wooing her jostle with
other Tamil-speaking citizens and compete with each other in corrupt
practices to seek favours in an alien land. Worth watching is the song *Paatu
Onu Paadu'* (Sing One Song) written by Kannadasan and composed by
M.S. Viswanathan. In it, we see Kamal and his unemployed gang on the
famous Rajpath in the capital city singing, 'When you can sing about the
greatness of your country, why do you need food, brother?' One cannot
imagine anything like this in today's Indian cinema.

The situation back home in Tamil Nadu at the time was aptly
summarized by John Keay in his book *Midnight's Descendants*:

There [in Tamil Nadu] the Dravida Munnetra Kazhagam (DMK), a
Dravidian party that was pledged to all things Tamil, happily added
the language issue to its secessionist portfolio of grievances. Strikes
crippled the Congress-led administration. From books to billboards
and timetables, everything in Hindi was torched. When Tamil
youths, four of them students, publicly torched themselves, the
scenario resembled that of the 1952 language riots in East Bengal.
The police opened fire, over sixty were killed.[1]

Kamal says, 'What troubles me is the linguistic bigotry being committed
by some vested interests. After all, we have accepted a song by a Bengali
as our national anthem. So, you cannot destroy any language in the name
of monocultural supremacy. Tamil Nadu especially was home to so many
films made in other languages, including Hindi. We were literally practising
the true significance of unity in diversity. Yet, all these language-based
clashes could be fuelled!'

The film was also strongly influenced by Ananthu, with whom Kamal shared a very close relationship. Though this film did not travel the festival route like the works of Satyajit Ray and Aravindan at that time, watching *Varumayin Niram Sivappu*, one will notice a distinct contempt for everything held as conventional and holy in the trade circles of the Tamil film industry. Just imagine two well-known actors singing a Hindi song in a Tamil film; a superstar fighting with his friends over a half-lit cigarette; a love song which sounds more like two lovers talking to each other; a film where Kamal does not dance or beat up villains or even romance the heroine! This is how a great mind like Ananthu who saw mainstream film conventions as superstitions broke them.

Let's look at another aspect. Generally speaking, this work of Balachander—though emotionally in sync with many other melodramatic films—has scant respect for the passage of real screen time and enters a kind of anti-narrative path. The film disregards questions such as how long the protagonists have been struggling without a job or how long Devi has been working in this theatre group under a crazy director or how and when they reached the picturesque hill resort to have the musical conversation. One could draw a parallel to this technique and its significance with what Richard Brody says about Godard in *Everything Is Cinema*:

> Through these decisions, Godard removed the scrim of convention by which cinema transmits time and space to the viewer; however, by flouting the principles on which classical cinema is based, he in fact ended by overemphasizing them. In appearing amateurish the film calls attention to the codes of professionalism and in the end highlights the fact that they are mere conventions; it denaturalizes them. [2]

To emphasize the stylized and dysfunctional narration, Balachander placed the climax of the film in the hands of Pratap, the eccentric theatre director with whom Devi works. Pratap wants Devi to marry him but when he comes to know that Devi loves Rangan despite his poor unemployed status, he chooses to walk away. Seeing an orphaned Devi, now also rendered jobless, Rangan takes up a job which demolishes his privileged upper-caste status. He settles down into a regular yet unconventional job, which will take care of him and Devi. The job is aptly revealed through his estranged musician father's eyes when he comes to visit Delhi for a music concert. He enters a saloon to get a shave and haircut and is shocked to discover that his son Rangan has now become a barber. This encounter becomes the punchline of the film and hammers in Balachander's rebuke of India's so-called development policies, along with a plea to honour dignity of labour as an essential component of modern times. The father sits down and lets his son give him a clean shave. A renewed relationship is announced in a saloon!

This film emboldened Kamal to believe that if the artist feels passionate about something and at the same time thinks it's important to communicate it, she or he must go ahead and trust that the audience will also feel similarly. And very often, such feelings may not come all tied up in one single story, reminding the artist that the time has arrived to disrupt and abandon formal/narrational compulsions. Added to that, the success of *Varumayin Niram Sivappu* in Tamil and Telugu convinced him that the angry young man could truly reflect the angst of an angry young generation in a narrative that could mix theatre, painting, poetry, music and dance without diluting the individuality of the artist in each of these arts.

6

RAJA PAARVAI AND *EK DUUJE KE LIYE:* TWO MILESTONES FROM THE EARLY 1980S

Ek Duuje Ke Liye: *Crossing over to Hindi Cinema*

The travails of the various states of a diversified country like India coming together can always be understood by a careful study of its films. And the rather insidious north–south divide can also be seen in the way both sides stereotype the 'other'. In the early post-Independence years, the 'over-the-top' portrayals of the Madrasi, the Sardarji or the Parsi more often than not helped diffuse lurking tensions in the newly formed nation. India was undoubtedly more of a cinematic imagination than a well-argued or properly articulated set of diverse citizens. In 1981, *Ek Duuje Ke Liye* looked at the grim side of this unfortunate national divide. Before I talk about this film and Kamal's foray into unchartered territory, let me give you a quick flashback to contextualize this syndrome.

I have always believed that post 1947, Indian cinema provided a major cultural foundation for the nation to set itself into a structure of conflict-free states. Even earlier, in fact from 1913 onwards, with the advent of Dadasaheb Phalke's *Raja Harishchandra*, Indian cinema has incorporated and transcreated traditional myths into modern constitutional strategies for self-governance and social decorum. Built by semi-skilled technicians from all over India and even technicians from Europe and America, the Indian film industry took into consideration, and paid obeisance to, the vibrant democratic freedom movement led by Mahatma Gandhi and scores of other highly qualified and talented political leaders. Last but not least, the 'rasikas' or the mass audiences just glued themselves to this virtual reality like bees around a resplendent honeycomb. Indian films lead to packed cinema halls, full of disparate people with no regard to gender, caste, creed or communal divides.

It has been such an unbelievable win-win situation for filmmakers and their audiences that despite a slim 15 per cent chance of getting their investment back, film producers continued and still continue to burn themselves at the altar of this highly inflammable popular culture.

In the South, from the mid-1940s onwards, the professionally run studios of Madras city and other southern metros produced cinematic fare which combined the business strategies of Hollywood, the artistic lighting sensibilities of the German studios and the socialistic fervour of Soviet cinema. A kind of nationalistic narrative field was developed which a post-Independence population could comfortably snuggle into.

Producers such as Nagi Reddy, T.R. Sundaram, A.V. Meiyappan and L.V. Prasad nurtured a sea of talented artistes and technicians to make films in all the Indian languages, with simple, family-oriented scripts soaked in a thick syrup of melodrama. By telling (and retelling) the same story six to seven times in different languages using the same actors, they managed to pull off cultural impersonation as never before witnessed in any modern society.

It is in this tradition of national intercourse that several screenwriters, musicians, choreographers and technicians migrated back and forth between Bombay, Calcutta and Madras. But the story of the on-screen icons migrating from the southern to northern zones requires careful attention. Legendary Carnatic music vocalist M.S. Subbulakshmi was indeed the pioneer as she crooned her way into the Hindi heartland singing the songs of the poet-saint Meera in a bilingual film of the same name (1945). Next came the daring Vyjayanthimala and Padmini. A few more women followed, but no male actor had dared to step into that 'other' territory till L.V. Prasad decided to throw Kamal into the ring after seeing the hugely successful Tamil–Telugu experiment called *Maro Charitra* (Another History; 1978) starring Kamal and directed by K. Balachander. Something provoked L.V. Prasad to remake this experimental film in Hindi with Kamal in the lead and Balachander as director.

From Prasad's point of view, such remakes were not new; from Balachander's perspective, it was a chance worth taking because he could always come back to Tamil cinema; but if Kamal the actor-star failed in such a crossover project, nobody would forgive him. Nevertheless, it seemed as if destiny was at play again. The very film director who had pushed Kamal into the limelight as an actor was now going to make him cross the border as a Tamil boy falling in love with a North Indian girl. The summer of 1981 was indeed tense for Kamal. Here was the chance of a lifetime, but the audacity of taking on the likes of Rajesh Khanna, Amitabh Bachchan and Dharmendra, after acting in more than sixty Southern films, was indeed a serious risk.

When Kamal landed on location in Visakhapatnam to make a shot-by-shot copy of the original Telugu/Tamil film, he was on tenterhooks. Everybody was on location getting ready for the first shot and several other locations were already booked. Uppermost in Kamal's mind was the thought of what would happen if he failed. Would the Tamil industry still respect and embrace him, and take him back into its fold? How was he going to manage the rest of his life as a has-been hero? Impulsively, he called up Prasad Productions in Madras and said that he would go on set only if he was paid double his rate. After a few hours of intense discussion with the financiers, they agreed and called him back to say that they would pay up, since they had no choice.

Yet, this film called *Ek Duuje Ke Liye* (Made for Each Other) became memorable with music composed by Laxmikant–Pyarelal and Anand Bakshi's lyrics. The song *'Tere mere beech mein, kaisa hai ye bandhan anjaana'* (What is this strange bond between us?) would virtually become the national anthem of a nation for at least five years to come.

Kamal's dilemma was similar to the dilemma in the film's story. Should one trust one's natural instincts and fall in love, or should one rely on conventional and proven elderly wisdom? A Tamil boy called Vasu and a Hindi-speaking girl called Sapna strike an immediate rapport in idyllic Goa and want to get married. But Sapna's parents have fixed up Chakravarty, a groom within their family circle. Despite the warnings from the respective parents, the young couple is not willing to budge. As fate would have it, after many days of separation, young Vasu meets Chakravarty and is told that Sapna has already married him.

Vasu cannot believe his accursed fate and goes away from Goa only to walk into the arms of Sandhya, a good Samaritan in another city. Her brother Danny is happy that Sandhya has finally found a match. But when Sandhya comes to know about Vasu's failed relationship with Sapna, she decides to bring the two together again. She finds out that her marriage to Chakravarty actually never took place and tells Vasu, who rushes to meet Sapna. But their star-crossed destiny does not allow them to meet again. Sandhya's brother cannot forgive Vasu for dumping his sister and arranges for some goons to beat him up. At a parallel level, Sapna, who comes rushing to meet Vasu, is accosted by some thugs who rape her.

When the two meet on the furious wave-slapped rocks on the shores of Goa, they have both been scarred for life. Society did not allow their natural desires to be fulfilled but forced them to drift away on antagonistic 'cultured' paths. Their natural selves can never be the same again. Instead of compromising with such a world, they choose to end their lives. They jump into the alluring sea, which was the sole witness to their promise, and thus dissolve into the eternal narrative of star-crossed lovers.

While Balachander wrapped-up the high-strung melodrama within four weeks, Kamal was also in shreds. He had exhausted himself doing everything to make the film worth watching. From pushing trollies to setting up lights to make it look like a high-value Hindi film, he had drained himself to please both his mentor and the great movie mogul of Prasad Productions who had trusted his capabilities.

All post-production work was done in Madras, but when L.V. Prasad screened the first print for some of his select Bombay distribution buddies, it was a disaster. They said that the film was a washout. There was no way that they were going to release it or even promote it. Octogenarian Prasad, with his long years of experience, was not going to give up. He called Kamal over to Bombay so that he could acquaint himself with the Hindi filmdom.

In Bombay, Kamal was put up in a small hotel. Later that evening, he put on a smart blazer and went over to Prasad's office, expecting it to be grand. Instead it turned out to be a modest flat on the third floor of a building. It was decorated with the most spartan of furniture—some chairs and a steel table with a black telephone.

After a cup of tea, Prasad got up and said, 'I will need your help now!'

Kamal wondered what he needed until Prasad pointed to a big ugly metal-strapped film box containing the fourteen reels of his magnum opus. He said, 'Can you help me carry that box into the elevator?' Strangely this great movie mogul had no office boy or servants that day. Kamal immediately said, 'Of course, sir, I will carry it for you. You are not going to lug that heavy and slightly rusty box. It might hurt you!' Kamal carried the 30-kg box into the elevator and yet again from the elevator into the boot of the ordinary Ambassador car waiting below.

The car took them to a special screening at a preview theatre for a Delhi distributor. Prasad introduced Kamal to the gentleman. After the first reel commenced, Prasad excused himself and left, telling Kamal to get their guest some sandwiches and coffee during the intermission. Kamal sat embarrassed next to this pot-bellied distributor, trying to make small talk. But by the fifth reel even that was not required, as the distributor had fallen asleep. After a few more such screenings, a dejected Kamal flew back to Madras. How could Romeo and Juliet, the most famous of all tragedies ever written, fail to win attention in this accursed city of

Bombay? Nevertheless, putting on a brave face, Prasad met with his dear friend Gulshan Rai, a prominent Hindi film distributor, and requested him to lend his banner for the first release. The North–South divide was not going allow for a risky film to be launched on a South Indian banner. Gulshan Rai agreed and the film was released in just one theatre called Roxy with minimal publicity.

Prasad sat through each screening that weekend to study reactions. He saw audiences come out with tears in their eyes. Some people would tell him, 'How could the world be so cruel to such a lovely pair? This is so unfair!' Prasad realized that everybody had seen a wholesome tragedy after a long time on the Hindi screen and there was no difference in feelings between the Tamil audience he had been close to and their Hindi counterparts. Now sure that he was on the right track, he immediately called his son Ramesh Prasad in Madras to order for another forty prints to be released all over India the following Friday.

The film went on to celebrate fifty weeks. Kamal flew down to Bombay yet again for a special function to celebrate the film's success at the Novelty Theatre. This time he was a superstar, while his mentors Prasad and K. Balachander were still the same down-to-earth film veterans. They reached the theatre early and while inspecting the lobby, Prasad remarked, 'The floor is really spanking clean and shining, isn't it?'

Intrigued by this remark Kamal replied, 'Yes, it's clean but what is so special about that?'

Prasad replied, smiling, 'Do you know, when I was twenty-six years old, as old as you are now, I used to be an usher here and between screenings I had to mop this very floor clean every day? I am happy such traditions are still being followed by the workers here.'

Kamal was deeply humbled, not merely by knowing this fact, but more by the casual way in which this great man had mentioned it to him.

The film also got S.P. Balasubrahmanyam the National Award for the Best Playback Singer. This foray by a Southern artiste into the Hindi heartland was very significant, for it soon opened the doors for Yesudas, Chitra and others. The Hindi belt had found the Southern accent agreeable to its ears. This cross-cultural influx would continue—youngsters such as Chennai-based A.R. Rahman went on to make huge inroads into Bollywood even as Hindi playback singers like Lata Mangeshkar, Asha Bhosle and Udit Narayan entered recording studios in Chennai and Hyderabad to record Tamil and Telugu songs.

A few years and many more films later, Kamal met the legendary L.V. Prasad at the Prasad Studios in Chennai, which now had in its compound a brand new massive 70-mm recording and mixing studio, the first of its kind in Asia. Prasad stroked the side of the big building and told Kamal, 'This big baby you see is thanks to you and all those who worked on *Ek Duuje Ke Liye*. I put all the profits that I earned from it back to serve the same film industry that had briefly lost trust in my capabilities to make a successful film!'

Raaja Paarvai: *A New 'Hero' Figure*

For the first production by his company, Raaj Kamal Films International, Kamal decided to make *Raaja Paarvai* (The Royal Gaze; 1981). To direct it, he chose a virtually unknown filmmaker called Singeetam Srinivasa Rao, with whom he had worked earlier on a Telugu film.

Rao recalls, 'My first film with Kamal was *Iru Nilavugal* (1978). It was originally made in Telugu [as *Sommokadidhi Sokokadidhi*] and then dubbed in Tamil. It was one of those popular comic forms—a double-role story with an absent-minded doctor and a small-time crook who look exactly the same. Kamal had a penchant for comedies resulting from mistaken identities. A few years earlier I had also made *Dikkatra Parvathi* (1974) in Tamil—a grim, realistic film based on a story by Rajaji [C. Rajagopalachari]. Kamal had seen the film and been taken aback by its realism. It led him to feel that I was the right candidate to direct his company's first production too.

'The decision to have me direct the film [*Raaja Paarvai*] was taken when we were both onstage in Bombay receiving our Filmfare awards! I had just finished a low-budget art film, which was not going to make much money, and then I get this offer from a superstar for my next. I was thrilled, until he told me that it would be about a blind Hindu violinist, Raghu, falling in love with an attractive Christian girl, Nancy. He made it clear that he did not want to play a sympathy-gaining visually impaired poor soul, as was the norm. I did not know how to react. He wanted to play Raghu as a self-confident person—a musician who, though blind, sustains himself well. He wanted the other "normal" characters instead to flounder around with all kinds of deficiencies! It seemed a sure-fire recipe for disaster.'

Kamal's elder brother Chandrahasan, one of the producers, was also unconvinced about its fate. 'With two big names like Kamal and Ilaiyaraaja involved, I could just about begin some business talk but everyone who heard the story was simply unwilling to lend any money.'

In fact, all of Kamal's well-wishers at that time were very sceptical about this first production venture. Moreover, no actor in his or her right mind would venture into film production to make money since times were bad, they felt. Many in the industry even believed that Kamal was behaving irresponsibly by throwing away his popularity built on the success of his acting career.

The films that Kamal did from the mid-1970s had positioned him as an archetype of the young Indian youth wanting to experience his independence through expressions of sexuality. Doing away with the sacred burdens of sacrifice, righteousness and patriotism, valourized by his senior Sivaji Ganesan, here was Kamal positing an appropriate antithesis to him by breaking through the conservatism, not as an indolent and sex-starved adolescent, but like a 'mature', thinking adult. Expressing their sexuality was a virtue for the youth of the 1980s, who courted the other gender without the constraints of moralistic family ties and social barriers. In a nation just emerging from the Emergency and an equally chaotic Janata regime, Tamil Nadu's filmmakers chose to break free and establish a new expression of romance. This was also the era when most Tamil films either had very self-determined women or those sunk in deep despair. The typical Kamal script of the 1980s revelled in encountering women who defied all orthodox behavioural norms to carve out their own paths. Was it the remnant of the typical mid-1950s Dravidian postures of empowered women? Or was it a response to the modern women of the late 1970s as initiated by mentors like K. Balachander and K. Viswanath? Or was it just an antithesis to Kamal's not-too-standard postures of the Tamil metrosexual?

Raaja Paarvai's storyline is straightforward. Its main character, Raghu, is a musically gifted blind orphan. When his mother passed away his father remarried but the stepmother did not care for this blind stepson. And when the father too passed away, the stepmother decides to send him to a blind-school-cum-orphanage. She presumes that one day she will inherit her husband's property which is still in young Raghu's name. Raghu's skills on the violin gets him to be a musician in the film world where he meets his trusted friend Seenu and they share a dingy apartment. Raghu adjusts himself to a world where his landlord is mean, and his friends spend all their spare time drinking. Instead of confronting these odds like a regular hero, Kamal chooses to ignore them all until a young girl, Nancy, played by Madhavi, falls in love with him. She becomes his first love. Any reference to this first production would also be incomplete without mentioning another of Kamal's mentors, L.V. Prasad. In *Raaja Paarvai*, this mogul of the South Indian film industry played Nancy's liberated grandfather who encourages her romance with the blind musician.

The film's climax has the girl's father refusing to let her meet Raghu. He actually nurtures the idea of marrying her off to another Christian. Hearing this, Raghu does (what for him is) the unthinkable. He gets drunk with his friends and creates a nuisance in front of Nancy's house, which forces her to shout at him to get out. Taking advantage of this fragile tension, Raghu's greedy stepmother tells the girl and her father that Raghu is going to marry another girl. Soon after, she also lies to Raghu that Nancy is marrying another man and thus breaks his heart.

From a screenplay point of view, this betrayal by the stepmother could be quite an abrupt strategy, but from the larger socio-political perspective it was bang-on. The stepmother was a rather common character in many of

Kamal's earlier films and she was always shown as possessive and craving for power. It seemed to resonate the larger anxieties of the Tamil people who were subject to the constant diatribe between the two Dravidian parties who would do anything to retain their ruling positions.

These basics in themselves, as per the Tamil film industry norm of the time, should have produced a tear-jerking potboiler. But to Kamal, here was a hero who would surmount the insurmountable for he had nothing to lose except his freedom to seek the hand of the woman he loved most. In every way, this first production of Kamal's was a metaphor for his unabashed love for cinema. Kamal was confident and felt that Raghu—blind and battling the intolerant world with its religious and work prejudices and the ever prevalent rich–poor divide—would provide the sentimental core of the film.

'It was obvious that he [Kamal] wanted to produce an offbeat kind of film within mainstream Tamil cinema,' says Singeetam Srinivasa Rao. 'It was a huge risk, but with him in the lead, I thought it a risk worth taking. And I hoped that Raaja Paarvai—incidentally his hundredth film—would be a lucky one.'

For a good part of the film, Rao tries to depict how a blind young man attempts to use his tactile and other senses to discover the world around and the physical beauties of a woman. Raja Paarvai thus required a new kind of acting style—Raghu could not see but Kamal, through this character, wanted his audience to realize Nancy's beauty even though he could not experience it visually himself. The image and sounds of Nancy on-screen seen by the viewer to the accompaniment of a song teases the audience to seek the inner, almost divine beauty of the human being. Bruce Kawin refers to such a point of view stating, 'A mindscreen presents the landscape as the mind's eye, much as a subjective camera presents what is seen by the physical eye. A mindscreen can show what a character thinks—the cinematic equivalent of 'stream of consciousness'.[1] Wearing a bikini, Madhavi addresses an entirely new Tamil youth's mindscape by letting them gaze at her, albeit through the point of view of a blind person. Raghu cannot see her, but we can all see and interiorize the raw sexual power of a new identity, which would get further enhanced a few years later with the films of Balu Mahendra and Mani Ratnam.

In the context of such nuanced acting, Kamal recalled conversations with the master thespian Sivaji Ganesan. 'You know, I used to ask Mr Sivaji Ganesan as to where he picked up those amazing nuances he would display onscreen. You see, he worked his way up from the melodramatic theatrical stage. He could swing from an over-the-top performance to under-the-table subtlety. He had an amazing range and I used to watch his performances with my mouth open and feel as though I was falling from a great height. I watched him so intensely and so, when I asked him who his source of inspiration and style was, he replied with two names: Laurence Olivier and, believe it or not, Orson Welles! I never knew that he even got to see any of their films, given his circumstances.

'Very emphatically he said [of Laurence Olivier], "That guy had style!", and I realized that these people had that kind of sense to recognize international quality. And Sivaji sir would talk about the genius of L.V. Prasad. He used to call him his guru! They learnt all their craft hands-on. It was as if they got into their cars, drove them fast and then went on pick up their licences!'

It is this antithetical position—an actor trying to establish himself not by mimicking Sivaji's charisma, but by making the necessary quantum leaps to create a new legacy for himself—that made the transition from the era of Sivaji to the era of Kamal so meaningful and seamless. Making this transition more significant was the sad fact that fifty-four-year-old Sivaji was still playing romantic roles opposite the same heroines as twenty-five-year-old Kamal. What would you expect a modern post-Independence generation to do other than simply reject the old and ring in the new?

For Kamal, choosing to play a blind man in 1980 was not merely an act of faith, but a way of seeing his own body through the eyes of a new nation, a woman from a different faith and the semiotics of a new melodrama.

The amazing songs by Ilaiyaraaja and some superb cinematography by Mumbai-based Barun Mukerjee also brought a new touch of realism to this melodramatic tour-de-force.

The strong plot-oriented screenplay also drives us to look at the factors that impelled this imperative—the need for an aesthetic point of view which could truly evoke the multi-sensorial way that any art form must approach reality. In front of good art we are all equally blind and the work demands that we open all our senses and enter its ecstatic zone. Kamal, like many discontented youngsters of the late 1970s, belonged to a new young Madras gang that frequented film societies and film festivals, absorbing all kinds of international trends like sponges. Along with Rao, Kamal and the team would sit through hours of VHS tapes to come up with new visions for this first production. *Raja Paarvai*'s script, written by his mentor Ananthu, reflects resonances from the East European delicacies served up by Milos Forman, blended with the unconventional brashness of Mike Nichols in the 1977 classic, *The Graduate*.

Addressing students years later in 2010 at IIT Bombay, Kamal reflected on the days that had led up to the launch of Raaj Kamal Films International and *Raja Paarvai*.

'You have seen some of the Tamil films, terrible ones,' he said. 'Do you think we are responsible people at all? I admit most of us are irresponsible. One or two guys raise a voice in between to make us seem responsible. Yes, there is a civic responsibility; as much as there is for a pedestrian, it is there for an actor, for a filmmaker too, but we seem to have forgotten it in pursuit of working for moneybags. I know that this is a management school and I must talk to you about compromises in management. You don't have to compromise. You still can make money. And I am standing proof [of it]!'

The last word lies with Rao, who has a way of assessing his work with detachment, unlike other directors: 'The film was undoubtedly a critical success, had great songs by Ilaiyaraaja, but somehow did not do well at the box office. The reason could be two-fold. One, audiences had got used to seeing Kamal as the glamorous and dancing lover boy. And so it was a big risk on our part to put him in a sort of unsentimental, serious role like this. Two, the film was not an "achievement" story. It did not give the hero a certain goal to pursue. Even his interest in Madhavi is seen more at the level of wanting a companion. So his running away with the girl at the end of the film was not probably what the audience expected in terms of heroics. The film was more typical of the "slice-of-life" film genre.'

But was Kamal exploring the reality of Tamil people at that time? When cineastes would ask Kamal what, according to him, would be a successful film, he often said, 'The success of a film cannot be measured by its box-office revenue but the way in which the film stays in the memories of its audiences much after the film has exited from its exalted status on the silver screen. You just have to ask a fellow Tamilian and I can assure you he would not have forgotten *Raja Paarvai*.'

7

SAKALAKALA VALLAVAN AND *ENAKUL ORUVAN*: VENTURES INTO POPULAR CINEMA

Sakalakala Vallavan

In 1983, my film *Ezhavathu Manithan* (The Seventh Man; 1982) received one National Award and was honoured at the Moscow International Festival. But back in Chennai, it was a struggle to get the film released, appreciated and keep the box-office coffers clinking every day. And one of the obstacles was a film called *Sakalakala Vallavan* (The Master of All Arts; 1982) starring Kamal Haasan and running to packed houses in a theatre right next door to the one playing my film. I cannot count the number of days my crew members and I spent hanging around trade union offices, convincing them to buy our film's tickets in bulk (the film was about the exploitation of industrial workers). We would assemble each evening to review the day's sales efforts and lament the poor taste of our audiences. We would reiterate how important it was to carry on our protests against the evils of mainstream blockbusters like *Sakalakala Vallavan*. We almost believed that commercial success was something of a curse that should not visit a good filmmaker, lest his martyrdom to a cause be snatched away by 'plebeians' who could lay claim to understanding those rare pearls of wisdom scattered over his laboured yet moving images.

The predicament of good actors like Kamal and others in mainstream cinema in that era (and perhaps even now) was often similar. They did not believe that they were acting in a 'bad' film, for they worked hard to deliver the intended narration, however formulaic. But when these films became blockbusters, many of them felt the need to apologize with statements such as, 'Well, that's what the people want, and we need to do one or two formula films like these once in a while to keep in touch with the common man and woman on the street!' The subtleties in their performances were intended for the 'connoisseurs of cinema', not for the 'vulgar masses' who sipped tea from the roadside vendor! Some Indian actors felt that they also needed to do English plays, participate in rallies for the underprivileged and host TV programmes for the physically impaired or at least become a member of the Rajya Sabha, mostly after being decorated with a Padma Shri.

Writing an objective and analytical report about Kamal and his relationship to *Sakalakala Vallavan* would have been inconceivable in 1983. The film had stormed across silver screens throughout South India like a hurricane. My so-called 'socially purposeful', 'politically sensitive', National-Award-winning film *Ezhavathu Manithan* could not hope to compete even in the slightest with this 'masala' film, let alone pack the theatres at every show. At that time we, the intelligentsia, simply distanced ourselves from this gross travesty and even admonished the millions who thronged the theatres to watch it. It was hard to stomach that Kamal, who had just done the delicate *Moondram Pirai* (1982), was an integral part of this awful piece of ribaldry.

Today when I revisit *Sakalakala Vallavan,* however, I can look at it very differently. I am able to contextualize the statement by its director S.P. Muthuraman who told me, 'I had to work hard to convince Kamal to act in a formula film *like Sakalakala Vallavan* and make him realize the importance of restoring the star value of an actor. After all, we were both part and parcel of the same context, which nurtured us. Kamal's first film, *Kalathur Kannamma*, when he was five years old, was also my first film as an assistant director when I was seventeen. We owed each other a certain right to enter the cinematic limelight!'

Let's ask ourselves. What is a film driven by a star? This narrative of artists traipsing through commercial/popular art forms is now, for me and I am sure for many other scholars, a site which reveals the complex socio-political layers of any nation's popular culture. Yet, why do India's mainstream films get so maligned when compared to Hollywood's popular cinema? How are they able to celebrate and seriously discuss their popular films and stars like Robert De Niro or Brad Pitt? Rewind and we shall know that this did not happen by chance but thanks to a concerted move by the Hollywood studio moguls in the 1940s to attack the censorship laws being imposed by the state. Studio owners like George Cukor convinced Iris Barry, director of the Museum of Modern Art in New York, that she should buy copies of good Hollywood films and preserve them like other works of art in their venerable collection. Very soon, American audiences felt proud of such acquisitions and select Hollywood films would be recognized on par with high-quality progressive art. Thus, the label of mainstream was not so 'vulgar' after all.

In such a context, it is important to study films such as *Sakalakala Vallavan*. First, the film works perfectly well in the larger narrative of the behrupiya or the disguised impersonator, a concept with which Kamal shares an immense bond. In this film, he uses make-up and multiple guises as he serenades and fights his way through the duration of the movie. It works as a metaphor at many levels while also functioning as a robust folk tale with solid doses of profanity to narrate the sacred text of the modern 'rural Tamil' hero in the post-Dravidian context of the 1980s. Second, Kamal had established himself by this time as a 'persona' on screen, having done about fifty-five films. He had essayed a variety of roles, gracefully taking over the space of his mentor Sivaji Ganesan. He epitomized teenage romance with his sensuous body, voice and intelligence.

Modern 'rurality' is not an oxymoron when it comes to Tamil Nadu, which is probably the most urbanized state in India. People still do live in mud-walled mansions, but with electric appliances and LED TV sets, while preferring to sleep and weave urban dreams on a wooden-roped cot. *Sakalakala Vallavan* is probably the most outlandish folk tale of post-Emergency Tamil Nadu, where the hero has to romance a state torn between the values bequeathed by an old English-speaking Presidency and the trying-to-be modern Tamil chauvinist identity. Kamal as Velu represents the landed rural gentry, which is forced to confront the cruel capitalist class in the form of a heartless woman landlord-cum-moneylender called Parvathi, played by Pushpalata.

Was she an allusion to Indira Gandhi, at least at a subliminal level? Her husband is henpecked but always criticizes her exploitative ways. Her Westernized daughter arrives in a big car and has nothing but condescension towards the rural folk. To balance this conceited daughter is a son, a spoilt brat who has a vamp tucked away in the city. Velu, on the other hand, has a slavish father, a gullible mother, an innocent sister and a dumb sidekick for laughs—certainly not the best soil for intelligent growth.

To confront the cruel landlady, Velu has to tame the Westernized daughter and also get his sister to marry/transform the wayward brother to accept his rural utopia. From a pure folk-tale point of view, the characters assume a near-perfect 'archetypal' balance and Velu has the heroic task of reconciling the arrogant urbanized rich with the wisdom of the rural folk.

At first, Velu, with his exaggerated long hairdo and an even more exaggerated rural Tamil accent, displays the 'symbolic' power of the bullock cart over the big car owned by the landlord's daughter. The conflict in the modes of transportation becomes the central trope to represent the power of the idyllic yet wealthy Tamil societal landscape, which had become capable of urbanizing itself without having to shift to the big cities.

This echoes an article written by Ashis Nandy, 'Science, Hegemony and Violence—A Requiem for Violence'[1], in which he explains how common people offer themselves for sacrifice at the altar of development. Nandy's argument can be extended to *Sakalakala Vallavan* in order to make us ask why Velu cannot simply ignore the car and leave the Westernized woman to her own quaint ways. Why does Velu have to get through two songs to win her heart? Is it just to pose a threat to the crooked ways of her mother, the evil landlady, and her brother? The actual task of the narrative is to enrage Velu into going and suffering in the city of Madras. But it takes a different direction—the insolent brother, instead of confronting Velu, goes and rapes Velu's sister, thus bringing Velu's family to the brink of dishonour and shame. In return, Velu chooses not to avenge his sister's rape but vows to get this errant rich man married to his sister somehow or the other.

In today's time, this proposition would be scandalous. But the laws of 'development' and the legality of the 'scientific/rational state' during Mrs Gandhi's days would not permit slaying one's own 'native' fellow in the face of a colonial legal system. The situation had to be resolved through artful compromise. The hero sacrifices his rural identity and metamorphoses into a rock singer, ushering in the new year in a big urban club by riding onto the stage on a motorcycle. The snooty girl's big car is now challenged by the motorcycle and the heroine falls for this dashing hero! By adopting the ways of a Westernized Sam, Velu entraps the arrogant landlord's family into conforming to the 'good old' rural ways of Tamil Nadu. Even after thirty-two years the New Year song sung by S.P. Balasubrahmanyam and scored by Ilaiyaraaja is still played in the most sophisticated clubs of South India.

In his avatar as Sam, Velu speaks in an American accent. His sister meanwhile transforms into a modern short-haired girl with outrageous glasses in order to lure the very man who raped her. The impersonation works well as the greedy mother readily agrees to the marriage of her daughter to Sam and her son to Sam's sister. When the weddings are completed, Sam and his sister reveal their original 'rural' identities to shock the cruel family. Now, the rich family's honour is at stake and the only way out is to kill the impersonators.

The climax of the film is entirely centred on outlandish car chases all over the city. The very automobile that enraged Velu becomes an agent of wanton destruction and mindless violence in the streets of Madras. Director S.P. Muthuraman has a tendency to stretch his fight scenes until he reaches a 'happy climax' scene.

Recalling the long list of atrocities in the name of capitalist progress committed through the twentieth century, from the two World Wars to the Iraq War, Claude Alvares in his article titled 'Science, Colonialism and Violence—A Luddite View' laments about how the dominant images (of modern development) are that of science and violence:

The former is considered as intrinsically good and the latter as universally evil. Yet paradoxically, the more science, the more violence. In our times, even nations at peace are economically at war: their economies are driven by war machines and war manias. Indirect wars are equally severe and devastating; the construction of a dam in the midst of a natural river course, the destruction of its catchment-area forests, the uprooting of thousands of living organisms and beings.[2]

So who were the Luddites? In 1817, much before Marx would talk about the grave threats being posed by the capitalist system, the Luddites were smashing industrial machinery because mechanization had snatched the jobs of common people in the name of growth and productivity. Studying *Sakalakala Vallavan* in this light, could one call Kamal and the entire system of mainstream cinema, especially in Tamil Nadu, a sort of Luddite offensive, which unsettled the capitalism and its supportive political organizational coordinates?

Mainstream Tamil cinema has always been engaged in a war with the larger hegemony of Hindi cinema and its so-called nationalist politics. Therefore, until 1975, it was intrinsically bound with the vernacular Dravidian movement to unsettle the pseudo-nationalist vision of the Nehruvian dynastic politics. In the spirit of the Luddites, both of these together smashed the Hindi-speaking culture and the dominance of the Brahminical Congress hierarchy, and abandoned their elaborate and ubiquitous temple cultures by embracing atheism in protest. Kamal entered the scene serendipitously during the Emergency in 1975, around the time of the ignominious betrayal of the so-called Dravidian ideology by both MGR and Karunanidhi.

Kamal was thus a Luddite, entrusted not only with the resurrection of the Tamil spirit but also keeping the Hindi mainstream monster at bay. And it was by no means an easy task to become an iconic symbol in such a turbulent period. Virtually working around the clock, gaining tons of experience, empowering himself by joining hands with fellow Luddites such as Bharathiraja, K. Balachander, Ilaiyaraaja, Rajinikanth and others, Kamal achieved this seemingly impossible breakthrough in just about five to six years. And when he chose to rest on his laurels by working in the films of his personal 'intellectual' mentors like Balachander, Ananthu and Balu Mahendra, S.P. Muthuraman jerked him out and brought him back to the 'popular' Luddite ways for which he had been virtually nurtured.

Reacting to the words I have written above, Kamal wrote back:

Fascinating. True, neither of us [Ananthu or Kamal] could have looked at *Sakalakala Vallavan* with equipoise in 1983. Even now I guess the scholar has contained the revolutionary and the Darwinian logic tries to settle the dispute in a still-ongoing battle for heading the food chain.

My honest confession: I was ready to use all the subterfuges of the National Socialist Democratic Party (Germany 1936) to gain power in the corridors of commercial cinema. Being an ardent fan of Chaplin and also seeing the film scholars of Cahiers du Cinema taking over from the old papa French cinema emboldened us. The 'us' were exactly two persons: Mr Ananthu and I. We decided to infiltrate the not-so-well-guarded citadel with as many Trojan horses as we could roll in. This is not an afterthought embellishment of plans gone astray but the actual plan.

The fact remains—commercial filmmakers are simple and honest beings, not governed by philosophies, either moral or ethical. Martyrdom is the first virtue or utopia we destroyed. We wanted to live to tell the story. G.V. Iyer was the first man who caught on to our strategy. He advised me to keep out of the so-called Kannada and the national art film revolt. He found that it would flounder for lack of feed. The counter-revolution is still on. Now with the distribution platforms, multiplying entertainment is entering a new era, like in the times of sound and colour entering silent movies.

I see infotainment as the latest political and artistic field of battle of ideologies and intend to be part of it. I see gaming and news interlacing into a núero-plastic platform. I am glad I am alive and healthy to be part of that paradigm shift. Time for Sophocles who will be the voice of the people! While Russia and China are opting for authoritarian capitalism and the capitalistic mantra has become equity they have successfully and subcutaneously exchanged ideologies. The next ten years of our lives are going to be exciting. Hope my system can bear it and be cognizant of it!

Sakalakala Vallavan was the booster rocket which propelled Kamal into secondary orbit, that is to say, shot his celebrity status sky-high and beyond, quite like the way our own Mangalyaan was blasted away from the earth's orbit into the Martian circuit!

Enakkul Oruvan: Karz *Revamped*

If K. Balachander was Kamal's intellectual pillar, S.P. Muthuraman, the quintessential commercial filmmaker from AVM Studios, was his mass-appeal springboard. His *Sakalakala Vallavan*, as discussed above, had placed Kamal firmly atop the blockbuster pedestal.

Well trained under several filmmakers, including A.V. Meiyappan, S.P. Muthuraman believed that every shot in his film had to convey a story in the simplest terms possible. Each shot must be produced at minimum cost and must make all the members of his unit happy! Muthuraman had released over thirty-five films between 1977 and 1982, marked by his unique formulaic style, and a staggering 75 per cent had met with box-office success. Yet, when faced with a star like Kamal, Muthuraman had to seriously think about ways—however bizarre and complex—of accommodating him in his style of cinema.

This meant getting Kamal to do a film that would appeal to both the actor and his unit at the same time. Muthuraman knew fully well that Kamal was drawn to films that provided unique challenges, rather than typical masala fare. He also knew that he himself had been identified by viewers as someone who would provide 'standard-variety meals' on the table in different ways. So, in mid-1982, he roped in Kamal's mentor K. Balachander as the producer and proposed to direct a film on the subjects of reincarnation and extrasensory perception, but without any of the superstitious shamanism usually associated with them. The story rights of the Hindi blockbuster *Karz* (Debt; 1980, starring Rishi Kapoor and Tina Munim) were acquired from director Subhash Ghai. This film in turn had been inspired by *The Reincarnation of Peter Proud* (1975).

Thus was *Enakkul Oruvan* (Someone Within Me; 1984) conceived. The details were then discussed and a package ironed out to ensure that everyone was happy. Kamal played Madan in the film, a so-called typical disco dancer who hallucinates about a Bharatanatyam dancer marrying a man who looks just like him. The man dies the day after the marriage in bizarre circumstances. Madan has no clue who the dancer is but is able to finally locate and put an end to the villain who is the cause of his psychological trauma.

All the above ingredients fitted into S.P. Muthuraman's formula. Choreography—Kamal was adept at modern/Western dancing; sex— there was ample opportunity for sequences with skimpily clad women gyrating around him; stunts—there was scope for over-the-top fight scenes where good would trounce evil; and locations—using the entire spectrum of lenses, filters, gadgets and new technology available at that time. Madan's lookalike character would provide the platform for a lot of stunts, while Kamal's two women co-stars (the heroine and the woman in the hallucination) could balance his Western dancing with their traditional dancing skills. The comedy quotient was to be provided by the parents and sidekicks.

To get Kamal's nod, the story introduced a psychoanalyst—a character not so visible in the real Indian medical landscape at the time—to play a part within a mainstream film. Even today there are just about 10,000 practising qualified mental-health practitioners in India. That was a calculated risk taken by Muthuraman so that Kamal, the logical modernist, would come on board. Kamal had to work equally hard in those scenes to make the concept of a character having the ability to undergo extra-sensory perceptions and not confusing it with a traditional flashback or trying to recollect a distant memory. The psychoanalyst was played by veteran actor Calcutta Viswanathan, who smoked a pipe or a cigar with British elegance and spoke Tamil with a clipped accent.

Next, the intriguing split personality of Madan's doppelganger had to be introduced with equal novelty and demanded some of Kamal's incredible resources, including his martial arts skills. The 1980s were incidentally the period when Bruce Lee, kung fu and the Eastern pugilistic modes stirred the imagination of the masses. So how was Kamal going to blend into that East Asian mould and still speak reasonably good Tamil? The solution was found in portraying the 'other' Madan as a rich Nepali businessman who was also a renowned martial artist and lived in Darjeeling. By default, this gave our 'bahuroopi' Kamal the opportunity to work on some prosthetics whereby his face could be stretched, the outer corners of his eyes pulled up, and all the special effects topped off with a wig. This look would export him into the northern Mongolian territories.

K. Balachander produced a story never told before in Tamil cinema, with some of his anti-Brahminical punches thrown in; Muthuraman got to make a star-based commercial film with his own AVM unit members; Kamal got to act in an unusual double role, enter new motivational territories and exhibit several of his well-known talents; and the audience got to see Darjeeling as never seen before, watch their superstar dance and fight, while also admiring some wonderful traditional dances by the two heroines—Shobana and Sripriya—to the music composed by maestro Ilaiyaraaja. Is this not a lesson on how a not-so-commercial film needs to be devised in a manner where it can easily be sold to a huge market of distributors across Tamil Nadu?

The film was shot in forty days and the post-production executed in another forty days. It ran for an average of forty days per theatre in the forty screens where it was released in 1982, to make enough money for another two films, at least. The reason for this deconstruction of the production strategies behind *Enakkul Oruvan* is to elucidate, for the benefit of the reader, the coining of a mainstream film in typical circumstances. It makes one understand how 'cinema' is like any other industrial product with competitors, market realities and customer choices. Cars or biscuits are not labelled 'commercial' or 'art'; so why should we label films in such a manner? I have come to realize that in order to produce and release four films a year, Muthuraman had arrived at certain templates which facilitated all 'vendors' in the production assembly line in providing their expertise within a certain budget and specific time schedule to deliver a viable product.

Such films make one realize the true industrial nature of filmic activity and the expertise displayed by Muthuraman in building up some wonderful teamwork. Certainly, such a film would not figure in any National Award category simply because there is no 'auteur'-like quality about it that could please the high-brow intellectuals sitting on juries. And the fact that a film is a successful venture can actually work as a deterrent at these screenings.

So why would Kamal want to do films labelled as run-of-the-mill by the intelligentsia that he identified with? Muthuraman feels, 'Kamal was as much my boy as he was K. Balachander's. Working in so many Balachander films at the start of his career, Kamal believed that as an actor, he was perfect only for such out-of-the-box films. But I felt that as an actor, he should not—and nor could he afford to—identify with the ambitions of a single director and his audience. He had to display his talents to the widest audiences possible with as many filmmakers available. So, I made him agree to work in my films too and I can confidently say that if audiences of B- and C-grade films ever got to see him, it was thanks to my films!'

Undoubtedly, it was thanks to films like *Enakkul Oruvan* that villagers saw Kamal play a Nepali man connecting with a Tamil Bharatanatyam dancer in picturesque Darjeeling; saw him perform some fine kung fu moves; saw him play a clown in the make-up of an old Brahmin dance teacher; saw what brain-scan equipment in ultra-modern hospitals looked like; and enjoyed Kamal's scintillating Western dance movements in the two songs assigned to him. Just imagine hundreds of young villagers going back home trying to mimic the dance of this unusual superstar all the way! And, by total default, if there is a film today which has documented for posterity the nooks and corners of Darjeeling in 1984, it is this!

Despite all the haloes created around cinema as an art, the routine of filmmaking is often tedious and monotonous for every filmmaker, much like the routines of a cashier in an air-conditioned bank or a site supervisor on the construction of a metro line. Now, one can imagine a day in the life of Kamal who has done nothing else over the past fifty years other than moving from one film to another. All the excitement of watching his films, produced over seventy days, happens in those 140 minutes of projection in a darkened space. Popular actor Vijay Setupathi said in an interview, 'We should not compare ourselves with artistes of yesteryears such as Thyagaraja, the great Carnatic music composer. We need technology, a lot of money and audiences to pay for this entertainment. And yet, we need to have a certain determination not to be engulfed in this matrix but struggle to move beyond the limitations.'

It can only be Kamal's passion for his art that has saved him from the actual trauma and drudgery of a typical filmmaker's life.

8

TWO UNIQUE LOVE STORIES: *MOONDRAM PIRAI* AND *SALANGAI OLI*

A Freudian Folk Tale

'Love is a state of temporary psychosis.'—Sigmund Freud

Across the world, folk tales tend to depict stories of the valorous, the witty and the heroic committed to a cause larger than life. *Moondram Pirai* (The Crescent on the Third Day of the New Moon; 1982) by Balu Mahendra lies at the crossroads of just such a heroic saga. In a screenwriting class, Balu described the plot thus: 'Just imagine, a zestful heroine meets with a road accident and loses her memory. In the local hospital, a stranger, claiming to be her relative, takes her away and sells her to a brothel. Next: imagine our hero, a young schoolteacher, is reluctantly brought into the brothel by his friend. Our hero meets the heroine here and is unable to bear the plight of a young woman with no memories, forced to live the rest of her life as a prostitute. With no personal motivation whatsoever, he decides to kidnap her, yet again! Now what?'

In this National Award-winning performance, Kamal plays Srinivasan aka Cheenu, who decides to rescue Bhagyalakshmi aka Vijaya (played by Sridevi) from an urban brothel to give her a better life. The story then shifts to the two of them living in an idyllic hill station, where Cheenu is a lonely, almost adolescent schoolteacher on the cusp of a new and precarious sexual awakening.

Cheenu brings her safely to his home in Ooty, where an elderly woman staying next door also welcomes this young girl. Although the girl lives with Cheenu in his quarters, the old woman's presence and proximity is intended to prevent the audience from having needless anxiety about the girl's sexual safety. They know that she is safe with the older woman when Cheenu is away at school and that the mother figure will probably infuse some ethical/moral principles into this rather precarious relationship. Cheenu seems to take care of Vijaya like an elder brother would, in an almost paternal way. The subliminal text makes us wonder how, through the passage of time, will this girl with the mind of a six-year-old manage to wear a variety of new dresses; who bathes her and dresses her up; how does this girl attend to some of the other issues attached to having a twenty-year-old's body?

But the narrative of a folk tale presumes that audiences are more bothered about the larger goal of the film—will she stay with him forever; will she regain her memory and marry him; or will she regain her memory and leave him, to lead her own normal life? The desire to see which of these three options fructifies ensures that the audience does not mind the rather frail storyline, the inadequacies of the doctor's explanations about amnesia, or the shamanistic saint who later claims that he can cure her amnesiac condition with some green leaves within six to seven hours. In sharp contrast to all this tension is the setting of the film—the idyllic cool hills of Ooty, photographed for the first time in misty conditions, to enhance the story.

The folk-tale mindset pitches for Srinivasan to save the girl from her temporary amnesia and then claim her hand in an honourable manner. The Freudian approach secretly desires that the pubescent Cheenu should give in to his sexual urges, and probably repent later after seeing the consequences. Watching the film, one realizes that Kamal is enjoying the battle of dual intentions. Duality is further amplified by the names of the two characters (both do not use their real names). Not knowing her real name, Cheenu decides to call her Vijaya and she playfully calls him Cheenu (the traditional nickname for Srinivasan).

For Kamal, this was indeed the role of a lifetime, with no make-up, costumes or any of the signature flamboyant song-and-dance routines that were a must in all his films at that time. Tamil audiences in the 1980s were showing themselves to be receptive of the slew of such new-wave films.

Balu Mahendra deftly weaves the two sides of Kamal's character into a masterful conflict between the morality-bound male ego and the pleasure-seeking sexual id. The conflict in this saga is provided by the strange predicament of the heroine, who is suffering from a sort of temporary amnesia caused by a road accident. Since that makes her one suffering from regressive amnesia, for most of the duration of the movie she is incapable of recognizing the efforts made by the hero to bring her back to normalcy. She is like a fairy-tale princess in deep sleep, waiting for Prince Charming to kiss her awake. Except in this case, once she awakens she will not be able to recognize Srinivasan/Cheenu, nor remember all the emotional struggles he has gone through for her sake. Such a situation immediately puts the audience in the driver's seat as they fully back the Samaritan efforts made by the hero to preserve the childlike innocence of the young woman.

This was Kamal's second outing with Balu Mahendra, after *Kokila* (1977). Balu told me laughingly, 'There was a simple formula here for creating the sexual vulnerability of this odd couple, namely, the tension of waiting for that one private moment where Cheenu would falter and make love. So, I just alternated the shots between close-ups of the two and extreme long shots of this paradisiacal landscape in the larger mise-en-scène of the film. The loneliness of the two gets entrenched in the mindscape of the audiences who already know what a popular hill station Ooty is, a place where so many young Tamil couples go for their honeymoon! But I don't show much of the touristy areas. This is how we deceive the viewers!'

Kamal recalls, 'What I learnt from Balu Mahendra during the shoot was the art of switching over from the operative cameraman to the director and back. And many say that the relationship between the cameraperson and the director is like a well-adjusted husband and wife where distinctly different jobs come together through an amicable mindset. Balu had the ability to take quality time in lighting up the space and framing. Once he had done that, he would just forget about it and focus entirely on the action and the performance. This lesson proved very valuable when I later started directing and acting in my own films. While giving directions I would be the tough taskmaster wanting everything to synchronize well and achieve the wanted portrayals. But once the camera started rolling I was focused on just the character I was supposed to be.'

Balu had a different perspective: 'My films always reflect my own predilections. My films were largely women-centric and I did not want to settle for the stereotypes commonly witnessed on-screen. Therefore, I decided to get unique ideas from the very talented women that I cast. This required focused one-on-one conversations with them to extract responses from their experiences and feelings. Therefore, many critics saw this film as a kind of autobiography where I am constantly exploring the inner thoughts of my female characters. But it is also my belief that this story was equally the journey of Kamal Haasan—a daredevil who adventured into the most dangerous terrains with no resources to back him up. Like Cheenu, he was just determined to do good in what he could do best—love his fellow beings at any cost.'

The folk tale additionally shifts into a parallel terrain of the Biblical narrative of Adam and Eve—two innocent children of God sharing a guiltless world of proximity with no libidinous tendencies. The Adam in Cheenu is so innocent and committed to this childlike young woman in his house that he cannot understand the overtures made by the wife of the principal of the school where he works. This character is played by the popular Silk Smitha, known largely for doing cabaret dance numbers.

At the level of the Biblical narrative, the frustrated school principal's wife has another crucial function. She is one of the Satanic intrusions, along with a lecherous ironmonger who tries to molest Vijaya, in order to disturb the innocent relation between the two. Fortunately, both these forces do not traumatize Vijaya enough to shake off the amnesia which traps her. They are unable to break the beautiful relationship between the two; instead, they strengthen their bonding. On the other hand, the libidinous proclivity of Srinivasan/Cheenu, at least from the audience's mindset, achieves its orgasmic culmination when they get to watch Silk Smitha seduce him, now as the bold Srinivasan, in an imaginary sequence, a song which would soon become iconic. Balu often expressed his embarrassment at having to include such an adulterous character and seductive dance due to the enormous pressure of the distributors. 'Hopefully, the heavenly photographic quality of Ooty's landscape and the minimalistic dance movements will make me forgive myself for making such a compromise,' he said during one of our discussions.

Amplifying this primordial mindscape is Kamal's superlative performance, as he acts like an enslaved monkey dancing to the commands of Sridevi's character Vijaya, who is the master. Kamal's animalistic antics, while reinforcing childlike innocence, also provided him the only chance to alienate himself from the text, don another disguise and play his signature 'bahuroopi' role. What must be understood is that Kamal had nurtured his audience to such an extent that they had come to expect that he would disguise himself at some point in every film to surprise them. Filmmakers had to accommodate this as a sort of internal ritual in the scripting process itself for his films.

Paradoxically, the narrative later resorts to 'divine intervention' in the guise of a holy man in the mountains who offers to bring Vijaya out of the amnesiac trance. Balu was never a believer, but he felt that it would be too conventional to resolve this typical melodramatic story through a bloody fight involving Vijaya or through some kind of rape attack/trauma that brings her memory back again. He did not even give too much importance to the saintly godman who does herbal treatment to revive her memory. Instead, he reserves the trauma for Cheenu at the railway station, where he comes as she is leaving, fully recovered, hoping to revive her memories of the time she spent with him in their idyllic house in the misty hills of Ooty. But Vijaya, seated in the train, is now completely back to her old self, Bhagyalakshmi, and fails to recognize Srinivasan/Cheenu as he tries his best to get her attention.

As the train starts moving, he follows her coach, trying to perform some of the monkey-like antics he would amuse her with earlier but suddenly he crashes into a lamppost and falls. The train chugs away into the distance, leaving him staring at it like a person who has lost his mental balance. Will he be blessed with some kind of amnesia, which will help erase the memories of the best days of his life? In the words of Freud, 'Unexpressed emotions will never die. They are buried alive and will come forth in uglier ways.'

In the public discourse, Kamal has always maintained his position as an atheist of a playful sort. 'I never said I do not believe in God. I only said that I wished there was a God up there!' With the Tamil landscape being literally packed with temples, mosques, churches, where stars have a fiercely ritualistic fan base cutting across all religions, Kamal is walking a tightrope. If he ever hurts the sentiments of his fans and loses his grip on their imagination, he could fall off that tightrope in an instant for good.

Kamal sides with the rationalism of the early Dravidian movement and its patron saint E.V. Ramasamy Naicker or Periyar, who was a serious and vociferous atheist. His religious audiences cannot snap their ties with Periyar, their political patron saint, and at the same time, they cannot desert their icon, Kamal, whom they have nurtured as a symbol of popular Tamil cultural identity ever since he offered his prayers to Lord Muruga as a five-year-old child actor in *Kalathur Kannamma*. He is part of their imaginary set of icons/leaders, enshrined as the various heroic characters he's played onscreen. Other icons include Sivaji Ganesan, MGR, Nagesh and Gemini Ganesan. Having acted with all of them, Kamal is seen as having been blessed by these patriarchs. The audience still expects him to break conventions and move forward, as would be typical of any heroic force.

The dichotomy of Srinivasan (incidentally, Kamal's father's name) and Cheenu represents precisely this dilemma between the old-world rationalist who strongly believes in women's emancipation and the naiveté of the contemporary character of Cheenu as seen by a Vijaya who has no knowledge of her identity. He is struggling to come to terms with his adulthood post Indira Gandhi's Emergency and the consequent capitulation of the Dravidian party politics. At the same time in our discussions, my friend Balu Mahendra told me that he did not see his role, while making this film, as a commentary on Tamil Nadu's politics of those times. I only believe that like true artists Balu and Kamal simply responded to their times with suitable abstractions capable of being articulated in the way I have done here. These were the nuances that got missed when *Moondram Pirai* was remade in Hindi as *Sadma* with the very same lead actors and locations, a year later. Joining me in agreement would be his protégés Bala, Sasikumar and Vetrimaaran who have emerged as strong commentators on Tamil politics in their films today.

Mention must be made here about another of Kamal's penchants, appreciated largely by his Tamil audiences. The point where Kamal defines his ideological position is very clear. There is a scene in *Moondram Pirai* where he discovers that Vijaya has run away from his home. With subtle acting he manages to convey how vulnerable she could be, his guilt at his carelessness, leaving her alone at home, the almost impossible task of searching for one lone young girl in such a desolate landscape, etc.

During the search for Vijaya, Cheenu stumbles upon a wayside shrine to Lord Ganesh. He goes down on one knee and tries to make eye contact to pray but is unable to do so. Srinivasan is a rationalist and will not break down even at this most traumatic moment, that too in front of an idol. The childlike Cheenu in him, however, sees the oil lamp fluttering a bit and decides to shift it closer, under the shadow of the big idol. But it is Srinivasan who gets up and walks off without any genuflection or turning back. In that one instant, his fans get the message crystal-clear: 'I never said I do not believe in God. I only said that I wished there was a god up there!'

A Homage to Classical Dance

I can unabashedly state that *Salangai Oli* (The Jingle of Anklets; 1983) is one of the finest melodramas made in India, made even more fascinating by the delightful performances essayed by Kamal and an almost divine Jayaprada. Even Satyajit Ray once remarked that she was the most beautiful face ever to have graced the Indian screen. It is also one of the most perfect examples of an operatic form in Indian cinema, from a rather unrecognized master of Telugu cinema, K. Viswanath. What makes this exercise stand out is its masterly control over the framing, lighting and lensing by cinematographer Nivas. At a time when the zoom lens was being used virtually like a garden hose, one can notice an amazing restraint in this film, so that the elaborate choreography is not squandered. Finally, under Ilaiyaraaja's musical baton, this homage to classical Indian music travels through some exquisite innovations.

Since the tale is narrated as a series of flashbacks, the audience realizes that the protagonist is a doomed person who has to redeem himself by paying back for something that he received far more of than he anticipated. Kamal plays Balu, a talented classical dancer but uncompromising when it comes to the demands of the market. The fact that he is poor and totally dependent on his mother who survives with her culinary skills makes life even more challenging. Destiny gets him to meet Madhavi (Jayaprada) who spots him dancing while she is taking photographs in a temple. Attracted by his talents, she goes on to fulfil his dream of becoming a 'recognized' artiste. Somehow, his immense admiration for her prevents him from expressing his desire to live with her, for he deeply believes that she gave him something much more than he expected. Sadly, she has to depart from his life when her once-estranged husband comes back, and Kamal completes the circle by photographing her as she boards the railway train with her husband. Symbolically, he has to be content with her 'photographed' image and not her real self. A distraught Balu turns to alcohol to drown his sorrows. Several years later, she comes back a widow and now wants him to make her daughter a 'committed' performing artiste just like he was at one point of time.

A heartbroken Kamal has to surmount multiple levels of angst in order to attain the liberation that the narrative sets him up for. It makes one wonder how an artiste who has played romantic, comic and playboy roles can take on such a tragic story with equal aplomb.

The complexity of *Salangai Oli* lies in the delineation of the viraha bhava (the sentiment of separation from one's beloved) within the context of sacredness, almost bordering on ideas of divinity. Such a narrative automatically disallows even simple expressions of sexuality between the romantic leads. Continuing within a powerful Telugu Vaishnavite tradition set by Bhakti poets such as Tyagaraja (1767–1847) and Annamacharya (1408–1503), director Viswanath subsumes Kamal's and Jayaprada's popular sex appeal to narrate an equally emotionally charged yet tragic drama.

The employing of classical Indian dance forms within a popular art form, such as mainstream cinema, can be seen as a contradiction. Surely the so-called aficionados of Bharatanatyam would be waiting to condemn the liberties taken by mainstream filmmakers and actors! But these experts would miss the point that within a certain geo-cultural zone of Andhra Pradesh, a classical dance performance on screen is a metaphor for the notion of sacredness.

Kamal has not been a practising classical dancer, as were earlier legends such as Vyjayanthimala or Padmini. Moreover, this film demanded that he transcend some of the conventions and archetypal behaviours surrounding such performances in order to redefine and allude to an almost sacred definition of the 'classical Bharatanatyam form'. About his ability to dance, Kamal reminiscences, 'Some say that I was inspired by my sister Nalini who studied Bharatanatyam. I was too young at the time when I would mimic my sister to even know that I was doing classical dancing. The fact is that my propensity to dance did help me get roles in the days when film actors had to lip-sync songs and do some minimal dance steps on screen. It was a job requirement then, quite like the ability to speak the language clearly. Fortunately, unlike for youngsters today, these were talents I could acquire outside of standard academia.'

The structural strategy of the screenplay helps Kamal define his character in the most apt manner. In the beginning of the film, he is shown as an old dance critic with some very strict ideas of what is 'proper', criticizing an amateur danseuse laying claims to excellence through an overdose of publicity. Next, we see this old man dance to show what is 'proper' to the young, now-repentant girl in the unanticipated confines of a newspaper office. Both these events prepare the viewers to look forward more to the 'notion' of what is true commitment to dance, not a demonstration of what constitutes excellence in classical dancing. The interpretation becomes more important than the intricacies of a classical performance, which in any case cannot be portrayed through a cinematic rendition of the dance form.

Fortunately for Viswanath, South Indian cinema had already adopted and appropriated the tragic *Devdas* narrative of star-crossed lovers. Unlike *Devdas*, this film is not about Kamal drinking himself to death while pining for Paro but struggling to restore her failed marriage to an estranged husband. Jayaprada is both Paro, forever in love with Devdas, and Chandramukhi, his devoted muse. And Kamal has to deal with these two sides of her personality and his relationship with her. He has to love and worship her at the same time. She is the unwed Tamil saint-poet Andal and the married Rajasthani princess Meera, merged.

Such a complex construct can obviously only be comprehended within the semiotic realms of 'pure Bhakti poetry', and K. Viswanath shows us that he is a master at dealing with the cinematic idiom more as figures of speech rather than dramatic dialogues. From the way Kamal walks in late, accompanying an empty cycle-rickshaw at the beginning of the film, to the way he protects the vermillion on Jayaprada's forehead from dissolving away on a rainy night, or the discomfort he experiences while choreographing a typical mainstream 'masala' film dance or while receiving the little money that his mother gives away while she is dying—all of it conveys an amazing command over his actions, allowing them to speak for themselves rather than expressing through conventional rhetoric. These traumas are very close to the narrative presented by the Polish master Krzysztof Kieślowski in the morality tales he narrates in *Dekalog* (1989) an adaptation of the Ten Commandments. Can we practise the ideal moral tenets suggested in these myths while struggling to exist in a world worshipping the lure of capital?

The piece-de-resistance in *Salangai Oli*, however, lies in the absolutely brilliant manner in which K. Viswanath uses the trope of the still photograph in a variety of ways. It starts with an impish little boy masquerading as a professional, only to provide shaky and random compositions leading to the precise images clicked by Jayaprada. The journey ends with Kamal clicking a picture of Jayaprada and her husband, which becomes a divine icon of sorts for him. Viswanath's enquiry into what constitutes the memory of longing and belonging as an exploration of still images virtually challenges the moving cinematic images where the larger story is played out. He seems to be asking, 'Could these stills contain more drama than all the footage of the final film?' In an extremely subtle way, Balu goes through the experience of darshan where the insight into the significance of life as an event is far superior to actually sighting the realities of life. His ethereal romance with Madhavi is a deep inner journey, full of true love, but which leaves behind untold scars on his outer body.

Playing an old man as well as a suave and dashing youngster in the flashback is always a dangerous game for an actor. His actions and reflexes can be seen through layers of make-up and stuck-on grey beards. Kamal had to exude the wisdom of an aged man and the erratic idiosyncrasies of a drunken old dance critic without the kind of exaggeration that usually comes with such portrayals. He also had to maintain the energy of the young man that he once was. It is a big risk, but probably it is this rather contradictory behaviour that grounds this interplay of roles. On one hand, there are his 'real-life' early days as a young struggling dancer desperately trying to achieve some meaning in his life until he chooses to be on-screen as an actor. And when he does achieve the image of a 'screen' celebrity, he seems to not know how to express his love for this rich and beautiful benefactor who, in turn, is dedicated to his commitment to pure dance. Was Madhavi a metaphor for the role that cinema came to play in Kamal's life?

Viswanath sums up this amazing spirit between Madhavi and Balu when they set up a mock classical dance rehearsal in an open mountainous landscape and end the show by miming their reactions to a wild and frenzied audience demanding their autographs as they come out of an imaginary auditorium. Kamal and Viswanath share an unusual connection till this day. Kamal says, 'At least once a year, I will call him up and talk nostalgically about some scene or the other in *Salangai Oli*, as if it was made by some other master filmmaker!'

The film was released in all four Southern languages and was probably the biggest ever combined success in Indian cinematic history. It went on to be screened at the Moscow International Film Festival in 1984 while maestro Ilaiyaraaja and singer S.P. Balasubrahmanyam won National Awards for their contribution. Most of the Nandi State awards that year were also swept away by this film. Few filmmakers have understood the value of cinema as a metaphorical figure of speech and fewer actors have managed to respond to such a call with such inexhaustible vivacity.

The late Mani Kaul, who was a big fan of Kamal's ability to play tragic and comic parts equally well, once remarked that despite a very agile and energetic body perfectly suited for romantic roles, Kamal had the saddest pair of eyes. Mani would say that here was a case where two very differently abled actors were rolled into one body. Could this be the reason why Kamal would often choose a grim story soon after a hit comedy and vice versa? *Guna* (1991) was followed by *Singaravelan* (1992), and *Unnaipol Oruvan* (2009) by *Manmadhan Ambu* (2010). But I wonder, can actors really choose, or do they choose, such a strategy in such a crazy market-driven economy? However, Kamal makes it possible.

9

NAYAKAN AND *ORU KAIDHIYIN DIARY*: EXAMINATIONS OF MODERN INDIA

A Turning Point

If there is a Tamil film that heralded the new phase of 'liberal India' post Rajiv Gandhi in the most definitive manner, it would be *Nayakan* (The Hero; 1987). It shook scores of filmmakers and made all the Bollywood bigwigs sit up in awe. What Kamal could not achieve with films like *Ek Duuje Ke Liye* and *Saagar* (1985), he did with this film. I remember how most filmmakers and technicians in Bombay unanimously felt that here was a landmark film. Kamal started this movie with a determination of experimenting with film noir in its truest manner, paying tribute to its founders such as Elia Kazan and Francis Ford Coppola, along with actors such as Marlon Brando and Humphrey Bogart. And he did it with the kind of confidence few actors of his era could exude. In the scene where he admonishes his aides on the terrace, one can also see him paying a warm tribute to M.R. Radha, an actor for whom he had very high regard.

This film was truly a 'glocal' experiment by a group of spirited Chennai-based cineastes like Mani Ratnam, P.C. Sriram, Raja Krishnamoorthy and Bala Kumaran, who joined hands with two superstars, Kamal—who had done over 125 films by then—and Ilaiyaraaja, who was scoring for his 400th film. Together they decided to reposition the cinema of Madras as the 'real' national cinema. Sriram's high-contrast imagery, Ilaiyaraaja's period music and Mani Ratnam's amazing control on sequential rhythm along with Kamal's controlled yet nuanced performance would set some of the ground rules for what would be soon called the global 'Bollywood' style of transnational Indian cinema. The theme song, *'Thenn pandi seemayilay'* ('On the borders of a southern Tamil landscape'), sung both by Ilaiyaraaja and Kamal, remains a benchmark for all Southern filmmakers when they compose for an idyllic rural throwback.

But how does this film fit inside Kamal's search for a new standpoint from which to enter the discourse of law and order for a nation on the cusp of rapid globalization? Secondly, what does it mean for a melodrama to move out of the classical 'virtue versus vice' syndrome into a world of culpability without really taking on the grey areas of the psychological zone? What is the larger intention behind positioning the southern/ Tamilian gangster narration in the milieu of a Hindi-speaking Bombay metropolis?

Is he a good man or a bad man? This question emerges constantly for Velu Naicker, a self-appointed modern gangster providing safety and security for all those who seek his guardianship. His answer lies in the belief that if some misdeeds can help people overcome distress, then they must be seen as good deeds. In short, the ends justify the means. Velu Naicker's son joins him unflinchingly but his daughter dares to question him about who decides what is good or legal. And what happens when someone's good happens to be someone else's evil? What if the evildoer is a Tamilian in a Hindi-speaking host society?

The narrative does not belong to the 'angry young man' variety, spun so well by Salim–Javed in various films in the Mahabharata metaphor, of a good guy (Karna) in a bad house (Kauravas) who yearns for his mother and a virtuous family. *Nayakan's* tragedy is a choice made by the protagonist, knowingly and willingly.

The film explores various shades of such non-judicial justice being delivered by Velu Naicker. At one level, his style of administering justice is all about delivering a safe existence for his immediate community, the Tamil-speaking proletariat in the slums of Mumbai where ownership of land is highly contested and even convoluted. Then he also helps his fellow gangsters in other illegally occupied areas to accomplish their crooked ends. Lastly, he assists a top-ranking cop whose daughter has been molested by beating up the scoundrel responsible. In between he helps out a few others in hospitals and a schoolgirl trapped in a brothel.

Interestingly, the film's meta-text claims that citizens are happy when low-level transgressions are executed, but when it comes to big-scale violations, it should be the responsibility of the super-ego state to provide justice. At no point does the film contest the existence of state institutions such as the court or the police station. Secondly, the film also positions the ethics of defending Tamilians even if they are wrongdoers in an alien and hostile environ like Bombay. And Velu Naicker's character does not seem to know or worry about the difference between the two wrongs. In fact, when challenged by his own daughter, he wants justice to be done for all the wrongs done unto him.

Nayakan marks the start of Kamal choosing films in which he plays the lonely hunter, the protagonist who realizes that the only way for social justice is to go out there all alone and deal the dice of justice. In his book *The Cinema of Loneliness*, Robert Kolker writes,

When they do depict action, it is invariably performed by lone heroes in an enormously destructive and anti-social manner, further affirming that actual change, collectively undertaken, is impossible. When they preach harmony, it is through the useless conventions of domestic containment and male redemption. The only way to deal with them [such films], therefore, is by examining the contradictions, keeping them present in the foreground, confronting the films formally and contextually, aware that no matter how such separation is made for the sake of discussion, form and content are inseparable.

It is the skilful balance between the wounded persona and the dog-eat-dog world out there, the two kinds of iniquities which the script deals with, that makes viewers support a gangster. One kind of iniquity deals with the kind of self-righteousness that Velu Naicker as a Tamilian is comfortable with, and the second deals with how he draws a line on what is a nefarious activity. Most crucially, will it shame him in front of his own children? He is afraid that his children will not respect him for whatever he is doing. In a way, the kids act as the conscience of the audience. While some will enjoy the way the son embraces his father's ways of ganglord justice, others will side with his daughter who has the courage to question her father's violent ways and even slap Selva, his most trusted aide, for his behaviour.

The film hardly has any large-scale action scenes on the likes of what we have seen in any of the three versions of *The Godfather*. It scores by bringing in family sentiment in various ways in order to tug at the viewers' heartstrings. From a son running from the law after avenging his father's death to the crooked real-estate dealer's wife and children who plead with Velu Naicker to spare their luxurious house and lifestyle; from the mentally challenged son of a slain cop to Naicker's own grandson who does not know his identity; from the father who wants to save his son from the cops at a whopping price to salvaging the pride of a high-ranking cop whose daughter has been raped by a politician's son, in every case it is the familial cry of 'lone and hurt' Tamilians in a hostile city, embalmed by Ilaiyaraaja's lament, which torments the viewer.

The transition from a young twelve-year-old Velu on the run after killing a cop to the death of Velu Naicker at the age of sixty, all in about 150 minutes, is not a smooth ride. The time-skips do not have any well-laid-out milestones of a nation coming into its own after a long period of colonial rule to transit from the 1950s to the 1990s. A few old cars and some songs in the background contextualize the historicity of Dharavi in Bombay, the biggest urban slum in the world. Certainly, a great opportunity seems to have been lost and yet there is no doubt that the credibility of the film rests heavily on Kamal's shoulders.

Kamal shows how a loner with no education, no associations and no martial skills decides to take on the might of the Bombay police, only to get beaten and come back to his slum undefeated. His singular strength seems to be his naïve Tamilian spirit—maintained largely by his donning a white veshti and shirt, a host of rings on his fingers and talismans around his neck. The brutal Hindi-speaking cop is unable to comprehend this Tamil spirit. Since the script does not provide any material to establish his connections in high places, Velu Naicker has to be imagined as 'political prowess' incarnate. He is the sheer body of politics and he is the virtual representation of all that can be powerful.

In a conversation with Baradwaj Rangan, published in *The Hindu*, Mani Ratnam says:

> It is such a pleasure when there's an actor who delivers more than you can imagine. I realized that I didn't have to stage a scene to prop up the actor. It was enough if the camera caught him. He brings credibility to the lines and makes it so effortless. Apart from his ability to emote so well, he is also a master of technique. He did quite a bit of make-up for the other actors in the film. He was really a part of the team that way. He would bring his own gun for a shot and save us from using a terrible dummy. He had this bottle made from sugar glass, which he had brought from the US, and he used it in the fight with the cop. It is such a big boon to have an extra mind on the set. [1]

True to his character, Kamal also resisted displaying his dancing talents in the Holi song, or when a choreographic opportunity presented itself in the form of an item song with a seductress on his smuggling boat. Kamal also marked a significant high point in Tamil cinema's journey when he experimented with unique body language and voice cultivation in the

NAYAKAN AND ORU KAIDHIYIN DIARY

scene where his character sees the dead body of his son. The disfigured and charred body of his son is not shown and has to be imagined by the audience watching Kamal's reaction. Audiences that saw this demonstration at that time went back deeply disturbed after watching a performance that was highly stylized and realistic at the same time. In fact, at that moment, every member in the audience perhaps imagines how they would have reacted had such a tragedy befallen them. When Kamal as Velu Naicker lets out an animalistic cry of pain, every sensitive member in the audience feels his anguish. Even those who cannot associate with such a situation are left equally speechless.

In a conversation I had with Kamal about this iconic scene, he answered, 'As is my wont, I do not think like an actor playing a character on location. I asked myself what the key transition could be here for the script. From the story point of view, I realized that this was the end of Velu Naicker's legacy. With his son dead, this gang lord had grown twenty years older, waiting for his own demise. So, I just let out a weakened scream of pain which could only come from a very aged man. That's all!'

In fact, so popular was this scene when the film released that during every college cultural performance or mimicry show in those days—even until today—you could expect a young man to come up in a dhoti and shirt and cry out like Velu Naicker. If it clicked, the young man would receive a standing ovation and if not, that would be the end of his acting life, at least on stage!

An Unusual Revenge Saga

Oru Kaidhiyin Diary (The Diary of a Prisoner; 1986) is probably the best film that director P. Bharatiraja, screenwriter K. Bhagyaraj and Kamal have ever produced as a team. This successful film was remade in Hindi as *Aakhri Raasta* in 1986 by Bhagyaraj with Amitabh Bachchan and Sridevi in the lead roles.

There is no doubt that a majority of Indian melodramas, from the days of Raj Kapoor to Kamal, have been obsessed with the search for a new urban India where they could rediscover the romance of their village. From *Mother India* (1957) to *Lagaan* (2001), we have seen this nostalgia being enacted over and over again. Though most of the filmmakers behind these moves weren't born, brought up or educated in typical villages, their stories hark back to an ideal yet mythical world of the Indian rural space of fruit trees, coconut groves and cattle sheds where the women dance and the men work hard. In these mythical incantations, the directors play the shaman, where the fundamental requisite of a storyteller is to share the anxieties of their viewers who were and continue to be largely located in the mindsets of their native rurality. In other words, there is a reality of rural Tamil Nadu which is now electrified, well connected with the cities by several modes of transport and where English-medium schools have become the order of the day. But in their viewers' subconscious, it is an idyllic rural society undisturbed by political speeches, divisive caste politics and domestic brutality. It is in this conceptually reconciled space that Bharatiraja's idea takes shape.

The counterpoints of such narrations also arise here. While the so-called native village boasts of clean air, fresh food and a simple lifestyle, it is also the space which takes for granted some of the fundamental pillars of patriarchy, caste and unshakeable religious bigotry. And from the observer's point of view, the village has also fitted itself into a somewhat coherent social space amidst multiple contradictions.

Kamal plays David, an illiterate agrarian leader who leads agitations against the Goliaths, namely exploiters and the government systems that they dominate. The film sets up David's conflict with three urban outsiders (a politician, a police inspector and a doctor) who intervene and get him arrested for creating social unrest. Not satisfied with his incarceration, they come into his rural space and rape his wife, Rosy, a qualified schoolteacher. Unable to bear the humiliation, she hangs herself. Sadly, an enraged but innocent David is framed for her death and sentenced to jail for twenty years. Before going to serve his sentence, David hands over his infant son, James, to Velappan, a trusted friend, commanding him to make his son a heartless killer who should wait for him and avenge the horrible death of his mother. However, Velappan decides to set the boy (also played by Kamal) on a legitimate path and renames him Shankar. Shankar is later enlisted into the police force.

The stage is now set for two journeys: that of Kamal as the elderly father, David, who silently endures his jail sentence like a penance hoping to finally witness the avenging of the urbanites' dastardly act by his son. And the second is the possibility of Kamal as the son, James or Shankar, who will commit himself to commit this barbaric act on his father's behalf.

Among the many elements in *Oru Kaidhiyin Diary*, I shall focus on one aspect to begin with. Why does David want to kill a doctor, a police inspector and a politician in a nation where justice is available, even if at a price? The idea of avenging by murder has undoubtedly been a mythological metaphor for locating several other malaises. The diary in *Oru Kaidhiyin Diary* hardly exists, nor do the memories stored in it matter, but the milestones in David's journey as he takes on the Goliaths in a corrupt urban world is indeed a great lesson for anyone who wants a course in post-Independence urban India. And as often played out in the films of the 1980s, the theme of political betrayal by the Dravidian parties haunts the narrative yet again.

Therefore, the urban world with its complicated systems of governance in this film sees the coming together of three Goliaths—the politican Suryaprakasam, the medical expert Unnikrishnan and the police inspector Viswanathan—as pillars of corruption who force David, the chronicler of the journey, to move from a pristine village to an impure urban environ and take up arms against them. At a very simple level, these three exploitative forces are aliens in a rural world where the corresponding local physician, panchayat leader and a guardian/caste-based community conduct their chosen activities virtually free of cost and, at the same time, happily absorb themselves into the social fabric.

So, when David comes out of jail after suffering twenty years of injustice into a free country run by criminals, he wants his alter ego, his son, to execute the wrongdoers who are enjoying their freedom and power unrepentantly. To his shock, his son has joined the same forces who had put him behind bars. Will David now kill his alter ego, even though the latter is his own blood?

This is where the melodrama plays up what Ashis Nandy refers to as the 'different form of social and political intervention that ends up being a mode of self-intervention too'.[2] Quite ingeniously, the standard melodramatic trope of national representation in the image of the mother gets eliminated by the suicide of David's wife Rosy early in the film. The space for the 'mother' remains temporarily vacated/ unoccupied only to resurge later. And so, right in time, the narrative gets Shankar, the younger Kamal, to fall in love with an upright modern Indian girl called Sharada, played by Revathy, who also happens to be the daughter of the clean and honest inspector-general of police.

At the second level of intervention, James aka Shankar has become a Hindu boy who is in love with a Hindu girl. The innovative screenplay by Bhagyaraj portrays their meetings through a series of confrontations rather than romantic propositions. And some thirty minutes later they get together over 'Pon mane, kobam yeno', a song which would resonate in every street corner during the hundred-odd days that this film ran. A new, transformed, prospective mother has been introduced and David, the angry old man, has to now take on the avatar of the conventional angry young man. The older Kamal cannot compromise with the younger Kamal, who has found new levels of comfort in the Indian systems of law and order. Unable to understand the majoritarianism of a new Tamil Nadu, he decides to fight and contest the system. But the two Kamals must meet before the final confrontation and the script opens up an amazing scene for this. David kidnaps Sharada and holds her ransom. To his shock he comes to know from her that Shankar is none other than James. An educated yet tormented Sharada puts David into a deep dilemma. Will he have to eliminate his own son in the process of avenging the death of his wife?

The long climax of the film works out the details of a taut thriller from this point onwards in one of the most effective ways that Tamil cinema has ever witnessed. But the tour de force is undoubtedly the last assassination, that of the politician who had raped David's wife. This twenty-five-minute-long scene sets itself in the context of the politician coming to inaugurate the statue of Chhatrapati Shivaji astride his trusty steed. David pretends to be the sculpture and, at an opportune moment, jumps off the horse and drives the sword into the politician. His son Shankar shoots him down instantly. Shocking, astounding, overwhelming ... yet the irony of the whole scene lies elsewhere!

Nobody in Tamil Nadu really knows much about the valorous deeds of Chhatrapati Shivaji, the Maratha warrior who, for all Indian political narrative purposes, commenced the war to bring down the mighty Mughal empire that was dominating the Deccan under the rule of Emperor Aurangzeb. But they all know about another majestic icon, the actor Sivaji Ganesan, whose mantle Kamal had virtually taken over. So, when Kamal as Shivaji steps down in slow motion with his sword drawn, plunging it into the politician who raped his wife and the mother of his child, and is then shot down by his son Shankar, a nation is avenged, and the state also emerges (hopefully) as a new, law-abiding zone. At the same time, a nation is also romanced by the father and son with their respective romantic interests, enhanced by Ilaiyaraaja's musical compositions and Bharatiraja's unique formulae of choreographing his dance sequences.

The saga continued eleven years later in 1996 when Kamal took up the role of Senapathi, a seventy-year-old freedom fighter who once fought in Subhas Chandra Bose's army and transforms into a vigilante silently killing off corrupt politicians. His opposition comes from his alter ego, yet again in the form of his son Chandru, again played by Kamal. The film was *Indian*, directed by Shankar, Tamil cinema's blockbuster-churner. Although the scale of the film is much larger and more spectacular than the 1984 *Diary*, Kamal's journey continues to chronicle his belief that there is still space within the Indian political narrative for the ideal Indian with his tirade against the corrupt rulers who are no different from the exploitative colonial rulers of the British Raj.

10

SWATHI MUTHYAM: PEARLS OF TRAGEDY

Swathi Muthyam (The White Pearl; 1986), the second outing by Kamal Haasan and director K. Viswanath, seems to embody the dramatic process of the making of a pearl. In this Telugu film, made soon after *Salangai Oli*, Viswanath and Kamal try to experiment by showcasing the world of a grown-up with the IQ of an infant, who is being brought up by his grandmother. The film begins with actress Radhika playing Lalitha, disowned by her rich father, who was opposed to her marriage to a person of a lower class/caste. Sadly, the husband dies leaving behind a son, but the girl's father continues his antagonism and refuses to let her stay with him. Fate takes her to a rural district to the compound of Sivayya, played by Kamal. In the same district is her brother's estate where she starts working as a servant. The household is dominated by her sister-in-law Radhika, a heartless landlady. Seeing her being abused by this landlady, Sivayya decides to marry her in a fit of spontaneity to give her and her son the required security.

Unfortunately, Sivayya, an orphan by birth, is himself 'autistic' (not in the authentic sense) and unable to understand the duties and responsibilities of a married man. Added to this is the fact that the script and the 'rural environment' do not believe that a woman is capable of living on her own but has to be forever dependent on a patriarch for survival. In this case, the patriarch is unable to manage a home, let alone provide marital security. Such a situation makes Sivayya incapable of even thinking about consummating the marriage or providing any kind of sexual response to his wife. The trajectory of the film is thus all about how Lalitha empowers herself and manages to accept/mother Sivayya as her own in the form of a 'son'.

The Vaishnava symbolism here operates in the form of the mythical relationship between Yashoda, the foster mother, and Krishna, the doomed heir to an empire. How interesting to see *Swathi Muthyam* as the antithesis to *Moondram Pirai,* which we discussed earlier, just by reversing the primary roles! But there is more to it than just this reversal.

The viraha bhava (the sentiment of separation from one's beloved) of its Bhakti poetry operates in full swing, except that the deprivation of physical/sensuous fulfilment is mutual in this case. They are so near, yet so far! He is the pearl and she is the shell. His soulful cry is inaudible, and her lament is meaningless to all around. The scope of this film, however, is very limited compared to *Salangai Oli,* as it operates within just two dimensions—how is Sivayya going to provide Lalitha marital security despite his mental deficiency, and how is Lalitha going to accept a husband who is mentally just a child?

Thanks to the slim script, the director goes about creating/staging obstacles to benchmark the development of such a doomed relationship. From a thematic and performance point of view, this process could be seen as describing/constructing the observance/enactment of a ritual. The screenplay is therefore lined with a series of superstitions in the form of religious sacrificial vows, which help negate and mutilate this 'impossible' coming together of two lovers, a mentally challenged young man and a rich yet destitute widow. Both Sivayya and Lalitha have in their own ways chosen their paths which shall never meet. They have disinherited their roots and inherited pain and suffering, so important to the passage of rituals. At one time Lalitha rolls down some temple steps and at another Sivayya runs over burning coals to perform this tragic opera. Sivayya whips himself while Lalitha starves to fulfil their wishes. Witnessing the ritual by non-participants is as important as experiencing it and at times it can be more cathartic and impactful for the those watching the ritual. Adhering to these ideas, the narrative has the rest of the cast remain unidimensional passive observers, watching the protagonists' trauma with no development in their characters. Be they the seductive washerwoman, his uncle's dumb wife, or the heroine's brother, mother and father, they all visit the script at frequent intervals but stay back, unable to help.

In a way, the ritualistic paradigm provides Kamal enormous scope to play this 'infantile' character with aplomb. His usage of hand gestures, the frequent slapping of his back, the shuffled walk, his delayed responses and the way he befriends his stepson are all examples of character study and embellishing archetypal details. Crew members remember how difficult it was for Kamal to dance and act out of tune and rhythm while essaying such a character. Radhika's demeanour as Lalitha hints at the lost potential of a young woman in her prime. Kamal, the foremost sex symbol of the 1980s, is unable to fulfil her most basic need, despite having tied the marital knot with her, making the viewer ask, 'Is such a denial permissible, especially with Kamal on board?'

Swathi Muthyam and its Tamil version called *Sippikkul Muthu* (1986) were both massive box-office successes and the film received the National Award for the Best Telugu Film. Kamal received the Nandi Andhra State Award for Best Actor. This film was also remade in Hindi as *Eeshwar* (1989) starring Anil Kapoor and Vijayashanti, and in Kannada as *Swathi Muthu* (2003), starring Sudeep and Meena. Yet again, these films also enjoyed successful runs.

Was this film one of the last works to talk about mythology in the background of Rajiv Gandhi and his push for liberalization and consumerism? Would it be the last ode to the cinematic Indian rural life and all its hagiographic paeans? This over-the-top melodrama certainly demands a second look to see how certain mythical memories lie ensconced in the larger narrative of performative arts. A small clue is available in the amazing song 'Suvvi Suvvi Suvalamma', picturized on a river front with a big sailboat in the foreground and temple spires in the background. As the title suggests, it is about the mystery of opening an ugly, nondescript oyster to reveal the gorgeous pearl inside.

The song begins with Sivayya trying to sing like a typical classical singer when Lalitha comes and corrects his musical pitch. But when she commences her classical song, Sivayya butts in to sing a folk song in the same raga and she gladly joins in. The song moves on to allude to the Ramayana where the king-in-exile, Rama, accompanies Sita into the wondrous forests, while the film is actually depicting the reverse. It is the bold Sita who has undertaken the responsibility of guiding her 'innocent' husband through the dangerous paths. The song ends with Lalitha (Sita) wondering whether she is really capable of bringing up her Sivayya (Rama) and discovering the true, hidden pearl in the oyster? Was that her responsibility or the community's? The ballad of Sivayya and Lalitha ends with a reversal of the old Ramayana. Lalitha comes home to her rich ancestral home when her mother falls ill, but the patriarch uncle asks Sivayya to banish himself if he wants his wife and son to live happily for the rest of their lives. Sivayya willingly leaves but Lalitha disapproves and comes back to live with him and make the struggle of her/their existence meaningful. The scene shifts to twenty years later, when an older Lalitha wants to breathe her last lying on his lap while he is seated next to a basil plant. An entire family assembles to commemorate her first death anniversary and to enshrine her memory, Sivayya replants a basil sapling in the presence of his entire family. This film can easily be called the Indian version of the operatic form.

We must also recognize the political backdrop of this film—the long reign of the Congress party had come to an end in Andhra Pradesh as N.T. Rama Rao, the iconic film star, swept the assembly polls in 1983 and the Lok Sabha polls in 1984. The people of Andhra Pradesh were ecstatic but, like Lalitha, they too doubted whether this newly crowned Rama Rao could actually handle the mandate that they entrusted in his hands. NTR went on to serve three terms as chief minister. I am therefore, tempted to believe that the undercurrent of this film runs deep at three levels:

A. The neighbouring state of Tamil Nadu had resolutely placed their superstar M.G. Ramachandran as their chief minister, trouncing the old DMK and their Congress alliances. MGR was often referred to as NTR's older brother. NTR had worked hard to nurture himself as the most definitive cinematic mythological hero and most people did see him as an avatar of the same. So why was this younger brother hesitating to take the plunge?

B. The dominant Congress party had made Andhra Pradesh a showpiece of public sector enterprises with the government spending lavishly on diverse sectors such as mining, power generation, defence labs, naval ports and several research institutions. What happened to local Andhra enterprise? Why were their landlords and industrialists keeping such a low profile?

C. Indira Gandhi's leadership had developed several cracks and was certainly not a people-friendly system of governance. Was it not time for a local icon with no connections at all to the earlier political schema to enter and wrest the reins of leadership and power?

I strongly believe that people saw *Swathi Muthyam* resonating, in very broad ways, with such a layered conundrum. Somewhere in their subconscious, it seemed to hint at an appeal to NTR that he should come out of the oyster and glisten like the most exotic pearl.

Kamal Haasan with his family

As a young boy about to make his mark in cinema

With Savitri in *Kalathur Kannamma* (1960)

In *Arangetram* (1973)

In *Aval Oru Thodar Kathai* (1974)

With K. Balachander and Rajinikanth

With R.C. Shakti

With Rajinikanth and Amitabh Bachchan at an event. (Photo © Punit Paranjpe/AFP via Getty Images)

A Selection of Kamal Haasan's Films

Manmadha Leelai (1976)

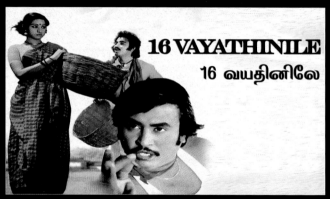

16 Vayathinile (1977)

Ek Duuje ke Liye (1981)   *Sakalakala Vallavan* (1982)

Moondram Pirai (1982)

Salangai Oli (1983)

Nayakan (1987)

Pushpak (1987)

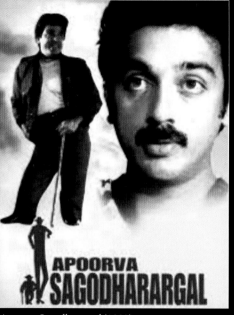

Apoorva Sagodharargal (1989)

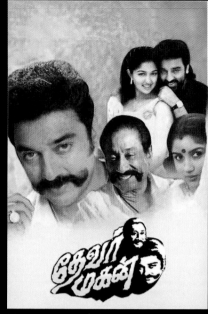

Thevar Magan (1992)

Hey Ram (2000)

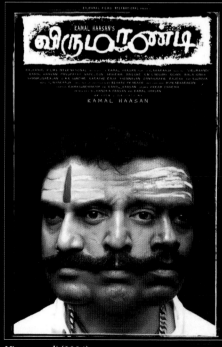

Virumaandi (2004)

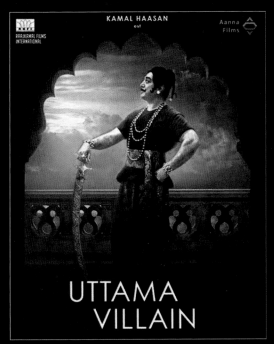

Uttama Villain (2015)

Vikram (2022)

Thug Life (to be released)

Indian 2 (releasing in 2024)

11

PUSHPAK: A COMEDY PAR EXCELLENCE

To attempt a film with no dialogues and songs within a strong commercial cinema framework is seemingly an oxymoron. Only the maverick team of Kamal and Singeetam Srinivasa Rao could pull off a film like *Pushpaka Vimana* or *Pushpak* (1987) with such daring. A large part of their strength was possibly the belief that if the legacy of Charles Chaplin was still alive in India, this film should set the cash counters ringing. Kamal had always been fascinated by Chaplin and saw him almost as a role model. Talking about the original idea for the film, Rao said, 'At first the script was called *Advaitha* and had a lot of philosophical innuendos about what it entails to be a human being in conflict with the real self and the spiritual self. It was a perfect recipe for an art film. Many producers, including Kamal, liked it but did not commit to making it.'

Rao worked on a renewed concept but believed that that this 'still' highly risky story could only be pulled off by Kamal. He somehow managed one day to persuade his good-friend-cum-screen-actor Shringar Nagaraj to finance this modestly budgeted film. They decided to shoot this film in a five-star hotel. When Rao started developing the idea further on location, the idea of a murder thriller combined with the comedies of mistaken identities germinated. Thus was *Pushpak* born. He explains, 'With this new narrative framework, Kamal agreed to be part of the venture. Yet despite scripting the film with great attention to detail, one had to be prepared for changes taking place on location. You see, Kamal, with whom I have worked earlier, was bound to come up with newer ways of interpreting the storyline. According to me, we in the film industry work with our intuition more than logic. We believe that audiences are forever changing their tastes and we should still have the knack of feeling the audiences' pulse on what they want. I have also understood that Indian audiences and the so-called idea of "Western" realism do not go hand in hand. Our audiences are extremely intelligent and can distance themselves from the work and also get emotionally involved at the same time. In the Telugu theatres I have witnessed audiences watch a tear-jerking scene or a sentimental song being performed and then, when the song is over, they get up and ask for a repeat performance! They want to cry again. Similarly, in the film, the psychology of the viewer is completely against the realism of the cinematographic image.'

Pushpak is the name of the five-star hotel where the main drama unfolds in the film. Kamal plays the modern unemployed lad, living in a pigeon coop on a rooftop with just a one-rupee coin in his pocket. Hope comes in the form of a drunk millionaire sprawled on the footpath with a key to a five-star room in Hotel Pushpak. After towing him away to his poor coop, Kamal gags and binds the rich man and decides to live the life of the rich and wealthy. The rich drunkard's wife, however, is shown having an affair with another man who has, in turn, engaged a contract killer played by Tinnu Anand to kill this wealthy drunkard. The killer, who uses an icicle as his murder weapon of choice, is unaware that Kamal has already replaced the rich drunkard in the hotel room.

This story of mistaken identities takes the story through a series of escapades for the rest of the film. In the meanwhile, Kamal befriends a rich girl (played by Amala) on whom he showers endless gifts with his hostage's wealth. And, in the end, when he finds out that the drunken hostage is actually a victim of another cruel love plot, he reunites the millionaire with his wife and goes back to live in his Chaplinesque coop and join the winding queues of India's unemployed youth.

Pushpak is like a tribute to a long list of comedy masters such as Buster Keaton, Harold Lloyd, Nagesh and, of course, the inimitable Jacques Tati, other than Chaplin. As a homage to all of them, Kamal holds mime conversations with his girlfriend Amala, standing far across the hotel enclave with a camera mounted with a telephoto lens. She looks at him through a simple telescope and expresses through sign language how she cannot leave her parents. And everyone in the audience understands the import of that conversation.

The unique quality of the comedy masters lies in the fact that they created humour not at the expense of others, but by the use of cinematic elements like props, timing and framing. Their brilliance is also demonstrated in how the characters in their films survive near-death circumstances around them which can be witnessed only by the viewers while the characters themselves remain oblivious to the dangers. In *Pushpak* the killer, played superbly by Tinnu Anand, is forever lurking around Kamal with a sharp icicle to execute the perfect murder with no trace left behind. And each time he comes close, Kamal inadvertently slips away on his pursuit to meet his beloved.

Rao reminisces, 'Those were the days when five-star hotels would let us shoot on their premises at very low costs with no "security" issues. And having a superstar like Kamal on their property for over twenty days was a big publicity attraction for the Windsor Manor hotel in Bangalore. The architecture of the hotel was perfectly suited to tell this silent story, for it provided multiple points of view. The comedy had to be constantly developed on [the lines of] "who saw what and when" so that the "why and how" of the connotation could be communicated simply to the viewer. Though it was a win-win situation, we had to work hard to get the mise-en-scène right. Every piece of action by multiple actors on the location had to be precisely timed and only I could see them all and certify it as an "okay" shot, for there was no playback tape system which Kamal and others could check out. It was a huge responsibility for me and there was no way we could do [any changes] once the shooting was completed.'

What we see in *Pushpak* is the continuous conflict between the international modernity of the five-star hotel, where the hero has surreptitiously come to stay in the guise of the 'kidnapped' rich occupant, versus the poor tenement that is his actual residence. We see what happens when aspirations of the marginalized get realized through the fake decorum of the rich. Everything is thus rendered cognizable only because of an inherent performance device loosely termed 'Maya'. We become what we are only because of how we appear.

In one of the finest scenes, the hero (Kamal) and heroine (Amala) come together holding hands in a long line of mourners assembled to pay their last respects to the late hotel baron. The girl's parents are searching for their daughter while the icicle-wielding killer is after the guy. But the two lovers gaze into each other's eyes and express silent sweet nothings to each other in this funereal queue and keep coming back into the same line again in order to avoid being caught.

Pushpak is delightfully controlled and contrived at the same time. Kamal's brilliant timing as an actor and Rao's playful detachment make this film a classic. To further accentuate the dark comedy, the father of the girl is a professional magician whose sleight of hand makes things appear and disappear. And it is during his magic show for a five-star audience that the icicle-wielding assassin keeps goofing up. The audience roaring in laughter at the magical tricks on stage is interspersed with Kamal inadvertently yet constantly evading the killer.

Few films have critiqued the standard romantic story that inhabits all our mainstream films the way *Pushpak* did. If filmed in a formal, dramatic manner, this would have been a dark and grim film on the futility of modern romance, which is nurtured inside a fake atmosphere of garish modernity where nobody really belongs to the architecture they live within. Instead, Rao's satirical approach and Kamal's blank look/unmotivated movements manage to subvert the emotional plane behind the tragedy of contemporary urban existence and instead get the audience to laugh and introspect at the same time. No wonder that we see the mirrors at different points in the hotel working as self-reflective motifs, forcing us to look into the various layers offered in the narration.

The fact that there are no spoken words in this film is a comment on the urban situation where there is little commitment between what is said and what is practised. A photo of Karl Marx, nailed to the wall of Kamal's character's cooped house, seems to watch over the unethical enterprise of looting the rich that the young protagonist indulges in. Is it in approval of the poor, asserting themselves to regain lost wealth, or in condemnation of the lack of a unionized force sanctioning this modern disruptive action? The black comedy finds itself offering a cynical perspective that in the long run, both the rich and the poor need to defecate each day! The young hero ends up collecting the shit of the rich drunkard, trashing it in a well-packaged carton, only to be envied by another person on the street! Semantics are merely formalities for modern business enterprises which are rooted in legal jargon and bureaucratic statements, while the vernacular expression silently weeps in long-winding queues in front of ration shops and employment agencies.

Kamal never made such a wordless, nameless, plotless film again but with Singeetam Srinivasa Rao at the helm, he would go on to make many more comedy films, which would establish him as the superstar of the Southern masses. Though the film was meant for an all-India audience, the exhibition strategy had to be done in a localized state-wise manner. The rule says that a talkie has to be in a certain language. Therefore, in order to release this wordless film all over India, it was certified the same year by the censor board multiple times, in all Indian languages, with titles changed and new censor certificates issued in all languages! A comedy within a comedy!

Pushpaka Vimana was the Kannada name, *Pushpaka Vimanam* in Malayalam, *Pesum Padam* in Tamil and *Pushpak* in Hindi; and, in the most ludicrous twist to this filmic experience, the film received the Filmfare Award for the best Kannada film that year and the National Award for the 'most wholesome entertainment of the year'. In almost every city that this film released, it celebrated a minimum run of a hundred days. And such a film has never been made again in India. This was a species which became endangered immediately after its birth!

12

SATHYA: A REMAKE THAT SURPASSED
THE ORIGINAL

Watching *Sathya* (1988), a remake of Rahul Rawail's *Arjun* (1985) that starred Sunny Deol, we see another facet of Kamal as a movie producer. *Sathya* was produced by Raaj Kamal Films International, Kamal's production house, which took the rights for the Bollywood hit scripted by Javed Akhtar to remake it in Tamil with Suresh Krishnaa as the director. We will get into the issues surrounding translating or even the transcreation from one language to another a little later. What we see first is Kamal's transition from the angry young man of *Apoorva Raagangal,* who has dangerous liaisons with an older 'motherly' classical singer, to another angry young man here, who has almost lethal liaisons with an older 'fatherly' politician.

Within the confines of a mainstream film it might be interesting to define who and what this 'angry young man' is, as opposed to the sad romantic in *Salangai Oli* or the comic, mentally challenged man in *Thenali* (2000). One does not see the actual process of how this character actually becomes angry or sad or romantic. We seem to take the character from a certain point in his lifeline, add in a few hints for the causation and quickly get into the act of questioning, 'What happens when an angry, jobless young man is given a supporting hand by a seemingly kind-hearted politician?' The angry jobless man becomes a category in *Sathya,* quite in the way the jobless mentally challenged boy becomes a category in *Thenali* or how a young upright military officer called Michael Corleone becomes a ruthless mafia don in *The Godfather* (1972).

Sathya starts off by defining 'who' and then goes on to show 'how' an unemployed youth becomes an angry young man—he has a heartless stepmother at home, his father is an incompetent accountant in a paint shop, his sister is teased on the streets by predatory goons and his friends are all as jobless as him, sharing cups of tea and playing carrom to kill time. All this is established as the status quo in one lower-middle-class ghetto until two events occur to disturb it. First, a bunch of gangsters arrive in Sathya's area demanding 'protection' pay-offs and even beating up a shopkeeper for not paying up. Second, a pretty young girl lands up seeking Sathya's help to retrieve her purse from a moronic thief. Both these situations are easily resolved by Sathya. He and his friends beat up the goons and unwittingly disturb a big pyramid of corruption and seedy politics, while Sathya pursues the young girl. So, for all practical scripting purposes, we do not ask why these thugs land up at that very moment or who is the girl and from where she comes into Sathya's life.

This strategy is often the foundation of melodrama where characters are categories of existence, as we see in a fable or myth. It addresses the rise of the hero through his/her courageous aggression (violence) combined with his/her faithful addresses towards the opposite sex. Through these two emotional positions, the hero ascends to positions of righteousness, valour and a kind of omnipotence that strikes awe in the minds of the viewers. By themselves these characters do not have an empirical or psychological position, but they allow the audience to access/manufacture their past and motivations in as many ways as possible. And when such free-flowing imaginary constructed processes are provided to certain actors, stars are born and stardom is sustained over a series of films, thanks to the efforts of the actor and the compassion of his fans in equal measure.

Kamal represents that kind of unstinting effort; it also elucidates the love of his fans in complex ways.

The 1980s were also the years when Kamal was releasing a film every month. Every town in Tamil Nadu had one of his films in the cinemas all the time. As a producer, this could seriously tell on the quality of the films in terms of attention to details such as make-up and set décor. The directors would have to rely on poorly paid art directors and craftsmen. Adding to this tension was the fact that Kamal's second production, a big-budget sci-fi venture titled *Vikram* (1986) suffered on both critical and commercial fronts. His company had to comfort the distributors who had shouldered the risk of such an ambitious film. Selecting a proven hit like *Arjun* for a remake must have also provided the encouragement for financiers to invest in his third production. Yet again, this film was not going to be a family drama or a comic caper for it involved a lot of action scenes and crowded sequences requiring a lot of sets, props and explosions.

That's probably why the good old 'remake' strategy works, since the matrix has already been properly pre-developed by someone else. It seems like all one has to do is simply copy most of the shots from the old film with the necessary indigenization to make it look new and 'Tamil'. But a closer look will reveal the complicated journey that an idea like *Arjun* would have gone through to manifest itself as *Sathya*. The writer in Kamal was very clear about constructing the protagonist's agency and how to make the audience invest in the eponymous primary stakeholder of the film, namely, *Sathya*. In *Arjun*, Sunny Deol is seen as a victim of circumstances, demanding deep empathy, and takes more than an hour of screen time to get himself into the action mode. In *Sathya*, Kamal gives up the brooding mood and gets into the action mode within the first fifteen minutes and makes clear his determination to root out the 'evil' forces manifest in the stereotypes of regional politicians. At times the hero is fooled and at times he takes the right steps. This trajectory is equally balanced by not providing agency to any other character in the story. So, while we see *Arjun* giving prominence and agency to smaller characters like the politician Trivedi (Prem Chopra) or the primary heroine Geeta (Dimple Kapadia), Kamal's *Sathya* casts lesser-known actors in these roles with minimal or nil agency. The character of Sathya takes upon himself the primary agency to structure the course of action while the rest react to the course laid down by him. This allows the hero in *Sathya* to have a wider scope to deconstruct either the heartless world of politicians or the romantic world nurtured by his lover. Kamal is clear that this is, ultimately, one hero's journey.

As producer, Kamal seems to have been attracted by the initial brooding loneliness of an unemployed youth. There is a wonderful opening song, which is a clear tribute to Robert Wise's *West Side Story*; a unique enactment of a public assassination on a rain-drenched street with hundreds of people holding black umbrellas; a clever staging of fight scenes in crowded urban spaces with multiple hidden cameras, with the 'real' public watching; and, most importantly, the conflict between two rival politicians which a youth gets sucked into. A perfect story to fit the Dravidian parties' conflict into a context, a conflict which leaves a young man confused as to what is the right path and wondering who shall be so selfless in showing the ethical way forward. *Arjun* does this bit effectively in a scene where the so-called upright politician (Anupam Kher) meets Arjun one night and advises him to join forces with him on the political battlefield. *Sathya* copies this scene in an even more effective way for the Tamil audience.

Sathya picks up this link from the Mahabharata and blends it into multiple religio-mythological strains, some comic and some serious. Kamal realized that his audience would come to watch his film to be provided emotional tones other than just anger. The introduction of Geetha Nair (Amala), unable to speak because of a severe toothache, is a hilarious tribute to *Citizen Kane*; Kamal's depiction of Sathya's character swings from being naïve to looking sad, from being ferociously angry to self-admonishing in ways that only he can portray with conviction. Kamal also roped in S.M. Anwar, the cinematographer who worked with him in Ramesh Sippy's *Saagar*, to match the skilful work of Baba Azmi in *Arjun*.

As one of the many filmgoers of the 1980s in Tamil Nadu, I can vouch for the one big factor that drew repeat audiences for *Sathya*—the musical score of Ilaiyaraaja. The opening song with Kamal and gang singing on the streets of Madras and the '*Valaiosai*' song which saw Lata Mangeshkar and S.P. Balasubrahmanyam singing together for the first time in Tamil cinema are noteworthy. Kamal's films were also reputed for ending on strong climaxes and this film was certainly not going to end in the tame way *Arjun* did, where we see the crooked politicians being arrested by the Bombay police. Kamal chooses to put on the 'invincible' sacrificial mask with which his character comes out of the hospital where he was admitted with multiple bullet wounds. Covered in plaster, Sathya carries the drip holder like a trident, escapes into the streets and enters the villainous den where the crooked politicians are celebrating. With the kind of effort that only Kamal can demonstrate, he assaults and stabs the two crooked politicians to death, calls up the police and waits, reconciled to spending the rest of his life behind bars. Was this Kamal's way of making peace with the Dravidian dilemma? Was it why he began the film with a glowing tribute to MGR who passed away on 24 December 1987, during the filming of *Sathya*?

As leader of the MNM party, Kamal was strongly critical of the ways the current COVID pandemic has been handled by the state of Tamil Nadu. To express this, he recorded and picturized a very emotional song depicting the plight of the unemployed migrants left to fend for themselves by the system that used to exploit them heartlessly before the pandemic hit. In each one of those migrants walking back home in hordes, there is the story of *Sathya* waiting to be told. Kamal pays homage to their resilience, tolerance and capacity to hope for better times to come. When he was asked by film critic Rajeev Masand about the impact the song had on his people, Kamal simply replied, 'Nothing. To elaborate further, the song can be equated to the gentle pat on a child's back by a loving mother. Isn't that pat something? If that small pat has helped us all grow to be what we are today, then I think that song was worth the effort.'

13

GUNAA: A STUDY OF ANDROGYNY

Gunaa (1991) is undoubtedly a screenplay far ahead of its time. From one standpoint, the script seems to require more maturation and clarification, and from another, it seems to demand complete surrender by the viewers to a story which is embedded in the metaphysical androgynous quality of the union between Shiva and Parvati (or 'Abhirami', as she is referred to in the film). But the story's origins are not so simple. In a *Film Companion* interview with its screenwriter John Era, a strange facet was revealed:

Kamalji and I had a broad idea about the story in which a mentally deranged person falls deeply in love within the 'beauty and the beast' template. But while travelling to the location I spoke to him about the disturbing relationship that I was going through. It was stressful but the passionate love that lurked behind was just too strong to give up the journey that we had already travelled. It was a trap full of love and agony at the same time. Kamalji listened to me patiently and encouraged me to contextualize my troubled emotions into the dramatic graph of the film. While writing the screenplay, I did not know whose story I was narrating![1]

In a nutshell, the plot revolves around a mentally challenged man, Gunaa played by Kamal, who believes that Goddess Abhirami shall descend to marry him on a full-moon day. But his uncle uses his innocence to get him to break open the temple treasury to steal its wealth. While coming out with the loot, Gunaa sees a rich girl (played by Roshini) coming to the temple for 'darshan' and believes that she is Abhirami incarnate. He kidnaps and takes her to a lonely house on a hilltop. The rich girl's guardian SK (Sharat Saxena) comes looking for her with his henchmen. In the ensuing struggle, Gunaa kills one of his men and takes the girl away into a cave. The police now tag along with a sympathetic doctor, Dr Ganesh (Girish Karnad), to get him to surrender. But SK has other plans. The film ends with the girl being shot dead and Gunaa leaping off a cliff in the presence of a rising full moon.

Let us look at some of the complexities located in the film's narration.

1. *Gunaa* demands that the viewer believe that the Shaivite (non-dual) concept is rooted in the non-separateness of the man–woman binary, quite like the coexisting unity of matter and energy. Such a union is supremely above the religiosity that accompanies the idol worship of the two deities, Shiva and Parvati, unified as one in the Shivalinga statue ('linga' means 'gender' in Sanskrit). In fact, we never see the idol anywhere in the film simply because the film is not about Shiva as typically described in the religious Puranic texts, but as a philosophical concept outside of its 'Hindu' reference. The development of the primary character as one seeking this 'divine' unity therefore gets a certain tweaking at the level of both the body and the mind. Such a desire or goal is definitely not the run-of-the-mill prescription for a Tamil hero!

2. Gunaa can probably be seen as a character with an acute obsessive-compulsive disorder (OCD), incapable of processing emotions of reciprocation like others. At the physical level, his gait has a simian posture and his gaze often seems deep and blank at the same time. Most importantly, despite being raised and residing in a brothel run by his mother, he has no sexual orientation at all.

For everyone around, he is simply a freak, a madman. And this narrative is happening at a time when Kamal, the star, was a sex symbol for all his fans.

3. Next, one has to realize that the main character is gender-neutral in symbolic ways personified and therefore free of issues that surround 'sexuality' and its pleasures. In fact, the film believes that Gunaa and 'gender-free' are synonymous. Therefore, the character Gunaa has none of the desires that haunt the average young man when he sees an attractive woman. Rosie, one of the women in the brothel in this film, is close to him and capable of fulfilling all his carnal desires, but Gunaa keeps telling her she is not his 'Abhirami'.

4. Abhirami is simply the 'energy force', which activates the inert physical mass called the human body. Her arrival in the film is concurrent with a criminal act to be conducted by Gunaa, namely robbing the temple treasury, and this is where the story's contemporaneity gets rooted. Her arrival comes on the heels of a moral dilemma, an area which Gunaa is completely ambiguous about. The pursuit of a woman as the 'completion' of one's spiritual identity is designed and located within the parameters of a criminal desire.

5. *Gunaa* the film seeks to question whether this form of altruistic/ platonic desire for a woman is tantamount to a crime in modern society. Is desiring such a person at a platonic level, without her consent, an illegitimate desire? Does the demand for an immediate and equal reciprocation from the other constitute a criminal activity? The story complicates it further by locating the young woman from an upper-class and North Indian background, thus removing Gunaa far away from any form of 'socially compatible' contextualization.

Positioning the primary character and the story's point of view in a so-called 'immoral' brothel packed with pimps, gangsters and thieves, the narrative shifts us into the metaphoric imagery of a society/nation gone awry in which only an individualized soul such as Gunaa can seek redemption, even if it is in the form of a gory death. But when the death does occur, it happens in the purview of all those who loved him, resented him, used him and even despised him. The death of an 'innocent' yet passionate individual makes us all feel guilty for not having acceded to a very simple fable, the amorous yet troubled relationship between Shiva and Parvati, which has unfortunately moved from its metaphysical essentials to religious and ritualistic observances.

Why was this film worshipped by all of Kamal's fans and completely rejected by the 'agnostic' rest? Why did Kamal choose to produce such a risky film, directed by Santhana Bharati and with an equally talented cinematographer in Venu, under his banner? At the time of its making, several stories of a troubled Kamal on location would make its rounds among the cineastes of Madras. But everyone realized that this was not any 'ordinary' love story that was being made in the hillsides of Kodaikanal for touristy pleasures but a film seeped in formative theories and principles.

To locate the idea in the most forceful and realistic manner, the film starts off with an extremely complex single shot with the camera on a jib, as if portraying God's point of view. Lasting about six minutes, it starts with Gunaa on the roof posing as Shiva the dancer watching the full moon, and the shot runs us through all the activities of a busy brothel. For all practical purposes, the film locates the audience into a realistic scenario and a brutally real one at that. In the next shot, we see a possessed Gunaa watching a marriage procession. He rushes down to claim the bride in the decorated car as his 'Abhirami'. The crowd pulls him out and beats him up, while a distraught Rosie, the only sympathetic woman in the brothel, comes to save him and take him away. The pursuit of this dream, the fuming cars and angry mobs continue right through the story till the end. Kamal recalls, 'I was once going back in a car after finishing a whole day's shooting of another film. A big crowd had assembled to watch us at the location and suddenly one young boy ran alongside the car with a blade in his right hand, slitting his left wrist and shouting out my name like a possessed person. I was shocked, even angry at this insane act of fandom. I stopped the car and rebuked him never to do such an act again. But today, on further reflection, I wonder whether the character of Gunaa took birth at that moment.'

This acute realism of Venu and Bharati has to match with the mythological fable of Shiva and Abhirami. The problem in doing so stems from the fact that film language has set up certain conventions in terms of set décor, body language, lighting, camera operations, etc., to distinguish the fabulous from the realistic. For a start, the film constantly grapples with transporting Gunaa from the realistic portrayal of a childlike adult and the character portraying the cerebral approach towards 'sexless' love. In the process of transportation and transcreation, the two distinct narrative trajectories of realism and surrealism occupy the same planes, devastated and dysfunctional. Be it the ramshackle brothel, the dirty prison, the decrepit temple, the abandoned house on the hill or the cave where Gunaa and Abhirami finally settle, they all look extremely realistic, yet they need to contain the mythical 'divine' fable.

Undoubtedly the last location, the cave, depicts the womb-like comfort of the 'garbagriha' where the duality of the gender can safely reside in harmony. Shiva and Abhirami unite most symbolically in the threshold of the womb, dissolving all differences, ignorance and knowledge in the process. In many ways, this film can be seen as an antithesis to Kamal's earlier film *Moondram Pirai*. If *Moondram Pirai* was about a young woman who suffers from a sudden mental aberration where she has forgotten most of her past, in *Gunaa* it is the man who suffers from a mental plight, except that his mind is obsessed with the mythology of Shiva and Abhirami. Both the films are located in idyllic landscapes and in that background, we see the unfolding of human tragedies.

The realistic abandoned house on a hilltop, symbolizing the mountaintop where Lord Shiva resides, is, interestingly, redeemed by the presence of a little bird hatching her eggs in a nest on the windowsill. Gunaa's concern for protecting a 'reluctant' Abhirami from the world around resonates very differently from the concern displayed by the bird for her eggs. Gunaa thinks he is protecting her but unknown to him, he has actually kidnapped her and is holding her hostage in this ethereal location. What would have happened if the emphasis had shifted from the protective Gunaa to a 'possessive' person, quite like the emotional vein displayed in *Beauty and the Beast*? On the other hand, is Indian melodramatic cinema so deeply caught in the Devdasian mode of 'unrequited love' that our star-crossed lovers have always to be sacrificed at the altar of nobility? Have the other locations like the temple/prison and their portrayal matched up to this concept?

The songs in the film, especially when sung in lip sync, set a dissonant note, considering the deeply entrenched realistic mode within which the cinematography operates. And yet Ilaiayaraaja's brilliant song composition '*Kanmani unodu*' picturized inside the paradisiacal cave reverberated around Tamil Nadu for months to come as an accepted favourite. The audience reminds us that they know how to accept what they like and reject what they don't. I still remember that my son, who was then about seven years old, saw the film and refused to eat for two days, crushed by the cruelty meted out to his favourite actor. Little did he know that this was just another make-up for the super 'bahuroopi', for very soon Kamal would release yet another blockbuster caper comedy called *Singaravelan* (1992).

14

TWINS, QUADRUPLETS AND KAMAL'S
PASSION FOR CHAPLIN

Any study on film spectatorship would conclude that there are two areas which Indian cinema has completely ignored: children's films and comedy. As cinematic genres, both could have played a serious role within Indian cinema, which has so far been the most definitive tool of modern popular culture in post-Independence India. The comedy genre has instead been adjusted within romance or action and adventure films. Any film with a comedy track and a happy ending, layered thick with a whole host of emotions and sentiments, has somehow got labelled as a comedy.

Kamal's contribution to the comedy and humour genre has been simply astounding. For all his seriousness, he has done a massive number of comedy films. In this area he is on par with giants such as Charlie Chaplin, Buster Keaton, Jerry Lewis, Bob Hope and Robin Williams. And when one sees him in films like *Michael Madana Kama Rajan* (1990), *Avvai Shanmughi* (1996) or *Kaathala Kaathala* (1998), one realizes why other producers do not attempt this format so easily.

Famous comedy playwright director and political commentator Cho Ramaswamy remarks, 'Writers like me got the audience laughing consistently thanks to repartees and dialogues, while Kamal works with situations in a highly Wodehousian manner. What's more amazing is the fact that he can come out of a serious film like *Nayakan* and jump totally into a slapstick barrel of fun and mirth. How difficult it must be!'

Kamal told me, 'If I had the guts to enter the world of comedy, the inspiration must go to the great thespian Sivaji Ganesan. During the time of heightened melodrama he had the courage to accept films like *Ooty Varai Uravu* (1967) and *Galatta Kalyanam* (1968). And his courage came from the amazing Wodehousian screenplays that only Chitralaya Gopu could write. One has to recognize the united strength in this. If timing is most essential to comedy, especially in serious films, then in that world K. Balachander was supreme, as he could precisely understand the comic presence within the ethos of tragicomic roles which I had to don often. I am also of the firm belief that he developed his art of handling the comic only through interactions with Nagesh. I was, and I am still, an unabashed fan of this great actor. For me, being a good "rasik" [appreciator] means imbibing the good qualities of the person whom you admire as one's own while still being able to acknowledge the source. I must also not forget that I could speak Tamil with a Coimbatore accent thanks to an amazing guru and fellow actor called Kovai Sarala. With wonderful writers and directors like Crazy Mohan and Mouli, I get to be seen as part of a big forest and not a lone tree that does everything.'

Making an audience laugh as well as forget logical issues in dramaturgy puts an enormous responsibility on the actors. The problem here is two-fold. First, unlike a stand-up comedian, one has to understand the fact that humorous cinema is itself an impersonal mechanical performance by a motorized apparatus, which needs enormous manipulation in order to make the necessary humorous impact. Second, the audience must be able to connect with the nature of film language first and then go beyond it in order to make the necessary humorous emotional contact. Imagine if the projection focus goes wrong or if the audio crackles during the screening of a film. All the hard effort behind the performance will come to naught. The key phrase becomes simplicity in complexity.

In a pure comedy film, the body language and timing of the primary actors is of utmost importance because one often expects the viewers to laugh at characters who are actually in deep trouble. The greater the difficulty in overcoming the challenge, the more humorous the story becomes, and the higher do audience expectations go. The role of an amazing gaffe writer like Crazy Mohan, the witty direction of Singeetam Srinivasa Rao or the foot-tapping songs of Ilaiyaraaja could take the film only halfway. The rest of the journey had to be virtually driven by Kamal, come rain or shine!

Most of Kamal's comedies are strongly laced with social criticism, as would be expected in a proper melodrama. Be it the way he ridicules urban godmen and dealers of modern art in *Kaathala Kaathala,* the double standards of the upper class in *Avvai Shanmughi,* or superstitious beliefs in *Singaravelan* (1992), every film provides an opportunity for Kamal to voice his larger concerns that examine the semi-modern/secular status of modern India. While some believe that social criticisms could get lost in the cacophony of laughter, I think that it actually gets better embedded in our subconscious as a truism through comedy and helps us in moments of social distress.

Comedy in films like *Singaravelan, Michael Madana Kama Rajan* (MMKR), *Sathi Leelavati* (1995) and even *Apoorva Sagodharargal* (*Strange Brothers; 1989)* has the centrality of marital alliances in common. T.G.A. Nelson remarked:

> Marital Comedy has traditionally offered its readers and audiences two complementary, almost contradictory, kinds of pleasure. One is delight in the prospect of successful marriages for characters with whom viewers identify. The other is laughter at disastrous or unsuccessful marriages, arising either from epigrams against wedlock in general or from particular disastrous unions which develop near the periphery of the plot. It is one of the paradoxes of traditional comedy that the leading characters, though confronted with a world filled with unfaithful, embittered or desiccated married people, by those in short whose flame has been dimmed

by marriage, still persist in their joint search for a paradise which they know to be elusive and perhaps illusory.[1]

While *Singaravelan* pursues the comic union of a handsome yet naïve country oaf with an educated, rich and spoilt city girl, other films where Kamal plays multiple roles seeking independent marital alliances provide a platform for mind-boggling combinations, which could easily end as narrative disasters if not handled competently.

Another area of versatility is Kamal's comic use of language. He speaks at least seven different Indian languages, all with a variety of accents, bringing an altogether new dimension to humour in his films.

At a much larger level is Kamal's unmistakable tribute to the duo of Buster Keaton and Charles Chaplin in their 'machine-age comedies'[3]. And I will take Singeetam Srinivasa Rao's two films, namely *Apoorva Sagodharargal* and *MMKR*, to articulate the process. Both these films focus on the fundamental dichotomy of modern industry and the impact of urban 'development' on human society. Kamal was also riding at that moment on the success of *Nayakan* (1987), *Soora Samhaaram* (1988) and *Sathya* (1988), which have stressed on the narratives of social injustice and the vigilante's response to it. In this context, when we see the two abovementioned stories from an objective point of view, it is about children who are victims of tragic circumstances. The mothers have been tortured and betrayed, the fathers have been isolated, the relatives have abandoned the children to their hapless destinies and, through some twist of fate, some strangers have picked them up and moulded them as per their wish. Sounds like the grim narratives of *Les Miserables* or *David Copperfield*. But Kamal spins a completely different approach.

Apoorva Sagodharargal

Kamal's spiritual mentor, who helped him navigate the essence of this story of tragic circumstances, is undoubtedly Charles Chaplin, specifically in his film *The Great Dictator*. Kamal combines Chaplin's burlesque with the counterblow of Alexander Dumas's *The Corsican Brothers* in this story of separated twins Appu and Raja. After their father, an upright police officer, is murdered and their mother poisoned, Appu is born as a dwarf with misshapen teeth and Raja grows up to be a handsome young man. They get separated at birth, with Appu growing up in a circus with his mother while Raja grows up in an automobile mechanic shed with Muniyamma, his foster mother. If Raja is the dapper twin Louis in Paris then Appu is the remorse-filled Lucien from *The Corsican Brothers*. If Raja is the ambitious Hitler of *The Great Dictator* (1940), then Appu is the subaltern barber with a noble heart. Undoubtedly, Kamal's heart was with the downtrodden character Appu when he thought of the original story plot and commenced production under his own banner with Singeetam Srinivasa Rao as the director.

The screenplay focuses on a storyline based on the life of Appu, a clown in a circus. The clown falls in love with two trapeze artistes, but sadly they do not reciprocate. So, in the end, it's supposed to end in a tragedy of unrequited love with a lot of trick shots and also a small heartfelt tribute to Chaplin's *The Circus* (1928); a simple strategy that could allow Chaplin's formula to work in Tamil Nadu through the characters of Appu and Raja.

The film went on the floor with P.C. Sriram at the camera and Ilaiyaraaja doing the music, and had a grand muhurat, where some of the biggest dignitaries of the film industry came to see producer Kamal acting in his own film as a dwarf. Undoubtedly unconventional!

However, after about ten days of shooting, everybody felt uncomfortable, realizing that this film was simply not working. Was it going to be another *Raaja Paarvai* about a physically challenged person struggling through the challenges of life?

That's when they took the story to a fine script doctor/confidante, Panchu Arunachalam, who was also a well-known producer and director. Panchu had written some of Kamal's earlier hits like *Sakalakala Vallavan* and was reputed to correctly gauge the pulse of the Tamil audience. So, he heard the whole story and asked, 'What does this wonderful and unusual hero achieve at the end of the film? Will audiences want to see Kamal lose?' And without changing the destiny of the dwarf he came up with two solutions—the first, to give a strong motive to the dwarf of seeking revenge on the crooks who poisoned his mother and killed his father; the second, to provide the dwarf's twin brother the scope to provide the glamour quotient necessary in a movie starring Kamal. The backbone to this plot is, however, the mother's search for the four villains who killed her husband (also played by Kamal). Aptly, these four represent the establishment, but she reveals them to Appu when he intends to commit suicide after coming to know that the young girl whom he loves is marrying someone else. Now, on realizing the cause of his mother's tragic circumstance, he prepares an elaborate plot to assassinate these four.

Thanks to the fateful discussion with Panchu on that day, *Apoorva Sagodharargal* went on to make box-office history all over India. What was destined to be a 'non-achiever flop' became a tremendous success, not merely in Tamil but also in Hindi and Telugu. The openness with which good filmmakers like Panju Arunachalam and Kamal function by exchanging ideas and other resources is the strength of our film industry.

Kamal always takes great pains to finalize the characterization of his roles. There are two areas he focuses upon. One is his 'get-up' and the second is the voice culture, also called the 'slang' of that character. Most of the big stars, including stalwarts such as Sivaji Ganesan, NTR and Ranga Rao, would simply absorb the character, develop a few gestures and behave as if they were that character. And they were very effective in portraying a variety of roles and ages without much work on their facial make-up or their voice and accents. But Kamal is not like that. He provides a unique dimension and, without doubt, the audience notices all the nuances that he adds by working upon himself.

Everyone wondered how Kamal 'cut his feet' and yet walked perfectly like a dwarf without any CGI effects. The ground had to be dug precisely to the height of Kamal's knees, on which specially designed shoes and pants were fitted to show him walking like a 'normal' dwarf. He had to even match the height and looks of his 'fellow' dwarfs from the circus company. When he was standing on a stool, some extra work had to be done because the open space below the platform was visible. That space was masked out in one shot and re-exposed in another, with it open. These two shots would be sandwiched on an optical printer to provide the required effect. The most enjoyable part, however, was when Kamal had to sit on a chair and swing his 'short' legs. For that effect, the crew had to remove the seating part and Kamal would stand in the gap. Inside there would be another person who would extend his arms at the right height, wearing trousers and shoes on his arms! Together they would create the effect of a seated dwarf. For one shot Kamal had to have his legs tied behind him, with a pair of shoes attached on his knees, and jump out of a jeep, only to land on his knees. With a slim smile, Kamal remarked to me, 'In those moments, when my knees would be sore with pain, I would only remember the grit and determination of my mentors Buster Keaton in *The General* [1926] and Charles Chaplin in *Modern Times* [1936]. If they could pull it off seventy years ago with even more primitive equipment, why could I not?'

Rao says, 'I have a small theory about exaggeration and our audience response to it. Our viewers are not satisfied with the image on the screen merely doing its job of showing the world as it is. They want the role not as it "will be" but as it "should" be, and that requires a touch of unrealism. If they see something which would anyway be seen when they come out of the theatres, they feel disappointed. And sometimes they even want to intervene. I have seen, in traditional Telugu plays, audiences wanting a repeat of a song or a scene and breaking the flow of the narration. So, looking forward to that element of the unreal is their artistic choice and not some form of escapism. It is at that level of expressive statement that you should see the usage of wigs, make-up or even excessive gesticulation. The psychology here is completely different. Naturalistic Realism is unbearable! It could be probably because our significant film history started with the talkies based on mythology with all its singing and dancing. So we are not able to come out of the photographed "mela" of our allied arts!'

When it comes to comedy, both Kamal and Rao have always believed that it must be based on action and not mere spoken words. And that is because of their love for comic strips in papers and magazines. Kamal would take a little sketch to another level altogether. For instance, when he was playing the character of Appu the dwarf, the focus was on how to make the 'unbelievable' look plausible. The entire effort that went into shortening his legs and hands, his smile with misshapen teeth and his big eyes, had to be invisible. The 'normal' character of Raja, on the other hand, required a lot more attention to make him casual yet equally important. So the narration had to be balanced by giving Raja the auto garage song, the song with the tiger mask and the song on the truck.

'I have a simple strategy on location,' says Rao. 'You see, I realize that I am working with a lot of high-profile actors, camerapersons, art directors and music directors on all these films. I have my own pet ideas, but I have to be careful not to thrust them upon the others. So, I begin planting my ideas in small ways during discussions or as suggestions to actors and technicians on location. And then invariably I would see them brighten up and execute them as their own. I was perfectly happy with people claiming credit, so long as they made the final film look good. My job was to complete the film on schedule within the budget and publicize it well before release. In the eight films that we did together, I realized that Kamal was excellent in micromanaging in terms of voice accent, make-up, developing small characteristics, rehearsing with other actors, etc., and I took care of the larger picture, namely, timing, continuity and keeping the integrity of the bigger story. I had to ensure that the chariot did not lose course by watching ahead and behind, while Kamal held the reins of the horses!

'One unit member who should be acknowledged on par with Kamal is Ilaiyaraaja, the music director. You see, working with someone like Ilaiyaaraja has to be seen in the context of the fact that his songs will reach the viewers before the film. And he knows that too! So, his contribution, along with S.P. Balasubrahmanyam's voice, sets the signature for the film, and they really work hard for that. Unknowingly they step into Kamal's Chaplinesque shoes and try to imagine what would make him and a song sequence shine out in an extraordinary way. It had to fit his star image and at the same time sound different too. In fact, the most popular song in this film, "*Raja kaiya vecha*", was sung by Kamal himself. Looking back, I feel Kamal seemed to have a certain kind of legitimate entitlement to these legends!'

As Kamal had imagined, the audience empathized entirely with Appu, the small angry man who shoulders the entire burden of seeking justice for his poor mother who was forced into such indignity by a callous establishment. In very calculated ways he brings down each of the villains, saves his twin from the jaws of death and even unites him happily with his sweetheart while he chooses to put on handcuffs and head off to prison. Appu was the new 'Nayakan'.

Michael Madana Kama Rajan

A few years later, *Michael Madana Kama Rajan* became Panchu Arunachalam's best bet on Kamal. He had bought the rights of a Pakistani film written by a person named Kashmiri. He took the basic subject of quadruplets separated and reunited from the original, and modified it to suit the Tamil audience's tastes. It was developed on the lines of an old royal folk tale, so Kamal asked director Singeetam Srinivasa Rao to open the film as a bioscope operator calling out to children to see the story being unfolded!

Undoubtedly the best character among the quadruplets turned out to be that of the Brahmin cook called Kameswaran. But the credit for that must also go to his romantic muse Tirupurasundari played by Urvashi, her kleptomaniac mother played by S.N. Lakshmi and his catering boss Palakkad Mani played by Delhi Ganesh. This unconventional Brahminical foursome brought the house down with their amazing chemistry and timing. You really cannot explain how this chemistry happens! The other three characters played by Kamal somehow did not reach the same peak and despite extensive analysis, one is not able to figure out why just one of the four equally developed characters managed to cross the boundary line.

The plot begins yet again with a wronged woman, Sushila, played by Jayabharati. She gets pregnant and her lover, Venugopal (R.N.K. Prasad), a wealthy industrialist, promises to organize their marriage. But his brother wants to usurp all the property and hires a goon to get rid of her. When the hitman goes to accost her, he finds that she has given birth to quadruplets under the care of a kind woman. Finding Sushila in a weak condition, he decides to kidnap the kids instead. But all of a sudden he feels remorseful and decides to keep one, leave another in a temple, the third in an orphanage and mistakenly leaves the fourth in the real father Venugopal's car!

The twins in *Apoorva Sagodharargal* and the quadruplet lookalikes in *MMKR* are all trapped, in some way or the other, in regular modern-day work routines. In *MMKR*, Madan grows up to be a stylish businessman, unaware that his foster father is actually his real dad; Raju from the orphanage joins the firefighting force; Kameswaran from the temple steps joins his foster father in the catering business; and the fourth, Michael, is a small-time crook working for the goon who had kidnapped him. Except for Michael, each of them gets involved with a partner, ably played by Urvasi, Rupini and Khushboo, to stage some memorable songs by Ilaiyaraaja, choreographed in a variety of locations by an equally amazing debutant Prabhu Deva who would go on to become a highly successful director in Bollywood.

The complexity of the conflict in *MMKR* begins when the routines of these characters are rendered chaotic through greed for money. Having disposed of Venugopal in an 'accident', the siblings want to inherit the wealth, now written out in Madan's name. But little do they know there are three more lookalikes who might become eligible for the same inheritance. Each time they think they are getting close to finishing Madan, one of them mistakenly comes into the scene and disrupts all their plans. The hilarious coincidences, made even more funny by Crazy Mohan's unforgettable dialogues, conclude with all four siblings reunited by their long-lost mother, who has been in search of them ever since they disappeared on that fateful night.

The array of simple, unsophisticated special effects employed in Rao's films that made thousands of viewers roll with laughter and remember them with awe came about thanks to an enormous amount of hard work and patience. One must remember that the filmmaker had no access to any of the computerized compositing and matting that is available today. Every effect had to be done on camera. So, if the four portrayals of Kamal in *MMKR* had to be shown on the same screen and time, the frame had to be understood by every member of the crew before it could be executed. It was even more complicated than in *Apoorva Sagodharargal*.

Rao concludes, 'Whatever happens, I had to have clarity on the overall picture, knowing full well that our viewers are capable of accepting a film even if they find it 70 per cent up to their expectations. Although I had the entire action plan in mind, I still know that my viewers are quite forgiving, you know! The last climax song in *MMKR*—when all four Kamals assemble at the tea estate looking like Madan, the foreign-returned rich boy—could have been anybody's nightmare. The song is primarily between Raja and the artistic girl, Shalini, played by Khushboo. And into this song arrive the other triplets in a variety of entries and exits, while a gangster wants to somehow finish Madan but does not know that he has three more clones all in the vicinity. The climax scene in the film was Kamal's idea as a tribute to Chaplin's brilliant scene in *Gold Rush* (1925) where the hungry Chaplin and his giant friend are trapped in a house balancing precariously on the edge. You can imagine the complexity of this crazy idea. Now, all the four similar-looking Kamals are trapped in the same small room on the cliff. At least the song was on a vast tea estate, but how was I going to mask out four lookalikes inside such a cramped room? I managed it because of my vast experience in doing trick shots from the days of *Maya Bazar* (1957) where I was the fifth assistant director. And mind you, we had none of the digital masking and zonal colour-correction systems available today.'

From a genre perspective, one could also see *Apoorva Sagodharargal* and *MMKR* as a continuation of the endless number of films made in the 1950s and '60s where the narration was built around 'lost and found' children who grew up to become unwilling products of their circumstances, starting with *Awaara* (1951), where Raj Kapoor is separated from his father as a child and grows up to become a petty criminal, to *Amar Akbar Anthony* (1977), a story about three abandoned boys who grow up to follow three different faiths. The three men in *Amar Akbar Anthony* are, of course, united at the end by a blind mother who miraculously recovers her sight at a temple, after a serious of comic events. I am sure audiences across India will recall such 'lost and found' films in every language. But on introspection, one realizes that they are all resonating with a part of Indian history which most filmmakers and other artistes were unwilling to directly talk about: the great Indian Partition of 1947. Millions died and thousands of families fled across the borders, leaving their loved ones behind or losing them somewhere in their journeys. More impactful than the loss of lives was the loss of one's identity. With the breakdown of all previous territories identified by monarchs, princes and presidencies by feudal caste moorings and places of worship, a population of around 400 million was suddenly rendered 'homeless'. The people could only hope that a small group of leaders from assorted political groups in Delhi would provide some kind of identity. But how could storytellers narrate these gruesome events when the new nation was just rearing to become an independent, forward-looking and self-sustaining entity? How could scriptwriters draft their narration without showing who was the ultimate villain in the partitioning plot? The British who drew the treacherous partitioning line had left the country. So, the choice was between calling either the Hindu or the Muslim as the perpetrator. And that choice was impossible to make. The best way, therefore, was to couch these stories into romantic comedies with a lot of melodramatic sentiment. This form of comedy could still refer to the great tragedy of separation, but at the same time embrace the idea of a Nehruvian India with a new Constitution enshrining equality for all. This is the successful post-Independence narrative that Kamal chooses to continue, albeit in his own style.

In his book *Machine-Age Comedy*, Michael North describes this aptly as a sort of nervous breakdown suffered by the narrative itself.[4] Commenting on *Modern Times*, he says about Chaplin: 'Of course his nervous breakdown also serves at the level of satire on several levels, on the implicit insanity of regularity pushed to the extreme, on the implicit insanity of the division of labor which reduces work to morsels, too tiny to sustain anyone.'[5]

Similarly, in *Apoorva Sagodharargal* and *MMKR*, we see how the denial of the mother's fundamental rights to her children has serious repercussions. It is only due to the satirical form employed by Singeetam Srinivasa Rao and the self-deprecatory style adopted by Kamal that such a serious drama gets converted into an insanely rollicking comedy. Kamal inherits an amazing legacy started by Chaplin in the silent era, which was admirably followed up by Walt Disney in the talkies era. If Chaplin was the quintessential modernist using the most minimal of visual cinema's compositional/linguistic resources, then Disney was the master of utilizing sound in the most complex contrapuntal manners, almost stretching his art to the level of surrealism.

Kamal brings Chaplin's visual minimalism while orchestrating himself into the rhythm of Disney. I am sure that this must have been the discipline to combine the tramp and Mickey Mouse.

What fascinates me is the penchant that Singeetam Srinivasa Rao and Kamal have for the automobile. The car chases are an absolute must, for the car is the most emblematic product of the greedy capitalist system. And we seem to have become complete slaves to the four-wheeler! How often do we see cars simply flying away only to fall and smash into smithereens? There seems to be an insanely childlike joy in creating and watching these car crashes which, in real life, could be so horrendous, something we do not even want to imagine. Just visualizing the fatalities caused by car crashes could make us nauseous, and yet, when it is seen as the human spirit redeeming itself in the face of the cold-blooded machine age, there is immense celebration by children and adults alike.

While working with Kamal, Rao was emboldened to set his stories in modern times and work with the narrative of the heroic adventure. That's probably why Kamal is seen in modern settings like a circus, the automobile garage, big hotels or high-rise buildings in his films. One can even conclude that filmmakers like Rao or Santhana Bharati were fulfilling their deep childhood desires to hit the highways, to run wild, run free when working with Kamal.

15

THEVAR MAGAN: COMING HOME

On 31 July 2016, in a village called Kallimeedi near Nagapattinam, the district collector had to stop the temple festival due to a conflict between two castes on how it should be conducted. The high-caste Pillais quoted the 'traditional' agamas (scriptures) and insisted that their way was the right one. The Dalits claimed that the temple of Goddess Badrakaliamman belongs to their area and so the function should rightly belong to them. Even as recently as 26 August 2019, a report in the *Hindustan Times* said, 'For the fourth year in a row Tamil Nadu's Nagapattinam district administration has cancelled the Sri Badrakaliamman Temple festival due to differences between various caste groups.'[1]

A similar temple stalemate was the focus of Kamal's film *Thevar Magan* (Son of a Chieftain; 1992), which was made exactly twenty-seven years before the latest real-life incident. This conflict raises the question whether this is the same Dravidian state that avowed atheism and chose to drop all caste names as a declaration of secularist and progressive values. Should we not ask what has gone so seriously wrong in our society? Don't we want to change ourselves and see sense?

Thevar Magan probes deep into the emotional reservoirs of the caste system and the Tamil home. It is a film that deserves to figure in top-ten lists, on par with the melodramas of Guru Dutt and Ritwik Ghatak.

The film starts by establishing a carefree funky-haired Kamal as Shaktivel, returning from London after completing his graduation, with Gautami playing Bhanu, a modern-era girlfriend, in tow. When he reaches home, the mere sight of Periya Thevar—his father, played by Sivaji Ganesan—in the front yard is enough to send him scampering away, speechless. Such was the obedience observed in the presence of a high-caste patriarch in villages, irrespective of one's relationship/kinship with him. This is something that continues until today in several feudal hamlets. Somewhere in the deep recesses of Shaktivel's 'modern' mind is the notion that his 'home' belongs to the caste leader first, and to his father later. Instead of rejecting or criticizing such a casteist position, *Thevar Magan* dives deep and tries to analyse how an ancient, time-worn, traditional social construct still manages to run in the veins of South Indian families and the extended society. The Thevar caste/community, consisting of the Mukkulathor, Maravar and Kallar sub-sects, has always been seen as fearsome, warring and extremely proud, and the film tries to reflect this ethos as it dives into the lives of a Thevar family.

The Tamil home space, as also seen in several agrarian settled societies, is defined by a common environ with traditional boundaries demarcating spaces for people belonging to the same: (i) caste; (ii) religion; (iii) language/level of education/erudition; (iv) gender; and, lastly, (v) economic status. The moment there is a discrepancy in any of these five primary commonalities, an immediate source of conflict is evidenced. In most of our melodramas, this understanding functions as a standard rhetoric, more so when placed within a set of post-colonial concerns.

The home is by and large considered the repository of everything that is 'warm and traditional', even if metaphorically so, while the world outside takes up the image of the distant and modern. In all Indian mainstream cinema, the notion of home is an extremely imaginative space burdened with symbols and contradictory sentiments. The home is the space that belongs to the patriarch, the benign mother, the rebellious son and the dutiful daughter. The role of the mother in the household is synonymous with an all-embracing roof, containing within the drama resonating in the authority of the patriarchal pillars. The contradictions inherent in this habitat invariably surface when the daughter moves into the home of another patriarch, her husband, and the future mother—the daughter-in-law—enters the home. *Thevar Magan* manages to take this discourse to a completely different level. In the movie, these factors surface within the few opening minutes when Shaktivel arrives, bringing with him the proposed daughter-in-law and future mother from an 'undefined' other caste and language.

The battle lines are then drawn, though in very subtle ways, in Periya Thevar's sprawling mansion. *Thevar Magan* functions at the level of caste and its interconnections with patriarchy. Understood is also the reality that women in such households virtually remain faceless, only providing all that is required to nurture and sustain their family.

All this is emotionally made available to us through the concordance or discordance between the patriarch and his offspring, who in turn develops independent relationships of peace or conflict with his siblings, lover and the other villagers. At the secondary level, offspring and siblings are stretched into another conflicting household—that of the patriarch's brother, a crippled old man who lives in another part of the same village. His son, Mayan, played by Nasser, has not seen the world outside his village and is therefore stuck in the archetypal politics of a superior caste leader, lording over his subjects. He is the type who has never learned to compromise or to even attempt to understand the rumblings of modernity sweeping across the home/country.

At this juncture I should invoke the insights provided by Rajni Kothari in *Politics in India*:

For any political system to become stable, it is necessary that its procedures are internalized and traditionalized; in other words, the new procedures and values must themselves be turned into 'tradition'. No society lives without tradition and the essential challenge of modernity is not the destruction of tradition but the tradionalization of 'modernity' itself. In the context of caste and politics, this means two things. First, those elements in the caste system that have a secular and integrative potential should be strengthened at the expense of the more obscurantist and dysfunctional elements. Second, the new modes of institutional articulation that secular democratic politics has provided to the social system must themselves become enduring parts of Indian tradition. [2]

I am not implying that Kamal as the writer and Bharathan as the director have consciously infused these thoughts into their work, but they seem to have the right progressive intentions to carry such a 'politically redefined' narrative forward.

Take, for example, the scene in which the Westernized Shaktivel wants to integrate himself into the traditional systems of the village. It is depicted as a song sequence in which Kamal dances with the villagers as they practise the traditional martial art of wielding the silambu (cane). This scene is watched by Bhanu and she takes photographs of his acculturation; at appropriate moments the routine of the dance is frozen into still images through the designing possibilities of the modern apparatus called the camera. In a very formal way, the modern gaze is turned back on the viewer and cleverly traditionalized. As the playful song ends, the violent strains of this tradition emerge as it unfolds into a caste battle. Shaktivel abandons the song, shifts into heroic gear and vanquishes the pugilistic oppositional forces, much to Bhanu's horror.

The family caste unwittingly dominated the discourse of the home. In the context of a post-colonial independent nation, it gains more relevance. In a nation which was hurriedly formed between 1945 and 1947, and quickly configured into a set of twenty-two new regional states, the average Indian citizen at that time had no way to really access his or her political status as a 'citizen' belonging to a new 'home/state'. And then with huge interstate migrations for jobs, education, etc., this identity conundrum did not completely resolve itself. Caste and its cultural affects, therefore, became by default the only identity that defined the 'self'. Sadly, all institutions of state authority and subjugation continued to demand caste and communal identities as reference, be it for educational or job opportunities, leaving several Indian citizens in utter dismay until this day, especially in the rural ecosphere.

With no recourse to any discussion or political negotiation in a public space, nor an 'active news media', Tamil films—like all Indian cinema—took this discourse in the form of stories and screenplays into the 'home' space and used the family to enact the surrogate state. However, the depiction of the 'home' in Tamil cinema too faced many challenges. Not only did Tamil cinema suffer the ravages of a suddenly supplanted national identity, it also had to wake up to the hegemony of the politics fuelling the Hindi-speaking culture. Hindi cinema became its most serious competitor, and the Tamil home needed an even more distinct identity. If the Hindi household remained entwined mostly within a modern context, the Tamil household harked back to the idyllic terracotta-roofed 'home' nestled in paddy fields swaying in the gentle breeze. 'Home' in many Tamil movies was imagined in a small hamlet that could only be accessed by a lone bus service and, in the case of *Thevar Magan*, by a big Plymouth car, thus drawing out the contours that converge tradition and modernity. Is this narrative some sort of ideal vision or does it mirror the realities of dynamic Indian societies?

From the world of the dominant patriarch in the feudal household of *Thevar Magan*, we need to see the dynamics of the women in their households to seek fresh solutions. The conflict in such a Tamil home is usually centred on marriage first and caste second. Thus, the kitchen/cooking space and the front yard (thinai)/social space become the two prosceniums of the social theatre in which the narrative unfolds. While the kitchen locates the womenfolk and their sagas, the front yard sees the men handling outside negotiations. Quite often, the two spaces have an uneasy relationship. The front yard becomes the space where the 'hero' is chastised and, at times, humiliated in 'public', while his poor sweetheart cries her heart out beside the burning hearth of the kitchen, either with her husband's younger sympathetic sibling or his aged helpless grandmother.

These spaces also serve a practical filmic purpose, since the rooms in most rural Tamil homes are not very big, making it very cumbersome to actually place lights and cameras inside. Not much of the film is physically shot inside these houses. So for all filming purposes, the central open-to-sky courtyard (the mitham) becomes the dramatic space inside where the codes of morality and ethics play out against the pros and cons of relationships. Even when sets are built inside studios, this practice of shooting in the inner courtyard is followed.

And it is this central courtyard where the patriarchal space of the home is often challenged by the womenfolk of the family. It is only after a lot of acrimony and compromise that the patriarch lets his daughter have her way, knowing full well that the stranger (her beloved) knows his girl better than him! There is a Telugu folk poem which goes: 'The flavours and nuances of a book are experienced only by a critic, what does the author know? The beauty of a woman is experienced only by her husband, what does her father know?'

It must be noted that the 'home' in Indian and Tamil cinema is not the romantic space as envisioned by Europeans such as Alfred Lord Tennyson, Thomas Mann, Charlotte Brontë, Jane Austen or Oliver Goldsmith. Those were homes to which men returned after war, from cities ravaged by industrialization, from colonial expeditions with booty in a rucksack. In an agrarian society like India, and in Tamil Nadu, which never witnessed the cold industries of modern twentieth century's advancement, nor the ruthless bombings in the killing fields of the Far East and Southeast Asia, the home is a space taken literally for granted.

As observed earlier, all institutions of state authority and subjugation continued to be intimidating and unfriendly post Independence. Tamil films, without a recourse to any discussion or political negotiation in a public space or an 'active news media', took this discourse in the form of stories and screenplays into the 'home' and the family space to enact the surrogate state. The parents and older members often became representatives of the three estates—the judiciary, the executive and the legislature—and, in this case, the 'Thevars', who were also the dominant caste in the growth of the Dravidian party movement in the colonial period.

In typical colonial fashion, the British had favoured the educated Brahmins down South and used the Thevars largely as mercenaries and marauders to frighten the common people, thus deepening the divide in the populace on already existing caste grounds. Even when Subhas Chandra Bose wanted volunteers to join his Indian National Army, the Thevars had offered themselves in large numbers as foot soldiers. Thus, the perception of the Thevars as machete-wielding, hot-blooded mercenaries did not change. It continued even into modern politics and still grips the popular imagination.

Thevar Magan's screenplay brilliantly locates the social bone of contention in the main village temple (shot at a Devi temple near Nagapattinam), which is the ancestral property of the Thevar family. Due to a variety of circumstances, there is a conflict between the two patriarchs as to who should be the temple's presiding benefactor. The fact that it is not clearly explained also mirrors the reality of many such conflicts in Tamil society today. This conflict is symbolically depicted by showing the disputed temple as being shut ever since Shaktivel went abroad to study in London. The onus of the temple's future is squarely placed on the arrival of the Thevar magan, the son of the chieftain.

Why did the story choose the temple as the location for enacting this family feud? Simply because the temple is one of the most important Indian societal spaces. From the Ram Janmabhoomi in Ayodhya to the Sabarimala temple in Kerala, is the Indian temple a religious space or a space primarily reserved for certain castes or genders? In the discriminatory practices during the British rule, which defined temples, mosques or churches purely as 'religious' spaces and therefore to be made available only to their followers, a social dilemma was born. And it was in this debate that a 'national' movement was generated from the early nineteenth century onwards, giving birth to 'nationalist' thinkers in the form of 'spiritual' leaders such as Dayananda Saraswati and Swami Vivekananda in Bengal, Narayana Guru in Kerala and Ramalinga Adigalar in Tamil Nadu. Later, even Mahatma Gandhi and Vinoba Bhave, with their spiritual stances, appeared like 'saints' to the people. Adding to this debate was the insertion of the term 'secularism' into our Constitution, probably with the intention to reaffirm that the nation continues to walk the spiritual path laid by such savants and not the religious paths being advocated by some.

In this context, *Thevar Magan* tries to study the ramifications of what happens when modern and secular-minded Shaktivel enters the scene after four years of self-exile. He faces the caste, religious and economic conundrums and is forced to decide which one of these forces has to be prioritized. In a very Gandhian approach, he chooses economic livelihood as the most important. Thus, the screenplay creates a situation which sees the large village being partitioned by a barbed-wire fence, at the behest of Shakitvel's cousin Mayan, which brings untold suffering to the poor underdogs of the village. Their daily life and jobs are disrupted due to the conflict between the two rival patriarchs.

Shaktivel convinces his father to give up his entitlement to the property to make Mayan happy, and orders that the barricades be brought down. Despite this, Mayan is unhappy because of the way the villagers express gratitude to Shaktivel. He decides to take revenge by inflicting yet another wound on the villagers. He gets his henchmen to blast open the check dam built around the nearby lake, thus causing a flash flood that ruins their fields.

The next morning when Shaktivel surveys the wanton destruction, his heart breaks and he is left speechless. How can a feud result in such extreme misery to innocent people? He sees a child dead and entangled around some bushes in the slush. Symbolically, he removes the shoes that he always wears (a symbol of the modern Western world) and puts his bare feet into the slush, announcing his entry into the murky world of feudal politics. Yet again, in another symbolic gesture, the story sees the passing

away of Periya Thevar, thus officially making the son the new patriarch of
the Thevar community, his village and his family, in that order.

The on-screen relationship between Shaktivel and Periya Thevar bears
close resemblance to the fond and parental off-screen affiliation between
Kamal and Sivaji Ganesan. Kamal recalls, 'One day we needed a solid
ornate wooden chair for the scene where the patriarch addresses the
villagers, and the set prop guys were out searching for one. Much to the
irritation of Sivaji sir, who was a stickler for time, we had to keep delaying
the day's first shot without telling him the reason. After some hours the
chair arrived, and a vexed Sivaji sir sat down and completed the scene. A
few days later, he left after he had finished all his scenes. And then we did
the scene where I sit down on the same chair as the new village chieftain.
Two months later, when we were dubbing the film with Sivaji sir, he saw
the scene in which I sat on the same chair to address the villagers. His
eyes looked amused and he exclaimed, "You little brat! Now I know why
you delayed that scene for so long. That ornate chair was not just some
gesture of respect for my sake, but it looks like you wanted to be seen
sitting on it too!"'

Kamal believes, on- and off-screen, that tackling an issue head-on is
more important than pontificating urban solutions for the upliftment of
the poor. His real and reel lives—like that of many genuine artistes, be
it filmmakers or others—have witnessed cross-pollination between his
personal world and the world of archetypes. Kamal genuinely believes in
the examples set by Gandhi and Periyar. And solutions in the Gandhian
tradition demand sacrifice of the personal world of desires. To find an
amicable resolution to the feudal conflicts, Shaktivel goes one more step
forward by marrying Panchavarnam (Revathi), a poor young girl from
Mayan's part of the village, thus emotionally binding the two patriarchs
together, possibly forever. And from Rajni Kothari's point of view, this
becomes a point where we witness the traditionalization of modernity
itself.

This one act by the character Shaktivel in the movie would have
provided fodder for discussion across hundreds of households in Tamil

Nadu. Should an individual sacrifice his personal commitment to one woman and marry another due to 'social commitments'? What future is Bhanu left with? How could he take the innocent poor girl for granted like this? How will he bring up the child that is being nurtured in his wife Panchavarnam's womb? What made Mayan so angry that he virtually got himself killed by Shaktivel?

And yet such incidents, in various shades, must have occurred within these and hundreds of other families across the state. The real/reel life of Kamal/Shaktivel must have resonated with the real lives of so many others and enlightened so many among the audiences that it makes Kamal, by default, one of the most important shamanic narrators in Tamil Nadu's modern popular culture!

The national resonance to this very 'Tamil' theme was made possible when this film was remade as *Viraasat* by Priyadarshan in 1997. In this scene-to-scene copy of the original, Anil Kapoor played the lead role while his father's role was essayed by Amrish Puri. With Tabu and Pooja Batra playing the female leads, this film went on to become Bollywood's highest grosser for that year. It will indeed be an interesting exercise to study cross-caste/cultural trends prevailing across India during that period.

This brings us to a very important question that has haunted Tamil popular discourse and several fans even in cyberspace. Whose film is *Thevar Magan*? The film won National Awards for Best Tamil Film, Best Supporting Actress (Revathi), Best Audiography (Pandurangan), Best Female Playback Singer (Janaki) and Special Jury Award for Acting (Sivaji Ganesan). In his forty years of unparalleled success as Tamil cinema's screen icon, Sivaji had never won a National Award for acting! And when he did, it was a mere 'special mention'. He declined to receive it and never made a noise about it. In 1997, he was awarded the Dadasaheb Phalke award, the highest national honour. So, whose film is this?

Kamal believes that it hardly matters, because the success of the film means more than just authorship of the story or the script. Artistes in the film industry know just how the journey to the film shown on screen has been negotiated, and who took which decision at what stage of the process.

It is common knowledge in the film industry that with regard to *Thevar Magan*, a detailed story was given by the producer, Kamal, to the director, Bharathan, who was undoubtedly an amazing craftsman and set designer but was often absent on location due to personal reasons.

In most films, in India at least, the final screenplay is always a work in progress with several contributors to the process of storytelling from the scripting stage to the last minutes of final sound mixing. Kamal wrote the screenplay for the first time on Movie Magic, a computer software, but should we equate the bound screenplay with, say, the final architectural design for a skyscraper? Can one not realize that the making of a film involves so many artistes, each with their unique talent, assembling to tell a story which the audience ends up seeing? How can that film/story have 'one' inviolable author? So, whose film is *Thevar Magan*?

From the ultimate consumer/viewer's point of view, it is Kamal's film, just as *Lagaan* (2001) is Aamir Khan's film. In reality, a film is the outcome of the efforts of many people, at various levels of hierarchy. Presumably, this must have been how shamanistic narratives like the Ramayana or the Mahabharata evolved. Popular myths are created by combining multiple ideational sources, packaging them under the aegis of one title and ascribing it to one author like Valmiki or Vyasa. From Kamal's personal point of view, the project must have started off with a very simple idea— his desire to work with the great Sivaji Ganesan and get himself maximum screen time with the legend. Deep in his heart he would have wanted to stake claim as the true inheritor of the great thespian's acting prowess, and he played the role of his son!

The film remains unforgettable thanks to some immortal musical compositions by Ilaiyaraaja, the performance by actress Revathi, who depicts the young bride singing a song (playback provided by the inimitable Janaki), the awkward Westernized portrayal by Gautami and the subdued yet brilliant cinematography by P.C. Sriram. And, last but not the least, the number of audiences in South India who cheered on this film even after Kamal had delivered some serious flops.

16

THE SPARTACUS TRILOGY: *MAHANADHI, KURUTHIPUNAL, INDIAN*

In our conversations, Kamal has often referred to the legend of Spartacus. The most famous version of this legend is the controversial Stanley Kubrick film, *Spartacus* (1960), starring Kirk Douglas. Kamal saw this film in his late teens and it certainly seems to have had an impact on him. Here, I attempt to connect this narrative—of a slave struggling to establish the contradictory positions of slavery and freedom—with three of Kamal's films, *Mahanadhi* (1994), *Kuruthipunal* (1995) and *Indian* (1996). The Spartacus discourse dominates them all. Kamal focuses the narrative of Spartacus on the conceptualization of faith and its attributes. 'What kind of faith allows the enslaved to move from one day to another when death by violence is written so clearly on the wall?' In fact, in *Mahanadhi*, there is a scene that is a straightforward tribute to [the movie] *Spartacus*. In it, Kamal singlehandedly beats up the crooked oppressor in the kitchen, where every slave collects a few morsels of food, their only access to something called 'personal dignity'.

Both Kirk Douglas and Kamal have a common desire to get back at the system however they can. Director Stanley Kubrick and Douglas chose to employ outlawed screenwriter Truman Capote to write *Spartacus* to get back at the treacherous House Un-American Activities Committee,

created to monitor suspicious activities of American citizens believed
to have Communist ties, which had demoralized the progressive spirit
of many a filmmaker in Hollywood in those days. Kamal, seeking to get
back at a system that was unprofessional, unimaginative and unwilling
to back his projects, ended up financing/producing his own ventures. In
both cases, their actions spurred a deep love–hate relationship with their
respective film fraternities, thanks to their decidedly naïve approach to
what they perceived as 'being a rebel'!

It is indeed intriguing to see how the image and social narrative of
Spartacus can be read in Kamal's three films at a subconscious level.
Within the melodramatic purview of mainstream Indian cinema, they
are more realistic in terms of incidents, conflict situations and human
relationships. The Spartacus theme weaves through these films through
the primary characters, who are enmeshed in powerful systems and are
also emotionally enslaved to the safety and well-being of their beloveds
or their progeny. This enslavement renders them enormously vulnerable
despite their 'visibly' superhuman strength. The emotional enslavement
also largely prevents them from any form of protest or rebellion. The
system may open up a few possibilities for escape, but no sooner than
these are revealed, other forces creep in to seal these options with even
more powerful repetitions of their fearsomeness. Ultimately, despite the
support of a few, these Spartacus-like characters played by Kamal do
manage to penetrate impossible barriers and redeem themselves. Though
still emotionally enslaved, they finally reveal their superhuman powers
and bring hope to their community.

All three films also share the common undercurrent of a father deeply
vulnerable to the insecurities he experiences regarding the future of
his wife and children. This mid-1990s marked a period when Kamal's
daughters were young. Was he reacting to some kind of fear in his own
mind through these films? There is a crucial line in *Kuruthipunal* when the
police officer Adinarayan (Kamal) warns a captured terrorist that everyone
ultimately reaches a breaking point when they have to shed their ideals to

face the realities of survival. Little does Adinarayan realize that these very words will ricochet on him.

As we explore these three films, we realize that Kamal has managed to incorporate some of his own socio-political concerns and advance their stories in an extremely symbiotic manner. He is always a very important contributor to all the films he acts in. His contribution to these films by doing more than just acting out a narrative also brings us to the question of ownership. Who owns these films? At whose door can the credit for these works be laid? For his part, Kamal feels that he gets paid and enjoys doing it too. 'I am probably the luckiest guy in Indian cinema to keep getting paid well to do what I enjoy and relish the most!' is a favourite statement of his in most interviews, whether on TV or in the print media.

Mahanadhi: *A Confluence of Rivers*

I begin with the first of this 'Spartacus trilogy', namely *Mahanadhi* (The Great River). The film begins with a scene on the Cauvery river, showing the faith that Indians have built around their multiple river systems. All the primary characters in the film are named after rivers. Kamal is called Krishna, his late wife Narmada, the woman who later supports his children is Yamuna and his daughter is Kaveri, the one who finally ends up enslaved as a prostitute on the banks of the Ganga river in the red-light district of Calcutta. These great rivers unite the maps of slavery, as did the landscape of Thrace to Rome for Spartacus. Directed by Santhana Bharati, the film deals with the story of a naïve village landlord (played by Kamal), who is lured and enslaved into the greedy chit-fund business in a metropolis. Krishna owns a betel-nut estate in a small town and is enticed by a city-slicker promoter (played brilliantly by Hanifa) with the promise of a high rate of interest from a chit fund. Unknown to Krishna, the promoter is connected to a bigger political mafia and before long, the company runs out of capital. All the depositors blast into Krishna's office, demanding their money back. Unable to pay them, Krishna is arrested and sentenced to imprisonment. While he is in jail, his daughter is kidnapped by the promoter's gang and sent off to Calcutta to become a prostitute. When Krishna comes out of prison and discovers the villains' treachery, he reaches breaking point, mutilates himself and kills the villains.

The heroic path is deeply connected to the idea of the father (Krishna) wanting to atone to his children for the poor standard of living that he has provided them thus far.

Krishna's cellmate in prison is a deeply religious old man who believes that the Almighty can only do good, provided man remains faithful. But Krishna is a rationalist (as is Kamal) and believes that blind faith has no place in a modern environment. This dialectic keeps playing back and forth, revealing a variety of contradictory shades.

The enslavement reaches its pinnacle as we see Krishna having to do menial jobs in the kitchens of the jail, as happens to Spartacus in legend. Kamal notes, 'The kitchen is the most basic space for any human being and becomes the site for revolt in [the movie] *Spartacus*. It is also there that I get my character to raise the "sword" in protest for the first time [in *Mahanadhi*]. Anger and violence are two qualities that I have zero tolerance for. And yet, that often becomes the only remedy available to the human species on planet earth. Spartacus is freed from enslavement to become an entertainer in the arena of gladiators. The rather exaggerated fight scene in the kitchen [in *Mahanadhi*] is the contradiction. I have to be an angry victimized beast but also an entertainer for the masses.'

The jail sentence over, Krishna is out again, hoping to reunite with his family, only to realize that his mother is no more and his children are missing. What happens to a slave's faith now? What happens when he falls in love in the midst of all this suffering? What happens when the slave realizes that there are still people who care for the slaves? The film has a good police officer who empathizes with Krishna's condition, a good nurse (the character of Yamuna) who plays mother to his children, a good street juggler who is willing to return his son to him and the religious cellmate who opens his doors to him. The rivers still exist, despite the dirty stinking Cooum sewage canal that winds through the entire length of Madras.

Director Santhana Bharati says, 'Undoubtedly, this film is largely Kamal's vision and we did our best to help his ideas take shape. Even though it is a very dramatic story, he wanted to make it as realistic as possible. So detailed was he about the jail conditions that we picked up several props [of] condemned [stuff] from real jails. The maximum attention was given to the sequence where he goes to find his daughter in Sonagachi, the red-light district of Calcutta. We went there a few days ahead and spoke to the women in that district and sought their help in doing the climax scene in the most realistic manner. After hearing the film's story, they were truly moved. Although the interiors were shot in Madras, the outdoors were shot in Sonagachi with real sex workers. I cannot get over those wonderful helpful moments in a film that is soaked in human deprivation and helplessness.'

'The idea of finding the daughter in a brothel came to me at that time due to a peculiar incident,' says Kamal. 'I heard rumours that there were some people in my neighbourhood who were planning to take away my little daughter who was about six years old. Of course, nothing like that happened, but it [the anxiety] kept obsessing me. Maybe that's why I chose to destress myself by staging such a scene.'

As in all good melodramas, the heroic slave slays the villains in a nightmarish encounter reminiscent of the climax in the film *Taxi Driver* (1976), where Travis shoots down all the crooks in the bloodiest shootout ever. The climax of *Mahanadhi* shows Kamal fighting the evil politician who headed the political mafia that caused his life savings to vanish, him to be jailed and his daughter to end up in a brothel in Calcutta. The fight takes place on the roof of a multistorey building with Kamal wielding a machete. The politician is pushed off the roof while fighting, but grabs Kamal's arm. In the blink of an eye, Kamal severs his own arm and the politician plummets to his death several storeys below.

Reviewing this film today, one can see the concerned Kamal taking early steps towards giving up escapist entertainment and moving towards creating meaningful cinema. When the film was released in 1994, it became the talk of the town, touching everyone's heart. Every women's college and social forum referred to the film with deep sympathy. Although not a financial success, the film certainly emboldened Kamal to make the next part of his Spartacus trilogy, *Kuruthipunal*, a remake of Govind Nihalani's *Drohkaal* (The Age of Betrayal; 1994).

Kuruthipunal: *When Treachery Is the Name of the Game*

In P.C. Sriram's *Kuruthipunal* (Streams of Blood), Kamal plays Adinarayan, an upright, fearless cop who, along with Abbas (Arjun), tries to nab a dreaded terrorist called Badri who gets away scot-free every time thanks to his contacts. Adi learns that his own mentor, an inspector-general, is involved with the powerful terrorist. And when that terrorist holds his wife and son hostage, Adi, emotionally enslaved, chooses to negotiate by virtually freeing the terrorist he had imprisoned. This leads to his innocent comrades being slaughtered. Adi rises to action and fights back. But when his valour runs out of steam, he tells his junior Abbas to shoot him dead and also to pretend to join forces with the enemy to keep the vigil alive and uncompromised. Spartacus, in this case, continues to live on through his young successor.

Kamal chose to produce *Kuruthipunal* under his banner Raaj Kamal Films International as he realized that in this narrative lay everything that modern Indian politics wallowed in, especially in Tamil Nadu. *Kuruthipunal* epitomizes the angst of the Tamilian's betrayal of his or her promised Tamil land. The film locates the narrative of fear as the key factor in driving everything, from the demand for devotion to the nation-state to protecting one's kith and kin at home.

E. John, one of the actors in the film as well as a creative associate, maintains, 'This was undoubtedly RKFI's [Raaj Kamal Films International] most ambitious and daring venture—no songs, no heroics and very little melodrama. The Hindi version [*Drohkaal*] had two character actors, Naseeruddin Shah and Om Puri, playing two sincere cops caught in the larger game of political violence and the counter-violence staged by anti-establishment forces. But in our version, we had two top stars in Kamal and Arjun taking on these roles, both of whom were doomed to die virtually from the start.

'Would the audience be able to see the undercurrent messages of the grand Dravidian betrayal in this story? Would the audience accept their superheroes losing in the face of adversity? We had to therefore buttress the emotion of their blind bravery couched in their implicit belief of the larger democratic system. So the Tamil version begins with the killing of innocent schoolchildren in a school bus by a bomb, which was meant to kill Kamal in his police jeep just a few metres behind. And ironically, our version ends with Kamal's little son firing away at two young urchins with his toy gun, vowing revenge.'

Directed by P.C. Sriram, with Mahesh providing the background score, Kamal pushed the envelope in this highly realistic format, shorn of all greasepaint and the manifold masks he always takes great delight in donning as a bahuroopi. Interestingly, the terrorist, Badri, is shown as an intellectual, a person driven by the same love for the nation as Adi and Abbas. Here is a villain with a rational motivation.

John helps connect this link, saying, 'We based this loosely on the activities conducted by the PWG (People's War Group) operating largely in Andhra Pradesh. They were an offshoot of the CPI (ML) [Communist Party of India (Marxist Leninist)] and Naxalite groups in West Bengal and worked largely with marginalized peasants and tribes. Most of the PWG members were highly educated and included young women too. That inspired us to bring a nice parallel to Adi and Abbas's married status in the form of a couple who are dumped on Adi's family by Badri [discussed later in this chapter]. The female characters play a kind of femme fatale, as we see in the all-male dominated film noir movies.'

Between shooting *Mahanadhi* and after a series of not-so-inspiring movies in 1994 (*Kalaignan, Magalir Mattum* and *Nammavar*), Kamal chose to get back to his favourite subject of deprivation, urbanization and violence, and the way they penetrate the psyche of the common citizen. Coming from a Gandhian position of non-violence and seeing the futility of violence in resolving any form of conflict, the enquiry becomes even more interesting when this subject is explored via the workings of a police corps dedicated to the quelling of terroristic groups in civil society.

Kuruthipunal is a strong critique of governmental institutions that confuse and condemn any sort of radical social activism as terrorism. The film also strongly critiques how the state—a democracy—openly supports the wealthy minority as saviours of the majority, despite their corruption and nepotism. The film also reveals how members of the government become selfish and greedy while paying lip service to the importance of duty and selfless dedication to the nation. In short, it informs us how the dissident and extremist forces are more sincere and committed to their cause than state officials.

Kamal, playing a Spartacus-like role, is a slave of the system, brainwashed to believe that the authorities have only the best interests of the people in mind, that the maintenance of law and order is extremely important to bring about a harmonious existence and that those who work as 'slaves' must equally exhibit ownership of the national cause. He posits the key players, the slaves or police officers, one Hindu (Kamal) and one Muslim (Arjun). The gladiator arena is the national space where the terrorists enact their plans. The head of the terrorist outfit is named Badri, a strong Vaishnavite Hindu name. Lastly, the traitors to this cause all hold senior positions in the police force.

Yet again, Kamal's Spartacus is a married man with a child. Obviously, this zone is going to be his challenge with regard to loyalty—will he choose the nation or his family? As the father, how will he resolve anything that goes wrong and as the husband, does he love his wife more than the nation?

The plot throws up yet another interesting dimension. The dissident groups succeed because they are capable of infiltrating governmental ranks through sympathetic officials or through blackmail and threats of death. So, the plot proposes that the most rational way to counter such a strategy would be for the 'governing' forces to infiltrate the ranks of terrorist outfits. Therefore, Adi and Abbas plant two of their policemen into the terrorists' group. One of them is caught and killed, while the second, Dhanush (played by Arvind Krishna), goes up Badri's ranks and becomes his second-in-command.

This system could be termed as treachery by anyone sitting on the other side of the fence, but from Kamal's point of view it is the best way out since it allows the dominant state force to empathize with its dissenters and hopefully bring an end to all animosity. Therefore, at the end of the film, while a policeman takes charge of the 'terrorist' outfit, out on the streets, Adi's son is attacked by the young orphaned children of Badri's men who were shot dead by the police force. Will Adi's son grow up to be an avenger and take up arms to continue the path of violence? Or will the policeman who has taken charge of the gang become the harbinger of peace and end all violence?

The women in this film have very interesting roles to play too. Although Kamal plays a married character, he is still a sexy poster boy for the Tamil audience. One of the opening scenes shows Adi coming out of the shower and talking to his wife Sumitra (played by Gauthami). During the conversation he casually slips on his underwear and gets into his work attire. As he exits, he gives her a passionate kiss. The scene uncovers several layers of relationships that take place within the film and outside. From Sumitra's point of view, he is her eternal lover boy and she does not blush at his amorous entreaties. From Adi's point of view, he needs Sumitra to be a buffer against the fearful world outside. He loves her and his son so much that he would be willing to forsake his colleagues and the nation, if need be. She is almost like a mother figure for him.

From the plot point of view, this almost sublime relationship is contrasted against a couple that Badri sends to watch over Sumitra and her son. Can we read this as a counter-position to Adi? Just as the executive state has its slaves, why can't the counter-state also possess its own slaves? Little does anyone realize that the new 'terrorist' who has forcibly occupied Adi's space is a lecherous person who is going to molest Sumitra after shooting his own partner.

John reminisces, 'I had several friends in the extreme left groups and I noticed that the few educated women who entered these groups were also the source of several internal conflicts among the men.' The character of Abbas's wife, Zeenath (played by Geetha), sends a secular message. Abbas and Zeenath are as much a part of the Indian 'traditional' landscape as are Adi and Sumitra. Secondly, the façade of Muslims being prone to terrorism is also ripped away. In fact, the anti-national character has a strong Vaishnavite name like Badri. Does this not resonate with Kamal making a very strong political statement in an election campaign when he stated that Nathuram Godse, a Hindu, was independent India's first extremist?[1]

Kuruthipunal deals with two kinds of slaves—those who are on the side of democratic authority and those who are pressured by extremist agencies. They are both vulnerable yet capable of resisting authorities. Loyalty and blind obedience can arise even under free conditions, as exhibited by Adi, who vows loyalty to his nation despite discovering that his boss is a traitor. The Spartacus in Adi can be seen in real life too, in every police officer who does his duty, and in Kamal himself who has a real fan base outside the movie theatre. In the movie, Adi chooses to die but leaves behind an equally dedicated young man to assume his 'patriotic' role of chasing the terrorist before he is assassinated.

The way the women characters related to the underlings in Badri's gang are treated is also interesting. The first underling is a good marksman on the rocket launcher but lives in completely impoverished conditions. His wife wants him to leave this boss who simply does not care for his well-being, although the underling provides him 'valuable' service. The wife of the second underling is a good cook and her food is so alluring that he is willing to take great risks to reach her.

The fatal meeting between this henchman, played by John himself, and his wife, is one of the greatest moments in Tamil film history. She waits for him in a typical tent cinema in rural Tamil Nadu. When he comes, she sneaks out of the tent and takes him to a vacant space behind the screen to serve him some fresh fish masala with rice. So, the backdrop of an old Tamil film (now seen on the obverse of the screen), is seen as the best place for him to relish his last delectable supper. This acts as a fitting tribute to the seductive powers of Tamil cinema, as a metaphor for Tamil film writers and their technicians who held political sway over the Tamil masses, and lastly as the space where Tamil women come to participate in such celluloid dreams.

Just as the Roman nation, which was supposed to be the refuge for all her slaves, became a concentration camp, from the Tamil audience's perspective, their dream of a Dravidian state, a utopian Tamil republic, had been shattered. They had been betrayed by their Dravidian leaders who had joined hands with the hegemonic Congress for their survival, letting down the motherland. In contrast, *Kuruthipunal* ends with Sumitra being requested to come up on stage to receive a medal of honour on behalf of her brave husband while her son battles 'other' kids in the car park.

In this process, subtly, the positioning of the character of Dhanush as an undercover agent is also problematized. Will Dhanush join forces with the so-called terrorist outfit or will he find the vital clues required to dismantle Badri's outfit? Will Dhanush continue to trust the police force which had betrayed his beloved commander? The audience is left wondering.

Indian: *When You Can't Beat Them, Join Them*

In Shankar's blockbuster *Indian*, Kamal plays a double role—Senapathy, an ex-army man, a patriotic father and an expert in Varmakalai, an ancient martial art from Kerala whose practitioners can disable opponents by hitting at certain nerve endings with the fingertips; and his son Chandru, a crooked government officer. Senapathy is emotionally enslaved by his love for his son and, in a way, oppressed by his wife, who shields the corrupt son from his highly principled father. The son thus grows up without ever seeing the power of Spartacus at home. The father fights injustice all over

India by exterminating wrongdoers using his traditional martial arts skills. One day he is shocked to learn that his own son is indulging in corrupt practices at the regional transport office. Chandru's actions lead to the death of innocent children in a faulty school bus. Will the old man mete out justice with the same measure now? Or will he remain a slave to the emotional bonds that tie him to his son?

The pairing of director Shankar and Kamal in 1995 must have been the best news for everyone involved in the business of cinema. Honestly, only Shankar can claim that every film of his is designed to be a blockbuster from inception itself. His films are always very well planned, pay meticulous attention to detail and include a lot of popular storytelling tropes. They usually entail several days of shooting. From exhibitors to poster designers, from junior artistes to buyers of audio rights, from make-up assistants to black-market ticket vendors, they must have all celebrated when they heard about *Indian*.

Indian was produced by A.M. Rathinam and had the biggest budget the Indian film industry had ever seen till 1994. When Kamal signed up for it, he realized there were aspects to the movie which would be in sharp contrast to the kind of serious narratives he was working on in *Mahanadhi* and *Kuruthipunal*. With an eye on the all-India market, he decided to cast Hindi actresses, and even the villains were from other regions. Shankar always worked with his pet formula—the split personality/Dr Jekyll and Mr Hyde—and his films always had spectacular songs and big fights. As Kamal would often admit, 'Money is a big factor in this industry and when you yourself are a product on the shelf, you have to do a clever balance. To run my production house, I need the money and I have just my body to depend upon! To balance this equation, I also chose to place a stronger emphasis on the old father's character rather than his son, whose role was also played by me. When you can't beat them, join them.'

Few films in the history of Tamil cinema could have been produced at such a vital political moment of history. If Kamal's earlier films resonated with the deep betrayals caused by the DMK–AIADMK rift, this film was shot during an era when Tamil Nadu saw the biggest and most vulgar display of wealth that a chief minister could have ever staged. Jayalalithaa, who swept into power as Tamil Nadu's youngest chief minister in 1991, following the assassination of Rajiv Gandhi on the outskirts of Madras, had risen to a level of autocratic power never witnessed before. Stories of her corruption in the multinational corridors of giants like Ford, Hyundai and BMW, who were setting up plants in the state, made newspaper headlines.

Unfazed by these allegations, she decided to hold the wedding of her foster son Sudhakar to the granddaughter of the great thespian Sivaji Ganesan in grand style. Money flowed like water and gold jewellery sparkled everywhere. For a leader who had sworn to take a token Rs 1 as her salary, this grandeur and lavishness left the common citizens shell-shocked. Was this the same person who had sworn to bring justice to the poor Tamil women by abolishing alcohol when she came to power? This betrayal was reflected in the film.

As mentioned in the beginning, Kamal plays the double role of father and son. Senapathy has retired and lives on an idyllic farm while his son Chandru is an agent/fixer in the road transport office, plying licences and 'authorized' permits for hefty commissions. To dilute his corrupt nature, the film cast two famous comic artistes, Senthil and Goundamani, as his sidekicks, who bribe their way through the bureaucratic corridors. The hilarious scenes in the RTO office help tone down Chandru's villainous aspect and even make us feel that it is cool to be a bit corrupt so long as it does not harm anybody. Was this an analogy of the corrupt state of Jayalalithaa, marketed as entertainment for the masses by the news media?

When corruption reaches its peak, Senapathy's beloved daughter dies due to the carelessness of a tainted medical system. All the Spartacus-like father's love for the nation seems to have been wasted by the actions of the son, to whom he is emotionally enslaved. The father finally chooses to rebel against this enslavement and puts an end to his own son.

So, how does the Spartacus strategy work out here? The opening scenes emphasize how the idealistic father takes a series of lethal actions against a lot of corrupt officials, but in complete secrecy. Since he just uses the power of his fingers to hit certain nerve endings, he does not leave a single trace behind. An alert police officer, played by Nedumudi Venu, is intrigued by the modus operandi and is anxious to nab this mysterious vigilante.

At home, too, the father wants to see justice and good behaviour. But Chandru does not agree and walks out. The rebel father is a silent predator, but the son, who chooses to be a gladiator, to fight for existence in the open arena, is an entertainer. From the audience's point of view, he provides the entertainment they have come for. Lavish song scenes in Australia and elaborately choreographed indoor sequences leave the viewers spellbound.

Yet, whenever you ask a typical Tamil audience about Shankar's films, they will state that his movies were about corruption and social justice. Why would they not want to admit the fact that the highlights of the film were actually the lavish songs and elaborate fight sequences? Though the entertainer is a corrupt character, Kamal has to portray the personality in a likeable manner. Although he is punished for his misdeeds at the end of the story, his presence in the film as his father's alter ego must be presented in an enjoyable way. This is the troubled zone of *Spartacus* and similar melodramas.

The core issue of slavery and human exploitation is very serious, but the onus of this troubled state of affairs cannot be placed on the shoulders of the audience who come from the very same society. In fact, the audience would have included a sizeable share of people from the police forces and other government departments. To point fingers at such an audience for its complicity in this grand charade of public corruption would not be palatable. Everybody in the audience would always like to believe that the crooked parasites are 'out there' and the audiences 'in here' have nothing to do with them.

Is it insensitive to be entertained by the very same element/emotion that disturbs and disrupts so much of our normal life? This troubled zone is also problematized by yet another issue: Chandru walks out of his father's home without giving a thought to the possibility of learning his father's skills, which could have helped him judge the world better, to sift the good from the bad. Joseph Campbell, in his master work on dramaturgy, *The Hero with a Thousand Faces*, says, 'Whether he knows it or not and no matter what position in Society, the father is the initiating priest through whom the young being passes on into the larger world.'[2] But in *Indian*, that is not to be.

Chandru disobeys his father Senapathy while his dutiful sister Kasturi stays back. Sadly, punishment strikes the father first. His daughter Kasturi suffers third-degree burns in an accident and he rushes her to the hospital. The chief doctor wants a bribe to attend to her, knowing the father's desperation. Senapathy refuses and traps him in a room. He calls for a TV camera crew and televises the killing of the doctor to the public, in the process revealing his other identity of the 'silent' killer.

This film set the trend for TV camera crews to appear in many films after, reflecting that TV as a medium has become concomitant with 'truth'. If it appears on TV, it must be the truth, even if it is a detergent soap that is being advertised. Images of Jayalalithaa and her clan decked in gold, parading themselves in a vulgar and grotesque manner, made her citizens stand up. Is this what 'entertaining display' was all about? While one set lodged cases of 'disproportionate assets' against Jayalalithaa, the rest were thoroughly impressed and voted her back to power with a thumping majority. Kamal and Shankar understood this new political truism very well and laughed their way to the bank too.

Back to *Indian*. The father is finally identified as the vigilante by the investigating police officer and through him, Senapathy realizes that the crook behind a lot of transportation frauds is his own son, Chandru. The father must now atone for the greatest sin he has committed—having fathered such an unscrupulous son. The gladiators' arena now shifts to the public sphere. The father confronts his son and cops inside a mortuary where the son bribes the doctors to get him freed. The cops nab Senapathy but he escapes once again to stage a dramatic encounter in an aerodrome with the cops. As the audiences at that time watched the pyrotechnics that followed till Senapathy manages to reach his son and stab him to death, for them it was entertainment that was worth every paisa spent on screen. This was the most expensive Tamil film made until that day, which also went on to become the biggest grosser ever among all of Kamal's films. Interestingly, this film also got Kamal the National Award, the Tamil Nadu State Award and the Filmfare Award for Best Actor; the National Awards for Best Special Effects went to Venky and the Best Set Design Award for Thota Tharani's work. The Hindi dubbed version with a few replaced scenes, *Hindustani,* also went on to become a box-office success.

But when we watch the Spartacus trilogy today, there is no doubt that the high-budget-dependent *Indian,* with all its technology, looks very dated, while the 'mostly' realistic *Mahanadhi* and *Kuruthipunal* still look reasonably fresh. It is also because the latter films have enormous empathy for their women characters while Shankar's *Indian* focuses entirely on the male protagonist, making the three main female characters cardboard cut-outs with zero soul in their portrayals.

Indian ends with Senapathy taking refuge in a foreign country and promising the decent investigating police officer that he will come back whenever the forces of evil in India should escalate to a high pitch. And at the time of writing, the sequel, *Indian 2,* is due for release.

17

HEY RAM: COURTING CONTROVERSY

'When I conceived the idea for *Hey Ram*,' recalls Kamal, 'it was developed like a crime thriller on the lines of *The Day of the Jackal* (1973). But after several readings, I felt that the approach of empathizing with the anxieties of Gandhi's assassin, Nathuram Godse, was very reactionary. I changed it around completely and made the story get some respect for the protagonist. Undoubtedly, the film got me a lot of respect, but it flopped. It's then that you realize that perceiving one's work is different from the reality of filmmaking, namely, this business of producing films and buying/selling tickets at the box office is not about respect.'

Kamal's screenplay narrates the story of Saket Ram (played by him), from the archaeology department who is working at the Mohenjo Daro excavation site along with his colleague Amjad Khan (played by Shah Rukh Khan), when news of the impending Partition of India comes in. They choose to go back, Amjad to Delhi and Saket to Calcutta, where his wife Aparna (Rani Mukerji) lives. When Saket arrives in Calcutta there is severe tension brewing on the streets. A group of Muslim rioters enter his house, rape and kill Aparna, leaving him distraught. That's when he meets a right-wing extremist, Abhyankar (Atul Kulkarni), who convinces him that the only way to save the nation is to make India a Hindu state. Saket goes back to Thanjavur, his native place, totally depressed. His uncle

and aunt convince him to marry a young woman, Mythili (Vasundhara
Das). On their honeymoon near Pune, Ram meets Abhyankar again who
reminds him of the solution. Ram is ensnared by his rhetoric and agrees
to assassinate Gandhi. When he lands in Delhi, he ends up by chance in
Amjad Khan's house and meets all his family members. A reluctant Saket
wants to get away from there when Amjad's home comes under attack by
Hindu nationalists. His friendship with Amjad wins over his feelings of
animosity towards the other and he defends the family. Amjad's family and
pregnant wife are secured first. A shootout begins and at a crucial moment
Amjad is shot, trying to save Saket. The next day Saket wants to seek the
Mahatma's forgiveness but another fate is in store for a frail Gandhiji.

The role of Mahatma Gandhi in this film is played by Naseeruddin
Shah, whose ultimate desire had always been to essay the character of
the Mahatma. Kamal set up the Gandhi assassination scene in the lush
green gardens of a colonial bungalow in Ooty, since it would have been
too hot to shoot in Delhi in July. Junior artistes were driven down from
Bangalore, wearing North Indian attire suitable to the period. One day, a
small group of musicians were rehearsing the hymn 'Vaishnava jana toh'
as they waited for Shah to get ready. When the camera set-up was finally
ready, Shah emerged from his cabin, made up like the Mahatma. The noisy
location suddenly turned silent as he walked towards the others like an old
man, with his palms joined in prayer. All the junior artistes and musicians
stood up unprompted, palms joined in deep respect. It was as if it were
30 January 1948 all over again. Kamal had goosebumps all over his body
as he hoped that the audiences would also feel the same when the film
hits the screens. Shah played up the illusion with aplomb until a young
sound engineer walked up to him to pin the wireless microphone inside
his shawl. By mistake the pin pricked his chest and Shah yelled, 'Oh hell,
what the fuck are you doing?' and decided to pin on the mic himself. In a
flash, the illusion was broken. A small pin caused a level of agony that the
ensuing bullet would not! Everybody got back to work.

Months later, truly constructed on the lines of a David Lean epic,
we see this film journey through the dark vicissitudes of a nation in

transformation and the struggle of an individual in realigning identities! Through the character of Saket Ram, played by Kamal, we see the various dilemmas in the Gandhian perspectives towards ethics and national freedom. In one scene, Ram declares Gandhi's autobiography, *My Experiments with Truth*, to be semi-fictional and the film goes on to show how the various narratives embodied in the work crisscross through Ram's life. At a dramatic level, it is Gandhi's ideological stance of strange mystic pacifism that traumatizes an enraged Saket Ram, who is reacting to the brutal massacre his beloved wife had to undergo during Partition. Why does Saket Ram turn fundamentalist?

I would now like to pick up a sample of the relevant visual layers opening up narratives and see how Kamal has gone about treating these layers. Symbolically, the film begins with excavations being undertaken by two archeologist surveyors, Amjad Khan and Saket Ram, at Mohenjo Daro, shortly after 14–15 August 1947 when Independence was declared and the creation of Pakistan had become a reality. A site once seen as the cradle of an entire South Asian civilization had now come to be precisely located within the political boundaries of a brand-new nation-state called Pakistan.

The site of the ancient ruins of Mohenjo Daro from the Indus Valley civilization is mythically the utopian South Asian space where the story of the Hindus, Muslims and Sindhis who came together here in their 'originating' cultural space takes place. Suddenly, due to a variety of reasons, this hallowed space is now politically reorganized through a bitter partition with mainland India, causing enormous acrimony, displacement and bloodshed. With the declaration of Independence or the 'pack-up' call for the British, the Indus Valley became part of Pakistan, but ironically is still touted as part of Ram's so-called Indian heritage. The common people, especially those living on both sides of the border, got no warning, and therefore were simply unprepared to handle the ensuing mob frenzy.

The film depicts this and shows this agony spreading into colonial Calcutta and even the smaller provinces of Maharashtra. Next is shown the small temple town in Tamil Nadu from which Saket Ram originates, and its Brahminical precincts. It seems to be blissfully ignorant of all the national turmoil. And then there is the Delhi landscape, which has seen hundreds of invasions, where we see a frail Mahatma Gandhi giving speeches about amity and compassion. Lastly, the story ends in riot-affected Madras, where the old Saket Ram, lying on a stretcher, is lowered into a dry stormwater drain under the pretext of escaping the wrath of fundamentalists in 1999. The dying old man was played by Kamal's older brother Chandrahasan, who in a strange way resembled Gandhi.

Was the ultra-disciplined Saket Ram another facet of Gandhi? Whose India was and is this anyway? Which of these visual layers/landscapes truly represent India?

The oft-repeated saga of Hindu–Muslim antagonism becomes the primary dramatic conflict zone for this film. While most narratives play up the minority card and often show Muslims as peace-loving and religious, this film tries to see what transforms an ordinary Hindu into a fundamentalist. And this fundamentalist Hindu wants to kill Gandhi, another Hindu, for not being able to stop the Partition, which racked the nation from August to November 1947.

Bringing a twist to the tale in the climax is Saket Ram's Muslim archeologist, Amjad Khan, who has chosen to live in Delhi as a genuine Gandhi follower instead of migrating to Pakistan. Shah Rukh Khan was so impressed by the vision of the film that he refused to charge a penny for his performance as Amjad, instead deeming it an honour to get an opportunity to work with a legend like Kamal.

Shortly after Partition, Saket Ram is able to meet up with his beloved colleague Amjad but gets trapped in Amjad's locality and is forced to fire upon Hindu militants who want to attack the Muslim ghetto. Credit must be given here to the meticulous attention given to the set décor by Sabu Cyril and his rapport with the cinematographer, Thiru. Together they brought alive a period which very few films have paid attention to.

The architecture of Amjad Khan's home and basement strangely resembles the Mohenjo Daro site, emphasizing the crucial narrative purpose of the film—a story can merely unearth some findings, but it depends upon the people who unearth it to decipher the codes etched into it. In short, the saga of the Mahatma's assassination can be unearthed, but it depends on the viewers to determine its significance.

At a cultural level of this conundrum, the narrative tries to deconstruct Saket Ram's Hindu space. At first, he belongs to a secular space, which allows him to marry his beloved with simple marital vows and no religious ceremonies; after her rape and death, the subsequent marriage with Mythili, a lady from a Hindu feudal household, has no element of 'choice' and is formalized with a ritual-bound ceremony. Then he makes an intoxicating entry into the politicized all-male world of Hindutva, where the gun is supreme. All three events are further discussed below.

Another facet of the story is when Amjad's wife, Nafisa, adopts Saket Ram as her brother, quite like the way Maulana Azad and Suhrawardy were comrades of the Mahatma. And then there is the in-between category of the Sindhi friend, Manohar Lalwani, neither Hindu nor Muslim, who is forced to beg for his survival in an estranged landscape.

The music in the film was designed to play a crucial role. Kamal initially selected the renowned violinist L. Subramaniam. Not much used to composing music for films, Subramaniam struggled, using up hours of precious recording studio time. A few songs did get ready, but Kamal was not too convinced of their emotional power. So Subramaniam and Kamal parted ways and he went back to his old friend Ilaiyaraaja. This kind of substitution had never happened in Ilaiyaraaja's career, but for Kamal's sake, he stepped in and did something which no other musician could have done. He retained the original voice tracks but replaced the melodic music track arrangements to evoke the right mood to seduce audiences into the multiple layers hidden in the film. To give it even more depth, Ilaiyaraaja went to Hungary and had the music performed by the Budapest Symphony Orchestra, a feat never before witnessed in Indian cinema.

Politics as a seductive agency dominates a big part of the film. From the beginning, Kamal decides to frame Saket Ram as being obsessively in love with a Bengali friend, Aparna, his first wife, in the backdrop of the relentless Hindu–Muslim riots all over Calcutta. In a subliminal way, Aparna represents the quality of an undivided Indian landmass, capable of living all by herself, at least in a poetic imagination. She waits, loves, asserts her rights and demands loyalty from her beloved. Yet, in the face of violence, she is vulnerable and capable of being destroyed.

Mythili, the young Iyengar girl and Saket Ram's second wife, is cloistered in orthodoxy but in the modern private domain with her educated husband, is capable of opening up and demanding affection from the 'other' partner. This brazenness helps Saket Ram to come out of his depression to be seduced once again into the lure of serving 'nationhood'. At the same time, behind this conventional heterosexuality there is the presence of an individual deeply in love with himself and his values, bordering on narcissism. Like the legendary Narcissus, he is deeply troubled at his image not conforming to what he, as a male, positions as ideal, ethical or Gandhian.

Saket Ram would like to see his reflection in Gandhi but the waters have unfortunately become too bloody for comfort. Is the gun that he embraces, therefore, a new phallus, devoid of any romance? Is the lizard on bloody waters a metaphor for his capability to survive and be hated at any cost? Or is it the auspicious symbol as revered by the Vaishnavite community, of which he is now an entrenched part?

Kamal proposes a paradigm that forces the Indian male to seek the 'collective citizen' status or, in other words, break the 'caste-based feudal family' bond. To commemorate Gandhi's 150th birth anniversary, a special screening of Hey Ram was held in Chennai. Moderating the discussion post screening, I asked him why he chose to eroticize Saket Ram's liaison with right-wing politics of that period.

Kamal replied, 'There are two levels. One was to metaphorize the orgasmic high that fanatics could build themselves up to feel in such rabble-rousing. The second was to posit Saket Ram as an antithesis to the Mahatma's avowed celibacy, which he claimed was a powerful source of inner strength.'

It is almost like saying that if sexual awakening is required to break away from the feudal family, then citizenship in the collective status also demands the willingness of the individual to bear arms and engage in 'public' violence to assert a modern nation state. Let us also not forget that sexuality has been the running theme and strategy in scores of films that Kamal has powered through over thirty-five years. 'So, if the Mahatma chose austerity and celibacy as an important pathway in the search for truth, I thought it would be appropriate to see the emergence of the antagonist in Saket Ram within the ambience of opulence and eroticism. Such a mood gives him a strong high to entertain the idea of assassinating a world leader. If you recollect, Saket is given a kind of alcoholic potion on his arrival at the Raja's palace and from thereon begins his "drunken" ruthless journey.'

Kamal also recreates a new mythos around the crucial days of late January 1948 when Gandhi was assassinated, depicting some more radical groups who were keen on eliminating Gandhi. Suddenly Saket Ram realizes he is not alone, neither as a fundamentalist, nor as a secular comrade coming to the rescue of Amjad Khan and his family in distress. Saket Ram's frenzy and irrational fundamentalism ceases when he sees Gandhi being shot in front of his eyes. To his shock and surprise, all that remains in the sylvan surroundings after this dastardly act is Gandhi's pair of slippers. He has to find a new path in order to cleanse himself of all the heinous thoughts that had consumed him.

To deal with such a complex transition from a 'normal' citizen who is seduced into becoming a politicized agent and back to the demoralized present tense, Kamal uses Abhyankar, a Hindu right-wing leader, as the seducer to transport Ram into the citizen/state diatribe. At first it starts with Saket Ram's inability to consummate the union with his young Iyengar Brahmin bride. He withdraws into a zombie-like state when he revisits the site of his first wife's rape in Calcutta. Next, he retrieves an image of Durga painted by her to resurrect a lost nationality. Interestingly, in popular culture, India is often painted as a mother goddess. He comes back home with the painting and this time he chooses to take his young wife along to meet Abhyankar and his royal patron somewhere in Maharashtra. They travel by plane and, nestled in the clouds, away from Mother Earth, his wife gets closer to him. The decadent palatial space of the maharaja is where Ram's surreal journey into the contested zone of nation versus state begins. The royal Hindu patron wants his followers to plot the murder of Gandhi, a secret wish which is already nestled in Saket Ram's id. To make it simpler, Saket Ram is given a strong alcoholic potion by Abhyankar, which transports him into a world of machismo as he watches Abhyankar valiantly ride a horse in a polo match. The horse stumbles and in the process cripples Abhyankar, which in turn results in Saket Ram having to take on/get seduced into donning the mantle of Gandhi's assassin. Training himself to be a marksman, abandoning his seductive wife and sending off his Sindhi friend into the comforts of a daily job become the starting point for the third act to begin.

From here on the narrative of seduction switches the film from a semi-realist melodramatic path into an expressionist journey where he travels to New Delhi and into the womb of a self-styled bastion of peace: the silent gardens from where the Mahatma attempts to orchestrate some kind of peaceful solution to the anarchy and mayhem that followed the declaration of Independence. Saket Ram has to kill Gandhi here, but fate in the guise of searching for his lost gun/phallus brings him into the womb of the Azad Soda factory inside a Muslim ghetto, where a young Muslim woman is giving birth. Here Saket Ram reconnects with Amjad Khan, his spiritual other, and chooses to stay back and defend the Muslims/his enemies of the subconscious from his own ego in the guise of the Hindu militants seeking bloody revenge.

The expressionist journey could trace itself to the visual stylistics employed by Edvard Munch in his painting *The Scream,* or the sensuous murals of the Mattanchery palace; from the weird sets of the classic *The Cabinet of Dr. Caligari* (1920) to the sci-fi visions of Ridley Scott. The imaging reaches a high point when the pregnant Muslim woman is located inside a basement which can be accessed by a stepladder. She delivers her child in a space surrounded by other women-in-support, while in the world outside of this womb-like space, her husband and other males battle out their ideological values. The father dies outside while the mother delivers his child inside. Saket Ram's ego is shattered when he hears the wails of the widowed wife overlapped by the cries of the newborn. And with those cries, his long surreal journey is over and the original Saket Ram is born again to share space with Amjad, who has fallen victim to a militant's bullet. Amjad dies with a smile, holding the arms of his comrade, his brother Ram. From Indus Valley to Azad Soda Factory, it has been a torturous journey for all Indians and in the film, Saket Ram is just one among the millions who has been affected.

On 30 January 1948, a repentant Saket Ram arrives at the Birla House to ask for forgiveness. In a brilliantly scripted scene, Saket meets the Mahatma along with the family of the slain Amjad Khan, who feel so touched in the presence of a great leader. Gandhi expresses his embarrassment at being called a 'Mahatma' and praises Ram's valour for saving a Muslim family from assassins. 'Even you are a Mahatma, my Ram,' he says. Saket is unable to tell him his real background but can only say that he is not worthy of such acknowledgement. The film comes back briefly to the surreal coincidence of three times and spaces. An ashamed Ram watches the Mahatma walk to his prayer meet; the old, dying Ram is trapped in the 1992 crossfire of Hindu–Muslim riots; the British overseer at the Mohenjo-Daro site in 1947 tells Ram that it is pack-up time. Cut back to the present—the next day Ram comes back with tears in his eyes to surrender his gun at the feet of the Mahatma, but he is already getting late for his prayer meeting. Suddenly out of nowhere Nathuram Godse appears and Saket Ram sees the Mahatma being assassinated. He rushes into the melee with a mind to shoot the assassin, but he cannot bring himself to commit another heinous crime. He moves forward to have one last glimpse but only manages to retrieve his slippers and spectacles. In real life, as Gandhi fell, some of his followers were supposed to have heard him utter, 'Hey Ram.' Kamal does not give us the pleasure of hearing this iconic utterance, which has become part of India's hagiography. The audience would anyway be uttering it in their subconscious.

Who is this Ram supposed to be anyway? What is so sacred about this icon that it enshrines so many codes of conduct, notions of governance and other values attached to social relationships for the vast majority of Indians? Can Ram, the mythological sacred image, overpower the potential of a real character's saga onscreen with all the emotions packed in?

Dozens of film reviewers, commentators and scholars have, of course, discussed and deconstructed the film. Ravi Vasudevan reads the film as a giant digital game, while others have rapped it as a blatantly right-wing partisan film. A few have lamented about why the RSS (Rashtriya Swayamsevak Sangh) never protested the depiction of one of their fellows being shown as a cold-blooded assassin. Often when I read their cries about the lack of historicity and rationality in dramatic films, I wonder whether they know how to watch films in the first place as another artistic recreation with a lot of imagination mixed in with some local specifics. Films like *Hey Ram* evolve on the sets in highly organic ways with multiple contributors and cannot/should not be ascribed to one filmmaker's intentionality.

Did Kamal anticipate this eventuality? Is that why the film pays no importance to what happened to our protagonist Saket Ram after the incident on 30 January 1948? Is that why the film locates the 'present' at a time when Hindu militants rent the air with shouts of 'Hey Ram' while they damaged the Babri Masjid on 6 December 1992? Why did Kamal choose to give the old, dying Saket Ram a last journey where he had to be hidden inside the gutters of the city in order to escape the same kind of marauders who pillaged the streets of Calcutta fifty-five years earlier? Was this just a part of the visual design which echoes the opening high–low levels of Mohenjo Daro, or was this the only way to redeem the guilt of the protagonist who could not protect his beloved, the nation, when she was being raped in front of his eyes? Is the film accusing all of us of inaction in the face of wanton vandalism and aggression where even the basic ideas of human dignity and civility are thrown away? Or is the film a warning that such a frenzy can erupt at any moment?

The hectic tension of writing, acting, directing and producing such a massive venture took its toll when Kamal set out to do the assassination scene. He was, in fact, seriously ill when the scene was set up in Ooty with hundreds of junior artistes and scores of make-up artistes and costumers ready for the final scene. Cinematographer Thiru had never done a historical scene such as this before, and Kamal was stretched out in a van, unable to get up.

'I cannot forget the invaluable help chipped in by Girish Karnad, who played the role of my father-in-law,' recalls Kamal with tears in his eyes. 'With his years of experience as a director, he ran back and forth from the van to the sets and executed the entire scene by himself. If it was not for his comforting presence, I too may have not lived to see this day!'

The film ends with the last rites for Saket Ram. Mourners are paying their last respects to the body which has been laid out, ready to be taken to the cremation ground, and into this scene arrives Tushar Gandhi, Mahatma Gandhi's grandson. In a strange cinematic confluence, the real person comes to meet the imagined character to see a veritable display of photographic memories set up in a spartan study. On the walls we Saket Ram's prized photos of Amjad and Abhyankar, along with many others. Love and compassion allowed Ram to overcome all prejudices, possibly in order to come to terms with himself.

18

AALAVANDHAN: AN ENCOUNTER WITH THE FANTASTIC

While 'popular' Indian films keep getting rejected at all the so-called important international festivals, film studies' academia all over the world have started analysing them very seriously, either as an exotic postmodern form or as an important method to examine post-colonial social reactions. The 'fantastic' in our melodramatic films seems, and probably is, largely improvised, non-standard and seriously dependent on the specific regional audience's ways of reading/enjoying the text and its subtexts. The bigger problem in such a deconstruction process comes when our films enter the zone of the 'fantasy' or the 'uncanny' but do not confine to their Western paradigm portrayed in films such as *Edward Scissorhands* (1990) or *The Imaginarium of Doctor Paranassus* (2009), or in science-fiction films like *Prometheus* (2010) and *Alien* (1979).

Tzvetan Todorov offers the following explanation of the 'fantastic' in his book *The Fantastic*:

In a world which is indeed our world, the one we know ... there occurs an event which cannot be explained by the laws of this same familiar world. The person who experiences the event must opt for one of two possible solutions: either he is the victim of an illusion of the senses, of a product of the imagination—and the laws of the world then remain what they are; or else the event has indeed taken place, it is an integral part of reality—but then this reality is controlled by laws unknown to us.[1]

Todorov explains the genre of the fantastic as distinguished from the surreal or science fiction due to the rather realistic nature of its narration, which balances precariously in a state of vulnerability, as if it is 'hesitating' on the threshold between the real and the fantastic. Todorov sees the characters in these fantastic narratives as almost being real, but the fact that they walk the thin, icy bridge called hesitation makes them unique, defenceless and poetic at the same time. The narrative therefore becomes a very uneasy experience for the viewers too, since they are all asked to keep awake while they are in deep sleep, in a manner of speaking.

Among all of Kamal's films, *Aalavandhan* (He Came to Rule; 2001) could be the most complex and complicated. Following the mixed responses that *Hey Ram* received in the press and among the public, Kamal decided to provide an antithesis by adapting a book he had written earlier, called *Dayam*, which he hoped would answer some of the enigmas of identity through this new film. He would play twins, one of them a nation-loving police officer and the other a mental patient living with the trauma caused by an evil stepmother. While *Hey Ram* works largely with the idea of politics encountering psychology, *Aalavandhan* (called *Abhay* in Hindi) deals with the inner world of the abused twin Nandakumar and his psychic space, where the sacred/innocent crosses paths with the vulgar/highly influenced mind; where God encounters the animal; where God is a flawed character because He is possessed by some of His own memories and therefore can exhibit no love whatsoever. In some ways Kamal seems to continue exploring the mindset of Nathuram Godse, the man who claimed to love India and yet assassinated somebody very dear to the nation. How did Godse justify his crime? Is there a criminal in all of us who wants to rule the world? In more ways than one, I am convinced that Kamal's strange Dostoyevskian psyche constantly vacillates between the mythological structures in his mother's Bhakti tales, his mentors' ingenious ways of transcreating their stories on films and his own sense of naïveté, which allows him to see the ever-changing world around him as adbhuta (wonderful) with childlike fascination. I am also sure that producer S. Thanu and director Suresh Krissna would have also joined the project just to see how Kamal journeys though this phantasmagoria.

For Kamal, the greatest strength of Indian mainstream cinema was its ability to reinterpret the tenets of European melodrama with some amazing indigenous twists. Thanks to the proven nationwide success of this approach, also read as 'formula/masala', which creates new archetypes in the collision between myths and modern realities, Indian film melodrama is now addressed by several scholars as an extraordinary structural device.

The character of Nandakumar is a kind of Quasimodo from *The Hunchback of Notre Dame* meets Norman Bates from *Psycho* (1960) and also Hannibal Lecter from *The Silence of the Lambs* (1991) within the confines of a mental asylum. It is also a kind of platform where Freudian archetypes meet with Indian mythical characters caught in the dilemma of Tamilians trapped at the crossroads of Dravidian chauvinism and liberal pan-Indian aspirations.

It is therefore relevant to study this film in the context of the films *Gunaa* and *Hey Ram*. The three primary characters in this triumvirate, namely Krishna (*Gunaa*), Saket Ram (*Hey Ram*) and Nandakumar (*Aalavandhan*), have one thing in common. They are romantics who are deeply content with living in an imaginary zone, possessing strong beliefs in the 'goodness' of humanity, but also people who would like to tear themselves away from the real world to go even deeper into the zone of the fantastic. They are all virtually two characters living in one androgynous body, where one of them sleeps snug in the primordial womb that provides eternal security while the other is furiously aware that the lover/nation/mother is being threatened and it is imperative that he moves out to destroy the adversary, even if it is at the cost of sacrificing the self-contented dreamer.

In all three films Kamal studies the position of 'hesitation' in a trance-like manner. Krishna in *Gunaa*, who has eloped with a beautiful devotee woman, wants to preserve the apparition of the goddess that he sees in her from being desecrated by her family. Saket Ram in *Hey Ram*, the newly married man, wants to ensure that the nation is going to be safe from those very fundamentalists who had raped his first wife. Nandakumar, who has escaped from jail, wants to protect the sanctity of his mother's image from the monstrous stepmother of his childhood. I believe that the strong sense of naïveté that Kamal claims as his most powerful weapon in real life surfaces very strongly as these three characters struggle to cherish their deep sleep while also having to wake up to slay the monsters harassing the nation/mother/lover.

'When we came on the sets of these films, I chose to dive into the deep end and immerse myself into the thought process of the audience. In such a space, I am neither aware of my creative processes nor their rationale. I sort of travel inwards and empower myself to make fantastic advances. Like a Jules Verne who wrote about space travel a hundred years before space shuttles came into existence, a combination of the heart and mind. I live between my two ears and there I can see an infinite space opening up. But whatever else happened, this film broke my back, while I wish it had gone to break other things too, like box-office records for example!' comments Kamal with his inimitable laughter.

And, like many of his experimental ventures, *Aalavandhan* left the audiences puzzled, wondering what just happened to their icon who had spun a superhit comedy titled *Thenali* (2000) just a few months earlier. The box-office response for this film was just lukewarm. And yet, after over twenty years of its inception, the film is remembered and even fiercely discussed. Many years later, Quentin Tarantino would see the film somewhere and decide to use the style of intercutting between 2D animations of action sequences with the live action version of the same scene in his films.[2]

Why do such iconic films remain relevant only in private conversations and not on the big screens? Are the intentions of the film more overwhelming than the executory capabilities/results? Should we also watch Indian mainstream films a bit more carefully for their intended aspirations rather than how it plays out at a sheer emotional and entertainment level? After a screening of Mani Ratnam's *Thalapathi* (1991), I was once talking to film studies guru Dudley Andrews who said, 'Do you realize that this film is just far too post-modern for the average Westerner's comfort?' I wish I could have shown him *Aalavandhan* and left him more aghast!

Aalavandhan starts off with an idealistic position where Nandakumar's twin brother, Vijay, is the perfect hero as an army officer successfully raiding terrorists who are holding a bunch of foreign tourists hostage. While Nandakumar gets mentally deranged, stabs the stepmother to death and is thereafter incarcerated for psychotic schizophrenia in a mental asylum, Vijay joins the army and qualifies to train as a commando. One twin thus internalizes the violence, while the other twin is able to rationalize and externalize killing in justifiable ways. Nandakumar's inability to come to terms with his memories results in an exaggerated body—big, bald and almost hunchbacked. But his perseverance to take revenge on the cruel stepmother is his only motivation to move forward in life. It is almost like if he ever forgot about it, he would die.

Where the film departs from the typical filmy sentimental relationship between estranged twin brothers is by probing into the subconscious of a modern schizophrenic mind instead. How does the mind construe what is violence, along with its associated modern-day images and sounds? Although this is a huge risk being taken in a mainstream film, one obvious area Kamal introspects about is the area of the entertainment media itself, especially through cartoons where there is a barrage of violence, as seen from *Phantom* to *Batman*.

Interesting to note is the fact that the film does not show the young Nandakumar absorbed in such books or shows. The film believes that these influences are virtually in the air and impossible to be missed. It instead highlights the kind of unbridled domestic violence in upper-class families which can have a shattering impact on vulnerable young minds. How does this real behaviour encounter with animated images of violence to form certain influences in a young mind?

Vijay's girlfriend Tejaswini (Raveena Tandon) and her parents are modern in their outlook, deciding to conduct their wedding after Tejaswini is already a few months pregnant. Nandakumar, however, is against this marriage. Like the maternally oppressed Norman Bates in Hitchcock's *Psycho*, he perceives Tejaswini as the reincarnation of his cruel stepmother coming back to take away Vijay, who is his only connection with the world.

As a powerful trope, the film introduces the memories of Nandakumar in the form of a diary where he has recorded all the trauma of growing up under his stepmother's shadow. Despite the dementia that has consumed him and locked him in an asylum under the care of a reasonably kind psychoanalyst, the diary seems to have sustained strongly in his memories.

Yet again, in parallel, the saga of the Dravidian betrayals reached its peak when the AIADMK led by Jayalalithaa crashed to its worst defeat in 1996, with the DMK sweeping all thirty-nine Lok Sabha seats and over two hundred Assembly seats. This time the Indian National Congress had allied with Jayalalithaa only to win four assembly seats in all. Who was ruling whom and how?

Aalavandhan can also be seen as Kamal's answer to Shankar's *Indian*, the blockbuster he was part of five years earlier. It was intended to be a multilingual pan-Indian film as well, capable of appealing to audiences across India with a mixed set of actors and locations set in New Delhi. The lead heroines, Raveena Tandon and Manisha Koirala, as well as other Bollywood actors like Milind Gunaji and Vikram Gokhale, could have been seen as a good marketing ploy to garner more finances. What differentiates *Indian* from this film is the characterization of the women who display an amazing range—a scheming stepmother (Kittu Gidwani), a progressive news anchor (Raveena Tandon), a kind mother (Anu Haasan) and a popstar (Manisha Koirala). That all these women navigated the narration in equal proportions to their male counterparts can be credited to Kamal's original story and the screenplay he generated from it.

Todorov further explains that the genre of the fantastic requires the fulfilment of three conditions. First, the text must oblige the reader to consider the world of the characters as a world of living persons and to hesitate between a natural or supernatural explanation of the events described. Second, this hesitation may also be experienced by a character; thus, the reader's role is, so to speak, entrusted to a character and at the same time the hesitation is represented in the process of becoming one of the themes of the work. Often, in the case of naïve reading, the actual reader identifies himself with the character. Third, the reader must adopt a certain attitude with regard to the text: he will reject allegorical as well as 'poetic' interpretations and seek his or her own ways to locate the state of 'hesitation'.[4]

The film has a rather ingenious way of getting the audience to enter the schizophrenic Nandakumar's mind. Nandu has been condemned by the system to be an animal, locked up in a cage. Tejaswini decides that grave injustice has been done to him and demands that his incarceration should be contested. Vijay takes her to meet him in prison. On seeing her, as mentioned earlier, Nandu hallucinates that she is his cruel stepmother. He is convinced that Vijay needs to be protected from the predatory stepmother. In a fit of fury, he manages to escape the prison, but he is so overloaded with anti-depressant medication that the urban landscape transforms into a fantasy. The entire urban landscape becomes a dystopic simulacrum where reality has been subsumed by media images and cartoonish virtual reality like a giant game. The city has now become the killing fields and the audience gets to sympathize with the weakened mind in a brutal animal's body. Is this what Nandakumar has come to rule?

On an entirely new axis, while writing out his memories, Nandakumar transcends the film to another level when the narrative of violence crosses paths with exquisite Tamil poetry, with flashbacks of his real mother reading out poems to him. These images are, in fact, very personal to Kamal—they echo his own memories of his mother, a wonderfully courageous woman wearing a six-yard khadi sari, educating herself by borrowing books from a nearby library in Paramakudi. She was instrumental in teaching him the nuances of Tamil poems and stories when he had stopped going to school, preferring instead to apprentice in a theatre group at just twelve years of age. Flashbacks of his mother reading poems are real for Kamal, but the conjunction with a stepmother comes from the new leaders of the Tamil state whom he witnesses betraying his dreams.

Nandakumar is out to kill that twenty-first century fatal attraction that has twisted young Tamil minds. Archetypically, the character of the stepmother is depicted in the film as a woman who smokes, drinks and has extramarital affairs without caring much for her stepchildren. She appears yet again in his imagination when he is grown up, as a fiendish dancing entertainer in the midst of a neon-lit shopping mall dominated by McDonalds', gaming arcades and drug dealers. His first weapon is the beauty of Tamil poetry and the second is a sharp knife he discovers in his maternal uncle's collection. One can cleanse the mind while the other frees his body. Both the weapons are somehow connected with the romantic notion of his mother and it is only through a schizophrenic position that he can use the two 'beloved' tools to kill his stepmother, the femme fatale!

But Nandakumar also suffers from a serious fear of the same stepmother and wants his mother to step out of his imagination and do something about it. Long years of sedation in an asylum also warp his thinking capabilities and he is unable to dislodge the memories of his wonderful Tamil mother and the tortures inflicted by a cruel colonial-looking stepmother.

The third act in the film sees the arrival of a surreal dancer called Sharmilee, played by Manisha Koirala. For quite some time the narration leaves you wondering whether she is an imaginary character or a real dancer with whom Tejaswini is desperate to get an interview.

The broader intentions of the film are obviously to implicate modern mass media such as television channels in splitting our identities and making us behave almost like schizophrenics in invisible ways. Our value systems sharply vary in how we behave and react to the 'amoral/ immoral' whims of iconic figures and in the way we react to similar behaviour in our domestic/fraternal folds. While we are tolerant about the excesses committed by our icons/virtual characters, why is it that we are unforgiving when it comes to our own near and dear ones? Modern mass media revels in the display and valourization of such icons, but the common viewer is forced to see it as 'mythology/simulacra' and chooses to remain a passive viewer.

And then there are media images in which rampant violence is taken for granted, accepted as falling within the normal parameters of entertainment. Kamal chooses to reflect critically upon this gross yet dangerous situation even if it affects his fundamental iconic position as a star. His star image had been bolstered with blockbuster movies like *Sakalakala Vallavan* (1982) and *Guru* (1980), where he played larger-than-life superheroes. How do we deal with a self-critiquing star? What is Kamal's way of redeeming his self-critiquing characters?

One strategy Kamal adopts in this film is to let himself loose in the manner that Bhakti poetry enters the huge imaginary ocean of simulacra and its associated mythical Hindu legends of reincarnation. That, according to me, is his greatest strength and he claims that such an affinity is only possible if an artist can remain distanced as an atheist. Brought up in a strongly Vaishnavite family, the stories of Vishnu's reincarnation on planet Earth in order to periodically redeem the people's imbalanced burdens of sin and virtues dominate several of his stories. In *Aalavandhan* the reference is to the Narasimha avatar of Vishnu, half-god and half-monster. He chooses to see the avatar of Narasimha not as a god but as another bahuroopi, a multifaceted person who is capable of changing his masks and, at the same time, remains untouched by the vicissitudes of the character's performance.

That, in essence, would be the way to approach this film and study it in the context of yet another important position in the construct of the Indian narrative, namely the structure of the Natya Shastra[5] and its rasa (emotions) theory, especially highlighting the rasa of adbhuta or wonder, which is the area Todorov calls the 'marvellous'.

Adbhuta is all about a feeling of wonderment that is akin to ecstasy. It is traditionally described as something divine, supernatural, even mystic, or that which has never been seen or imagined before. Adbhuta is also a very conscious dramatic position where the character sees the world and all its wonders, but at the same time stands still, as if in hesitation, without proceeding forward to risk immersing themselves in the magical zone of death. Like all the emotions on the rasa scale, adbhuta is the character creating this state in an active position; the character who experiences a state of trance, and also is the passive observer of the same. Such an appreciation of the marvellous is truly adbhuta.

Focusing exclusively on adbhuta, we can see the emotional validity of the three characters played by Kamal in *Gunaa*, in *Aalavandhan* and in *Hey Ram*. One wonders whether Kamal the actor should necessarily have to go through this emotional state of hesitation on the brink of adbhuta in order to communicate the 'fantastic' state of death and violence to the audience.

In *Aalavandhan*, Nandakumar plays the combination of the questioning son, the arrogant father and the monstrous vigilante. He is the boy in search of a mother and the father; the person who thinks he dominates over virtual reality and, in the end, chooses to destroy/consume himself by blasting himself in a backyard full of cooking-gas cylinders, the very source of fire that allows billions of citizens to cook and consume their daily bread.

The overall conceptual strategy seems to be very clear in terms of its narrative approach, but why did it remain cold to so many of the viewers? Kamal the ideator and Suresh Krissna the director seemed to have all the chips in the right place, but in totality the film seems to veer off-course and land itself a bit short of its goal. A very obvious reason is the overloading of Kamal the actor. Should he have played the double role of Vijay/Nandakumar? Besides stating that Nandakumar has a 'normal' brother, the film does not play on other 'twin' conventions like sharing of emotional pangs and extrasensory reactions. Somewhere through the film, the half-god/half-monster becomes more fascinating than the sedate brother, making one feel that another actor could have well played the secondary role. This particular portrayal of a double role was also for the purposes of special effects, where the efficacy of motion-control cameras gets demonstrated. It surely gives the audience a lot of thrills momentarily, but does it have the strength to emotionally engage?

Another area where the film goes unconventional is when there is an expectation that Vijay will somehow reconcile with his brother, help him transform and make him see the world of reason. There is also a glimmer of possibility that Tejaswini would want to resolve this issue of her identity, which has provoked so much revulsion in Nandakumar. Finally, the character of Nandakumar is also given an evil twist when he kills two fellow inmates who actually helped him escape from the asylum. If the overall ambit was to develop an emotional affinity for the traumatized child now grown up to be unmanageable, then this dimension of making him a wanton killer works against his charisma to some extent.

It is also possible that the reasons for these non-logical positions could be discovered in the 'edited-out' box of unwanted and extraneous scenes not fitting the three-hour duration limits of theatrical exhibition. Relevant connecting scenes could have been removed to handle the excessive length. And yet *Aalavandhan* went on to become a legend by itself, like many of Kamal's films that work with strong themes.

Audiences left the theatres perplexed and deeply disturbed. It reminded them that there is a Nandu lurking in each one of us. But do Indian audiences like to be reprimanded, to be told that their silence makes them accomplices to the dystopia that they are living in? Unlike *Indian*, this film was a complete failure. Shankar–Ehsaan–Loy's music could do nothing to elevate the phantasmagorical quality desperately needed. The graphics seemed to demand much more in terms of resources to look striking enough. Yet this film told the viewers the truth of their Tamil ecosystem and revealed their inabilities to challenge it. On par with the macabrish power of the theme song from *The Phantom of the Opera*, the film is still remembered for Kamal's rendition of a song about the spectre that haunts the Tamil mindscape,

> *'Half demon, half divine*
> *concocted together am I*
> *Animal in the open*
> *God while indoors*
> *an incomprehensible endless poem am I.'*

19

ANBE SIVAM: WALKING THE ROAD OF COMPASSION

A question that Kamal faces at almost every interview is, 'Sir, you have a rather complex disposition towards God. Do you believe in the existence of God or not?' He always replies that he has never said that God does not exist, but that he only wishes a god had existed! Kamal's young audiences feel that he is truly cool, while the senior intelligentsia, however agnostic they may be, feel that a superstar like him should not misguide the young generation with such blasphemous remarks!

In 2002, after giving three big comedy hits in a row—*Thenali* (2000), *Pammal K. Sambandam* (2002) and *Panchathantiram* (2002)—Kamal was about to ruffle some feathers again. The process started innocuously enough, with him announcing a new film to be directed by Sundar C., widely reputed for making successful comedies. Producers backed it because they firmly believed that it was impossible to go wrong with Kamal, the most powerful Tamil film icon of the twenty-first century, as often acknowledged by his dear friend Rajinikanth. But in this breakthrough film titled *Anbe Sivam* (Compassion Is God/Bliss; 2003), Kamal decided to take the road less travelled, a road that charted pathways to spirituality.

In the film, he plays the role of Nallasivam (Sivam for short), a mad devotee. In early Tamil Shaiva Bhakti poetry, such a person used to be called pithan or the mad lover/devotee who identified selflessly, completely with the Absolute. A pithan sought nothing but a form of pure compassion equivalent to bliss. The question is: was Kamal also asking his viewers for such complete compassion towards the film? Was that a tall order?

From the screenplay's structural point of view, the film makes no attempt to define what the main protagonist's motive or goal is. Sivam is depicted as an ugly yet funny person with a scarred face and crooked teeth, who wears thick glasses and limps. Recalls Madan, the dialogue writer, 'You should have seen the excitement on his face when the mask arrived. It would show him as a person with a scar wearing big, high-powered spectacles. He opened the package like a kid unwrapping a birthday present, took the mask into the anteroom and in five minutes emerged with the new look. I could not believe my eyes—there really was a transformation. Was he the same Kamal?'

Kamal's Sivam is an irritating yet charming personality, disarmingly disagreeable and a strange combination of an extremely sharp Chaplin and a super-witty Peter Sellers who must have the last word on every conversation. He decides to help Anbarasu (Arasu for short), a young, upwardly mobile metro male played by Madhavan, when fate traps them at the Bhubaneshwar airport thanks to an ugly cyclone that is ripping through the state of Odisha. Travelling through the flooded streets, they end up sharing a room and thereafter the journey back to Chennai.

Arasu is a bundle of nerves since arrangements are underway for his marriage with Balasaraswathi (or Bala) in Chennai three days later. Since Sivam has no overt motive to help, he does not pry further about the girl that Arasu is getting married to, or her family. On the other hand, he mischievously watches Arasu bumbling from one disaster to another from behind his soda-bottle glasses.

Why does Sivam choose to be a 'good' Samaritan? Is he atoning for some wrong that he has done earlier? That is the tone of this unique road film, starting with this odd couple battling one of nature's adversities and moving on to encounter a range of characters in the world. A true spiritual journey, which enquires into the epistemic constitution on which the tenets of that elusive zone called 'faith' are established.

Just as the fury of nature brings Sivam close to a stranger called Arasu, an equally ferocious bus accident had separated Sivam from the girl he loved. In a rather filmic coincidence, Arasu's to-be-bride is the same girl with whom Sivam was deeply in love before the bus accident scarred his youthful face and post which her father separated the two. Not having seen Arasu's Bala, and since Arasu doesn't mention her to him, Sivam doesn't know that she is the girl that he loves. The two components of this narration are later revealed in flashbacks.

Throughout the film we also see Sivam devoting his time to the labour wing of a communist party by staging provocative street plays (a tribute to the brilliant stage actor and director, late Safdar Hashmi) which criticize Kandaswamy, a big factory owner, for underpaying and exploiting his labourers. Considering the long history of the communist parties in India, one must admit that our left-wing leadership has completely ignored the potential of popular culture and the aesthetic use of the media. The founding communist party did have an autonomous theatre wing called the Indian People's Theatre Association (IPTA), virtually defunct now, but as far as cinema is concerned, the party was simply blind to its potential. Was this Kamal's way to provoke the left wing to do something about recognizing the significant role that performance arts can play, especially in a diverse nation such as India?

Coming back to the film, we see that Balasaraswathi, the young love interest, played by Kiran Rathod, happens to be the daughter of the factory owner Kandaswamy, the 'heartless' capitalist played brilliantly by Nasser. The daring Bala gets Sivam to paint a giant mural on a wall in her father's office lobby. Kamal pays tribute to Diego Riviera by imbuing the mural with various symbols chastising the capitalists for their cold-blooded attitude towards the working class.

As expected, her father, the boss, gets furious and prohibits his daughter from meeting Sivam anymore. The labour union members are also equally unhappy about Sivam's liaisons with the rich girl. He has to choose between his ideology and those emotions which are considered 'personal' and even bordering on carnal. Sensing this double-edged conflict, Sivam asks Bala to escape to Kerala and he would meet her there travelling via a different route. The bus in which he travels runs off the hilly road while trying to avoid a stray dog. Several people die and Sivam is seriously wounded.

The critically injured Sivam is taken to a nearby Christian hospital. Can and will he choose to live or die? Will the world outside manage to save him, or can some evil forces prevail and terminate him? The cruel Kandaswamy also comes to the hospital to snuff him out but decides to let fate take its course when the doctor tells him that Sivam has only 10 per cent chances of survival. Kandaswamy traces his daughter in Kerala and informs her that Sivam died in the tragic bus accident.

In the background plays an austere song sung by Kamal himself, which declares Sivam to be the follower of unbridled compassion and nothing else. An angelic old nurse nourishes him selflessly and treats him lovingly to move on to the less-travelled path. A few months later, when he recovers enough to be able to move independently, the first thing he does is to adopt that stray dog on the hillside. When he goes next to meet Bala, her father is shocked that the 10 per cent chance given by the doctor actually worked for Sivam.

When Sivam expresses his desire to meet Bala, the father lies that Bala has gone abroad after marriage and is in fact pregnant. Kamal walks away from the comfort zone of the two systems (the labour union and Bala), quite unperturbed like the Buddha, henceforth to take life as it comes. One could also see him as the weak and helpless Sivam choosing to become a pithan, the mad devotee. Yet, the film makes no references to the Buddha or other philosophical sources. Yet again, was Sivam seeing his unfortunate plight as the result of having abandoned his dear Bala to her own fate for which he has to repent now and transform into a more mindful person?

Dialogue writer Madan admits, 'It was Kamal's dream and vision all the way. He was less a highly trained symphony conductor and more like a mom at home who can put together a delicious meal in the most casual of ways. I don't recollect him quoting the Buddha or any other philosopher to make his point of view clear to every member of the crew. With his gentle persuasion, he could get everyone on location to bring out their best!'

In a recent interview, director Sundar C. was asked about how he got involved in such a complex film. 'I got a call from Kamal's production house to come over for a meeting,' he recalls. 'I was clueless about the intent. When I reached there, I was taken to Kamal's room and I did not anticipate that he was going to discuss the screenplay he had written for this film with me as the proposed director. I was dumbstruck when he started narrating the screenplay in detail. It was just me and Kamal in the room and just that was enough to make me so thrilled that I almost felt like announcing to the busy world outside that I was being considered to be a part of this great legend's project. That meeting is still so memorable!'

Reflecting on the characters he notes, 'Sivam was this enigmatic yet funny guy who always saw the humorous side of life as one gaffe followed another with this equally comic Arasu character in the stormy weather. I took the script home and worked hard on how to make it more laughable in my own style. And then, just a week or two before shooting, Kamal called up and confessed that there was a vital flaw in the characterization of Sivam. He said, "How could a serious communist party functionary suddenly become so comical just because of a road accident? How could it match with the flashback where issues of wage and labour rights were being argued by a talented street theatre artiste who is also deeply in love?" I was dumbfounded by this critical objectivity and the script went through a radical change to attain a new level of quiet sobriety.

'Every day on location was a learning process with Kamal as I directed the film. On one occasion, dialogue writer Madan had used the term "tsunami" with reference to the torrential downpour in the scene. I had never heard of such a term before and yet, three years later, the tsunami struck Chennai, leaving a long trail of death and destruction,' remarked Sundar.

The audience too had never seen their icon in such a narrative before. His high-powered spectacles could even give the viewers a headache. How did he wear those glasses for such long hours? Sundar recalls that Kamal had taken care to acquire a set of contact lenses which he wore to counter the heavy-powered lenses! Madan recollects, 'I had known Kamal when I was a journalist editing the popular magazine *Ananda Vikatan*. But when he asked me to write dialogues, I was dumbstruck. The industry grapevine was abuzz with how Kamal would interfere in every department, flattening everybody in the way. But when I started working on his screenplay, I found him extremely gentle and nurturing. I wondered whether he behaved like this due to my rather senior position in the popular media. On the contrary, he was like this with each and every one on the shooting floor too.'

Among the many details entrenched in this film, it is important to note two rather insignificant characters. They help us understand the larger philosophical context of *Anbe Sivam*. The first one is the stray dog, which Kamal adopts as his own son. Through this trope, Kamal chooses not to abandon the worldly animal instinctual drive as would have happened in a typical Buddhist mode. Instead, he adopts the Bhakti model which believes that the test of human endurance lies in its ability to deal with the existential while also realizing a higher mode of redemption. To make this more understandable, Sivam insists on taking the dog along with him in the car and asks Arasu, 'Is it not interesting that dog is god when spelt in reverse?' And a vexed Arasu snaps back, 'Do you have to see some extraneous symbolism in everything that you encounter?'

The second and more significant aspect of the film is its discourse on God itself. Sensing Sivam's rather cynical nature, Arasu asks, 'Are you an atheist?' and Sivam replies, 'I have never said that. For me you are God. Just look at how you helped a complete stranger by donating your precious blood. I see God in that act done by you. It's as simple as that.' Arasu asks,

'Then what about you?' and Sivam casually replies, 'I am also God.' But he does not go on to elaborate how he too had helped a stranger like Arasu with no motive or desire to get anything out of it.

This is similar to Thomas Aquinas who believed that 'love is the ability to do good to others', resulting in God seen as *Actus Purus* (Pure Act). Or Sankara who propounded that God is a concept which has no gunas (attached) qualities, or even Marx who sees the universe pulsating within the dialectics of a continuing set of oppositions. In sharp contrast is the character of the factory owner, Kandaswamy, a deep believer in a monolithic God but steeped in greed and apathetic to the very workers who toil and give him back more than he deserves. The point of the film is not to deride him but to keep up with questions of human struggle and to also fight for human rights rather than choosing to abstain from 'material' action to pursue a pure spiritual journey.

Sivam arrives with Arasu at the marriage hall where Arasu is to marry his bride. This is when he realizes that the bride is actually his beloved Bala and that her father had lied to her as well, telling her that Sivam had died in the road accident. As he is about to walk away and let the marriage take place with no disturbance, the guilty father Kandaswamy spots him and drags him into a room, begging him not to mess things up. Sivam chooses this opportune moment and warns him of dire consequences if he does not sign the workers' wage revision before the wedding takes place. Finding himself in a spot, Kandaswamy agrees. The union leaders assemble quickly and the deal is signed as we see Arasu walk away from the marriage hall.

The evil Kandaswamy sends his henchman to follow him with a big machete and assassinate him on a lonely street. Sivam senses the presence of a stalker, turns around and stops, willing to die. The henchman comes close but drops his big machete as his eyes well up in tears. 'It was I,' he says, 'as a loyal dog to my master, who wanted to kill you in the hospital. I had nothing to do with you and yet I wanted to terminate you. And fate chose to take my precious daughter away in return a few months later. Now I want you to do me one last favour. Please go far away and disappear. If my boss comes to know that I have not killed you, he will surely shoot me dead. I want to live and only you can give me back my life.'

Sivam says calmly, 'Go on, I shall let you live.' With that he limps away into the sunset, no plans or agenda in mind, his adopted stray dog accompanying him. Was he making that statement to the large number of his beloved audience who had chosen to stay away from the cinema theatres showing this film? Or was this Kamal's way of stating that if Chaplin was alive, this is how he would have ended his film, walking away into the sunset?

Madan recalls, 'Three days after the release, I got a call from Kamal. He sounded deeply disappointed that the film was not doing well. Like Sivam, he had to move on without trying to do any post-mortem. I could only say, like most journalists, that this film should have been released by working a bit more on the promotional drive to get the viewers better prepared for such a bold experiment.'

He says, 'It is untrue that Kamal is not conscious of audience expectations. In fact, the entire flashback with the suave moustachioed street-theatre dancer romancing with a pretty girl on a swing and later fighting off a horde of goons with an umbrella à la Jackie Chan was all done with an eye on the expectations at the commercial window.'

Many years later Madan would interview Kamal for a TV channel on his achievements, to which Kamal replied, 'One cannot blame the world outside for one's failures. I should have made such films ten to fifteen years (before 2003) when I was bursting with such themes and the audiences were ready for unique experiments. For example, I should have made *Chachi 420* (1997) and *Avvai Shanmughi* (1996) much earlier. I should have had the guts like a K. Balachander or Bharathiraja to storm the walls of a conservative market. Working under massive market compulsions, I have just hesitated too much. And as a result, I can claim to have achieved just about 25 per cent of what I set out to do.'

Despite his apologetic tone, the theme song of *Anbe Sivam*, sung by Kamal and composed brilliantly by Vidyasagar to sound like the Gregorian chants of a Catholic church, continues to ring in every Tamil mind to date, as a nostalgic relook at the atheistic precepts left behind by Periyar and his modern interpretations of Catholicism and Marxism. Madan's brilliant dialogues are still recited by Tamil cinephiles and quoted by young progressive writers.

Another unsung contributor to the film is Prabhakaran, the set designer. His amazing recreation of a massive train accident alongside a real railway line made jaws drop. Yet, the producers of the film wondered why Kamal would want to spend so much money on an incidental scene in a so-called 'road' movie. Looking back, we realize that it is to empower the scene where the selfish Arasu witnesses the agony of the injured masses being helped by the small number of medical staff led by a missionary nurse and this transforms his attitude and faith towards the world at large.

Eras come and go and like many bewildered humans, Kamal continues to wonder about the grip that religion and godhood holds over the multitudes inhabiting this planet. The film *Anbe Sivam* may not have been successful for a variety of reasons, but the large number of madly passionate South Indian filmmakers that this film triggered off, post 2003, is testament to the fact that contemporary Tamil cinema is probably the most vibrant and experimental of them all.

20

VIRUMANDI: A WHODUNNIT SAGA
OF CASTE POLITICS

'Politics should not be a business and it is not my business. It is my extracurricular duty. I will continue to act. It is my job. Until you, the people, give me a good office to sit in, I will not stop acting,' Kamal announced at a press conference held after the release of *Virumandi* (2004). Recalling this incident, he told me that his brother, producer Chandrahasan, later asked, 'Are you serious about entering party politics?' When Kamal brushed aside such a suggestion, Chandrahasan reiterated, 'Something tells me that you shall surely start a political organization. I can smell it!'

The elder brother's concern had several layers to it. Why was this film such a frontal attack on the judiciary, the police, the corrupt political system and, most importantly, the TV medium itself? Whose point of view was getting communicated to the public at large when it came to the decadent caste systems in Tamil Nadu? And while writing a script for such a critique, whose point of view should Kamal be taking? Is there anything called objectivity in telling stories?

Most serious films made by Kamal provide rabble-rousers grist to their mill. So, the moment they came to know that he was ready with a film

called *Sandiyar* (the earlier title for *Virumandi*), they called it an attack
by him, a high-caste man, upon the Thevar community, as 'sandiyar' is
supposed to be a derogatory word for someone from the Thevar caste.
But the fact is that the term has been in use for a long time in the villages
of Madurai district to refer to a bully in general. However, the controversy
was blown out of proportion, receiving coverage in the national media.
Kamal, stuck with the dilemma of being unable to release an already
complete film, decided to change the title to *Virumandi,* the name of the
main character. And the rabble-rousers duly blew the victory conch.[1]

Virumandi truly heralded the new 'new wave' of Tamil cinema in the
twenty-first century. Young filmmakers from M. Sasikumar to Shanmugha
Raja aka Mysskin, from Prabhu Solomon to Vetri Maaran, all confess that
this one film gave them the courage to go back to their grass/caste roots
and catch the Dravidian bull by its horns, quite like the way Bharathiraja
summoned the courage in 1975 to launch a frontal attack on conventional
Tamil cinema with *16 Vaiyadhinale.* From playing the blundering Chapaani
in that film to playing the crazy dimwit *Virumandi* in this one, it has indeed
been a long journey for Kamal.

With *Virumandi,* not only did Kamal interrogate his own filmic journey
but he also tried to tell the saga of Tamil citizens at multiple levels. In the
opening sequence, interestingly, the film questions the Indian judiciary's
continuing endorsement for the death penalty, based on evidence provided
mainly by the police and television news. This so-called objectivity is
supposed to prove that the point of view of any complainant or defendant
will always be limited, not just because of the very experiential nature
involved but also because of the varied sociocultural contexts that colour
our perspectives through the media. In this manner, the death penalty
seems to get justified.

Virumandi interestingly begins with a radical retired Supreme Court
judge, Justice V.R. Krishna Iyer, challenging the system of death penalty,
to locate the film into the nation's larger politics. But what can a judge
do when the 'democratic' citizens of India are themselves bloodthirsty,

seeking to avenge one life with another? How do we reconcile the objective reports of the police forces with the subjective temperaments of citizens? The supposed reality of the Tamil village versus the myths that envelop their narratives? To enquire further into this imbroglio, *Virumandi* attempts to provide two points of view of the same story to let the audiences judge for themselves. While many cineastes would point to the *Rashomon* (1950) influence, I would say that here, at last, is a film that transcends Kurosawa's masterpiece by a few miles.

The film begins with Dr Angela Kathamuthu (Rohini), a civil rights activist, and her cameraman interviewing prisoners in a jail. One of the men Angela meets is Kothala Thevar (Pasupathy), who is serving a life sentence for assisting in the murder of twenty-four people. He tells her his version of the story, blaming it all on Virumandi Thevar (Kamal), a happy-go-lucky rogue who had once supported Kothala in his fight against the village head, Nallama Naicker (Napoleon). Virumandi was in love with Thevar's niece Annalakshmi (Abhirami) and Thevar did not object to this because of the large area of fertile land Virumandi owned. But there was an assassination attempt on Virumandi, blamed on Naicker, for which Virumandi went to take revenge one night. Kothala and his gang were forced to save him, which led to the death of the twenty-four villagers. Kothala then refused to let his niece marry Virumandi. After this, as per his narrative, Annalakshmi was abducted and raped by Virumandi. She managed to escape from him and tell Kothala the whole story but then she committed suicide. A clash between Virumandi and Kothala took place in which six of Kothala's henchmen were killed. Virumandi then killed Naicker but was caught by the police. He testified against Kothala and his gang, getting them all fifteen-year sentences, while he himself got five years for raping Annalakshmi and the death penalty for murdering six people.

Dr Angela then meets Virumandi. At first unwilling, he later tells her his version. He had gone to Naicker to apologize for insulting him and other village elders, at Annalakshmi's behest, but Kothala and his men, thinking he had gone to take revenge, went and hacked innocents to death, despite Virumandi's pleas not to do so. He and Annalakshmi got married and went away but Kothala's men found them and abducted Annalakshmi the next day, when Virumandi was away. She was forced to marry Kothala's nephew Kottaisamy (played by O.A.K. Sundar), who was told by Kothala to consummate his marriage immediately. Annalakshmi committed suicide to save herself from such a fate. Upon hearing the news, a distraught Virumandi went to Kothala's house to take revenge. He murdered four of Kothala's men, including Kottaisamy, but Kothala escaped. Naicker then sheltered Virumandi but Kothala and his men cornered and killed Naicker. Due to Kothala's influence, Virumandi got convicted of having raped and killed Annalakshmi, Kothala's men as well as for the murder of the twenty-four villagers.

The twist in this story is the fact that Virumandi, this powerful sandiyar or bully, has his own point of view, which sees him as innocent of all the crimes he is accused of, having transformed himself into a pacifist thanks to the sweet words of his beloved. What does this woman signify in this film? Why does this character have to listen to her? We will discuss it a bit later. Let's get to the structure first.

The narration begins with Kothala's recollection about the caste-ridden machismo of his village, where Virumandi rules the roost at the local bullfight event. Then comes the rather complex sequence of several flashbacks, where Virumandi mourns for his grandmother, refuses to part with his newly inherited agricultural lands, his 'needless' rhetoric about being a farmer committed to his soil, his incessant drinking, his angry outburst at the panchayat meeting with Nallama Naicker, finally leading to the massacre after which Virumandi abducts Annalakshmi to escape the police. All these images are skilfully stitched by Thevar in order to convince the judiciary that Virumandi is a dangerous killer and a very bad influence, who needs to be hanged in order to put an end to the needless violence that his sheer presence triggers.

In Virumandi's own flashback, he comes across as inexperienced and naïve in worldly matters but quite rational when it comes to business.

The sequence of events coincides perfectly with Thevar's except for the reasons that led to the massacre. The background to his and Annalakshmi's relationship is shown as Virumandi approaching the pretty Annalakshmi with a lot of respect. Although he does serenade her openly, it is done with a lot of the typical Kamal panache. Virumandi's spontaneous gesture of proclaiming his love for her also results in an equally impromptu marriage in a local temple. In short, the portrayal is very realistic and mythical at the same time.

Every film that Kamal works in after 2000 resonates with concerns expressed in his earlier works. A first look at the film will make you feel that it is about Velu Naicker from *Nayakan* (1987) meeting Shaktivel Thevar in *Thevar Magan* (1992). Interestingly the grandson of Naicker in *Nayakan* is named Shaktivel! The two urban and suave characters of 1987 and 1992 converge into a highly self-critical narrative of the caste problems in Tamil Nadu in *Virumandi* in 2004. The film dares to rip off the mask of 'Dravidian' identity, something that started in 1972 with the strongly metaphorical films of Kamal. Balachander blasting the betrayals which rocked Dravidian political parties now enters the sinews of the Tamil identity to reveal the extent of bad blood that dirty politics can generate. Caste is such a strong influence in Tamil Nadu that it lives on even among Hindus that have converted to Islam or Christianity. There are Christian Nadars and Muslim Vanniyars. Yet again the film counters and extends the narratives of his rural encounters, to name a few, from *16 Vayathinile* (1977) to *Sakalakala Vallavan* (1982) to *Thevar Magan* (1992) allowing Tamil viewers especially in Tier-2 and -3 towns to develop a roadmap of the dynamic changes in the identity of their citizenship. Last but not least, caste wars in rural Tamil Nadu are always perceived as completely spontaneous and extremely chaotic, with no one knowing how they started and what really happened. Everyone involved seems to be in a stupor and killings often are reported as if they were akin to orgiastic collective outbursts. How does one construct a sequence of events that describes which incident led to which conflict? How far can one actually go in order to trace the beginning of these conflicts? When the long hand of the law enters the frame, how does it begin the enquiry, especially when law enforcers in the area could have also been party to the massacre?

To quote Justice V.R. Krishna Iyer who appears in the beginning of the film, 'Our legal system, including the police, is anti-Dalit and anti-poor. The death penalty laws' wrathful majesty, in bloodshot equality, deals the fatal blow on the poor, not the rich; the pariah, not the Brahmin; the black, not the white; the underdog, not the top dog. The law barks at all but bites only the poor.'

Virumandi examines the kind of changes that have happened or not happened in the rural districts of Tamil Nadu. One thing that the film affirms is the corrupt nexus that has developed between the police and the landlords, making a mockery of the judicial system. In a very subtle way, the character of Virumandi places himself between the colluding/ compromising forces of caste-driven villagers with another group who have given up violent means to play the straightforward village 'panchayat'—groups that have chosen to be disruptive versus groups that have chosen the peaceful path.

What makes Virumandi run amuck? What makes the entire community's mindscape violent? Is it a sheer case of caste stereotyping or is there meaning beyond that? Is the film much more than what we see on the screen? Most people I have met swear that this non-linear story film has to be seen at least thrice in order to completely understand the chronological and logical connections therein. Still, it leaves several concepts in a state of enquiry. For instance, what were the other motivations to go into the dual points-of-view narration other than to validate the idea of debating how much a 'first-person' confession is a valid mode of authentication, especially when it comes to crime?

The film's poster portrays the three lead actors—Kamal, Pasupathy and Napoleon—as playing equal roles in terms of the narrative scale. Somewhere it seems Napoleon has been truncated, possibly because he is the odd man out, having given up violence and thereby chosen to be the usual village headman. The story is akin to a Chekhovian narrative where one begins with certain preconceived ideas of morality and identities revolve around behavioural and societal levels of violence. Quite akin to Munshi Premchand's rural stories, the narrators in this film too begin with the premise that certain rustic castes have a propensity to settle internecine conflicts through acts of violence, in the same way that Kurosawa's samurais draw swords at the drop of a hat.

The narrative works on the primary premise that caste in India dominates over one's religion and the resultant behavioural characteristics of individuals in the context of their caste are almost part of their DNA. The issue of caste often escapes conscious logic and in modern independent and secular India, everyone aspires to rise to the level of the dominant upwardly mobile caste in their specific environ.

The second premise is a mythological one as proposed by 'Palagaara Kadai' (the snack shop), a blog site. In Tamil folklore, we have quite a few stories portraying the conflicts between various popular Hindu deities. The story here of Kamal as Virumandi could be seen as representing the deity Brahma who is sandwiched between Peykkaaman (the local name for Vishnu) as Pasupathi and Shiva as Napoleon, along with Parvati as the caste-free Annalakshmi accompanying them, forever playing the game of justice. Quite like the two versions in the film, these characters represent the same inside the prison too. Kamal plays Virumandi, sandwiched between the violent deputy jailer Peykkaaman (Shanmugarajan), the ascetic peace-loving IPS officer played by Nasser, and the caste-free Angela. The myth seems to play out the love–hate drama which mankind has inherited as though from the gods, to constantly demonstrate positions of the just versus unjust.

The third and the most complicated premise is Kamal having to play the 'commercial/mass-appeal' card. Kamal certainly did not make this film for the jury members at Cannes, Venice or Berlin. He had local financiers risking their investments, along with other players such as Ilaiyaraaja, poet laureate Muthulingam and a host of others. The film has songs, fights, comic interludes and some sex too. And all these needed to be modulated in unique and original ways. Fortunately, after *Hey Ram* and *Aalavandhan* flopping, this film brought some returns at the box office to compensate.

I found it amazing that a film which protests strongly against the death penalty has the most sympathetic character, Annalakshmi, kill herself by hanging. Her empathetic attitude is further emphasized by the fact that she is constantly surrounded by the animals that she rears as pets. Despite the fact that cows, bulls, dogs and birds are her close companions, she is extremely tough and dominates the menfolk like a 'goddess'. Annalakshmi is certainly one of the film's highlights, combining the mythical with the real. Her first appearance in the film has her arriving at a bullfight arena with her bull, wearing dark glasses. Virumandi accepts the challenge to tame it and, in return, win her hand in marriage. Whenever she appears later, she is shown as dominating like the proverbial Shakti over all the domestic decisions. When I spoke to Kamal about this characterization, he said, 'I think it was Abhirami's [the actress] sheer talent to take on such a role that inspired me to sketch her character in such a bold manner. Only she could balance this persona with so much conviction. She had acted in a few Malayalam films before but after this film she was determined not to accept any work if it did not provide a similar weighty challenge.'

This film is certainly one of the most powerful commentaries on the Indian caste system, where 'typical' memories and behavioural tendencies are perpetuated as if they are socially valid norms; where caste bonds are often stronger than bonds of one's own blood. Transgressing caste lines, especially by the poor, can often be tantamount to crime. Somehow the affluent and Westernized Indian seems to have forgotten about these inviolable lines and from his/her point of view considers them regressive and even inhuman. The roots of Virumandi's conundrum goes back to 1911 when several castes and tribes were notified as 'Criminal Castes and Tribes' so that the Salvation Army could step in and reform them with schools for the young and useful jobs for the elders.

For such progressive Indians who framed these laws and continue to enforce them, Kamal chooses to question and interrogate the depths of what constitutes 'real' politics prevailing in Tamil society.

How do we give up this prejudice and erase the idea that there are castes who are intuitively 'wedded' to 'specialize' in crime? The film seems to also express that this 'killer' complex, which somehow permeates even among the affected castes, should be removed. It is only in a society where the 'outside' perceiver and those perceiving from the 'inside' coalesce into a single unit that we can hope for peace and tolerance.

For Kamal, the change in heart cannot come through education or by listening to some peaceful sage. Like for many of our Indian heroes, it comes through losing one's heart to a beloved. And most importantly, it should be full of syneresis, with no logic or rational explanation to explain one person's love for another. It should happen in the most natural way.

21

THE MASQUERADE TRILOGY: *DASAVATHAARAM*, *VISHWAROOPAM* AND *UTTAMA VILLAIN*

To better understand the set of films discussed in this chapter, it is important to redefine the idea of the masquerade. Quite often, the word indicates pretension, duplicity and putting up a false front. But we will see it here as the essential formal device of a 'bahuroopi' or a performer who uses facial and bodily alterations as their formal performative device. Be it the traditions of 'Jatra' in Bengal, 'Theiyam' in Kerala or the 'Yakshagana' in Karnataka, performers use make-up to change themselves in radically different ways. Over his long career, Kamal has continued this tradition into cinema and often used make-up and prosthetics to portray different characters in his films. The character on screen and the real actor bear no resemblance to each other, thus creating quite a disruption in the realistic dramaturgy within which most films are constructed. And this is further complicated in the three films we shall talk about in this chapter, as they narrate the story of protagonists who have no personal motivation to resolve the do-or-die clashes they are pushed into. The unique aspect about mainstream Indian cinema is that while 'conflicts' exist in the socio-political framework, the hero needs to confront them based on an individual provocation. Certain movies, like Ram Gopal Varma's works, can function with 'uninvolved' characters playing motivated roles but in a big film, the protagonist must have someone in his or her family or a very close friend/associate to be a serious victim in the conflict, which in turn would propel the heroic force into remedial action. In such a narrative, the audience identifies with the cause at a personal level, seeks a resolution and thus feels the subjective emotional impact.

Kamal, on the other hand, moves off this path in a trilogy which imbibes political and judicial subjects with a strange mythological flavour. In *Dasavathaaram* (Ten Avatars; 2008) he plays Govind, a secret agent tracking down a demonical organization specializing in biological warfare. In *Vishwaroopam* (2013) he moves into the war-ridden zone of the Al-Qaeda in Afghanistan playing Wisam Kashmiri, an Indian Research and Analysis Wing (RAW) agent in disguise who infiltrates the militant organization to surreptitiously track down leaders of terrorist outfits. Lastly in *Uttama Villain* (The Supreme Villain; 2015) he plays the role of Manoranjan, an ageing film superstar who decides to play Uttaman, the myth of a folk hero who wants to revive his youthful days by donning the mask used in a very traditional dance form called Theiyam from Kerala.

Unlike most mainstream films, these three movies don't tell us anything about the main protagonist's family, the staple for all Indian melodramas. None of his buddies are affected by the perpetrators of the crimes in these movies. The victims are simple fellow citizens. From the conventional and mythical storytelling perspective, this unconventional formula would be considered a recipe for disaster. Imagine Ram going to destroy Ravan just because he is believed to be an 'evil' king. It is crucial that his wife, Sita, be kidnapped and his brother Lakshman almost die in the battle for Ram to sever the ten heads of this cruel king.

So, what is the motivation for the characters played by Kamal, and what is the chance that his viewers are going to identify with his non-personal concerns? Virtually none! Yet, many of his films managed to do reasonably well at the box office and enticed more producers to work with him. How? At the top of the list of reasons should be the unwritten fact that for film fans in Tamil Nadu and neighbouring states, the popular culture of cinema is the borewell from which they draw their regular refill of what one could safely call the 'emotional quotient'! And it is beyond doubt that there is no other icon in Tamil cinema to deliver this vital 'good' with such regularity and sincerity as Kamal.

Secondly, Southern audiences expect Kamal to do something radically different in every movie. Whether his intentions of enlightening his film audience about global issues are successfully fulfilled or not, whether the seriousness of the viewers gets intensified or not, or whether such a discourse is necessary or not are no longer the questions. The viewers all seem to need it like a plant needs water.

For Kamal, this trilogy—*Dasavathaaram*, *Vishwaroopam* and *Uttama Villain*—also became the fertile soil to sow the seeds of an upcoming revolution, namely his entering the grimy world of electoral politics. In the past decade, the political soil in Tamil Nadu had become infertile with virtually no options left for the common man, other than choosing between two parties, one run by the memories of an ageing patriarch (M. Karunanidhi) and another by those of an unyielding matriarch (J. Jayalalithaa). A fantastic dystopia seemed to be the only answer. With the family drama genre having become the preserve of unrelenting dysfunctional TV soaps rather than of real-life politics as it once was, the audience had no choice but to pray that Kamal, their virtual political hero, enters politics.

Dasavathaaram

In this film, Kamal provides the audience a package that encases the supra-real of epic/political proportions. In the Bhagavata Purana, the ten avatars or dasavatharam are a metaphor for the cycle of dharma to be established periodically by the hero (Lord Vishnu) who becomes the saviour of this planet. In each avatar, the hero kills the oppressor, reforms the evil forces and evokes an emotional response from everyone. However, from the perspective of an epic, there are no villains and heroes. We merely see the interplay of various dynamic forces as part of the leela or magical creation of the cosmic force for its own entertainment. The idea is that the Creator watches His/Her own creations over various 'yugas' or epochs. We humans experience these yugas in chronological order, but they all happen simultaneously from the Creator's viewpoint.

The film *Dasavathaaram* begins with Kamal playing Govindarajam Rajaswamy or Govind, a biotechnologist who explains the chaos theory with the historical story of Rangarajan Nambi (Kamal's second avatar), a persecuted devotee of Lord Vishnu in the twelfth century, who was thrown into the ocean with his beloved idol of the lord. Back at his lab in the US, Govind realizes that his boss is planning to smuggle out a lethal dose of a virus in a vial. Govind gets hold of it and runs, pursued by Chris Fletcher, a CIA agent (Kamal's third avatar). Before boarding his flight, Govind dispatches the vial to his friend Andal (played by Asin). Fletcher ends up killing the wife of Govind's co-worker who helped him escape, a Japanese woman, Yukha Narahazi. Shingen, Yukha's brother (Kamal's fourth avatar), sets out to avenge his sister.

Govind arrives in India only to be intercepted by a RAW operative, Balram Naidu (Kamal's fifth persona), but Balram lets him go. Meanwhile, Fletcher also arrives in pursuit. Fortunately, he is interrupted by a huge crowd welcoming pop idol Avatar Singh (Kamal's sixth avatar). Govind comes to know that the vial and Rangarajan Nambi's Vishnu idol are safe with Andal. He reaches her place and, with the help of her grandmother Krishnaveni (Kamal's seventh avatar), they escape with the idol in which the vial has been hidden. In the attempt to avoid Fletcher, they get trapped in a sand quarry run by a mafia. A fight ensues and Vincent, an activist (Kamal's eighth avatar), saves them. They run to the highway where Khalifulla, a very tall Pathan driving a big van (Kamal's ninth avatar), helps them. A long-drawn-out climax takes place with all the avatars battling it out for the vial when a tsunami hits the coastal town, dissolving the potency of the virus in the vial in its concentrated salt. Govind is felicitated for his bravery by none other than President George Bush (Kamal's tenth and final avatar) to a standing ovation!

This is the dramaturgic context that *Dasavathaaram,* whose screenplay was written by Kamal, is positioned upon. The avatars do not represent the various ages of mankind but deal with all the qualities of these troubled ages in the present against the background of a maniacal evil force that wants to extinguish mankind with a biological weapon. And only Kamal, the hero, can find out where the weapon is hidden. Ironically yet aptly, it is kept inside a bronze sculpture of Vishnu, which keeps escaping Govind's hands intermittently.

From an epistemological perspective, the story is about Vishnu's avatars narrating their own births and deaths, but the combination of Kamal and director K.S. Ravikumar provides a completely new perspective by taking the serious academic and theological veneer out of this narrative and making it a folkish comic full of songs, extreme fight sequences and plenty of colour.

The script is also a backhanded tribute to Kamal's mentor, thespian Sivaji Ganesan, whose film *Navarathri* (Nine Nights; 1964) sees the lost heroine Savitri move from one festive night to another during the nine nights of the Navaratri festival, encountering Ganesan in different forms. We the audience know it's him all along, but she does not because her fear prevents her from recognizing him as the same man she saw the on the first night. In the film, Ganesan shows off his acting range by donning a variety of faces and costumes, peppered with a lot of gags, songs and dances, while his serious fans spend quality time reading meta texts in between the lines.

All the avatars in *Dasavathaaram* cannot have an equal impact on all audiences. Favourites are bound to emerge, and in a wondrous concurrence the character of Naidu, who plays a comic RAW officer, gets the maximum applause. So much so that Kamal has decided to write a new film script called 'Sabash Naidu', based on this character, and will spin this Pink Panther trail into possibly another box-office hit.

Kamal explains the rationale. 'Apart from Rangarajan, the first character set in ancient times who sets the tone for the perennial human conflict of vested interests, the rest come from a wide variety of global diversity. The link character is a scientist called Govind and through his eyes we visit the other nine: from a powerful American president to an Indian Dalit/ Untouchable; from a devout old Hindu woman to a pious Muslim; from a Sikh entertainer to a Telugu-speaking government official; and, last but not least, a martial artist from Japan. Of course, from a producer's point of view, I have to work on characters that are doable and at the same time not miss out on the challenges of a "bahuroopi", which is the stuff that my dreams and I are basically made of!'

The film, released on a grand scale across the world in three languages, was a blockbuster, proving yet again the invincible combination of Kamal and director K.S. Ravikumar. It was shot in the US, Malaysia, Thailand and all over India. Unheard of in any Southern film, 1,300 film prints were released globally, raking in record collections. After this, Kamal's fans rechristened him 'Ulaganayakan' (the global hero), which was also the title of the main song in the film.

Vishwaroopam

Vishwaroopam deals with the global war on terror. Predictably, most part of the film is situated somewhere in Afghanistan, dominated by tribal warlords in possession of the most sophisticated weaponry. Kamal as Wisam Ahmed Kashmiri is planted there, disguised as a local, by the Indian military intelligence to infiltrate the warlords' ranks and find out more about their plans to attack peaceful and democratic nations. When Wisam is about to nab the boss, an explosion occurs, and the leader, Omar Qureshi (Rahul Bose), manages to escape to New York, where he plans to plant his next neutron bomb. So Wisam heads to New York too with Col Jagannath (Shekhar Kapur), this time in the guise of Viswanathan, an orthodox Brahmin Kathak teacher married to Nirupama (Pooja Kumar), a scientist in a pharma corporate.

Coincidentally, his wife's boss in New York happens to be the link in transferring some medical secrets and money to the terrorists. The wife lands up in the terrorists' lair where she discovers her husband has been trapped. In between a stunning fight sequence where the couple tries to escape, she comes to know that her husband is a Muslim and intends to wipe out the mastermind. From here on the story deals with how she joins forces with Kamal. They finally manage to defuse the devastating bomb, but the terrorist leader gets away in his private plane to an unknown destination, which was revealed in the sequel that was released in 2018.

Though modelled more on the lines of a Bond film with stunning production values, special effects, unusual escapades and a rock-solid love story built in, *Vishwaroopam* is also about an empathetic person with a social vision. Wisam sees the cruelty meted out by terrorist groups on their own kith and kin, their involvement in the drug business, their cold-blooded attitude towards voluntary doctors on the warfront, the way they switch their loyalties and above all use religion as a weapon to draw gullible compatriots into a gratuitous global war. All these make him more resolved to fight on. But what would have been a perfect recipe for box-office success faced serious setbacks when the release dates were announced.

After being officially certified by the Central Board of Film Certification, a self-styled group of conservative Muslims in Madras decided that this film was essentially anti-Islamic. Based on this assumption, they demanded that the film be screened for them. Sensing something strange here, Kamal called me over for the screening as well. 'Legally speaking, I don't need to show this film to anybody for approval, since I have a certificate in hand. But experience has taught me to face conflicts fearlessly and arrive at solutions through dialogue. I have to struggle through this alone,' he said with a touch of anguish.

The screening began, and the group saw the film like any other audience, reacting at the appropriate places to Kamal's sense of humour and acting skills. During the intermission it was obvious that there were two factions—some typical Kamal fans who talked to him and another lot that stayed away, whispering to each other. When the screening was over, there was silence and a group of about fifteen audience members trooped out without even the slightest acknowledgement of the host. Kamal looked at me and said, 'You can now expect some fireworks!'

By the following evening, this group had met top officials in the government and Chief Minister Jayalalithaa had all the district collectors across Tamil Nadu send 'restraining orders' to the exhibitors who were going to screen the film. If the collectors had chosen to, they could have refused to issue such a 'fatwa' due to its illegality. On the other hand, it was not a legal 'ban', which meant that Kamal could not take this unwarranted disruption to a higher appellate authority. The media and the film industry, though, clearly saw this as a 'ban', one where a motley group of 'official state-appointed' conscience-keepers could hold a film to ransom.

Hundreds of screens which had been blocked across Tamil Nadu for the film went empty. But in neighbouring Kerala, Karnataka and Andhra Pradesh, the film was released. Even the Hindi version was released across the northern belt, making this 'local' ban a complete political farce. The Tamil media took up this issue and in his first open interview Kamal burst out, 'If this is how a sincere Tamil artist is going to be treated, it is not worth living as a resident of Tamil Nadu anymore. How can anybody call me of all people anti-Muslim? This film is about an international problem that the entire world is facing. How can we as Tamilians keep quiet?'[1]

Television interviews showed the Muslim lobby expressing their anger on some strange issues. One group wanted to know how he could show terrorists talking Tamil. How could he show devout Tamil-speaking Muslims shout 'Allahu Akbar' and then kill others? Why should he, as a Hindu, play Muslim characters? Was this not insulting to God, they wanted to know. How incredibly flimsy could such arguments get? This was a fictional film about issues in Afghanistan and the insurgents in the film would certainly not say 'Hey Ram' and fire their AK-47s. Most people realized that their arguments were hollow and that this face-off was merely to get the spotlight on them, even if it was for just a few days! The TV news channels milked this controversy, making Kamal a soft target over an entire fortnight, trying to be as 'objective' as possible. There were no such reactions from Muslims in Hyderabad or Lucknow, where the local Muslims also spoke the language in the respective language versions. Very soon the protestors' steam ran out and the Tamil audiences finally managed to see the film on their big screens, after some dialogues were deleted.

Recalling this incident, Kamal said in an interview, 'She [Jayalalithaa] has been watching me, my political stands and seen me as a potential threat. I didn't realize this, probably because I was naïve.' With the entire publicity build-up and release expenses down the drain, producer Ravichandran hoped that the sequel, which had already been agreed upon, would bring in some new financiers to compensate. The National Awards for Best Choreography and Set Design were small morale boosters, though, but not enough.

The original plan was to start the sequel immediately, since Kamal had canned quite some footage for *Vishwaroopam 2* during the earlier shooting. Since the sequel required a lot more money, the producers put the project on pause to raise fresh funds. It was tough.

'I can raise more money only when I show my face on-screen and not across a negotiating table. At the same time, artistes also have the responsibility to sensitize and not sensationalize!' Kamal would say.

Kamal released *Uttama Villain* (2015), followed by *Papanasam* (2015) (a remake of *Drishyam* [2013]) and *Thoonga Vanam* (2016) in quick succession while his brother Chandrahasan was raising money for the sequel to *Vishwaroopam*. With very limited funds, he decided to keep his promise to Ravichandran, raised the necessary funds, took over production and directed *Viswaroopam 2* himself, which released in 2018. In a unique twist to the story, two events changed the course of Kamal's trajectory. On 6 December 2016, Jayalalithaa passed away. The political resolve of Wisam Ahmed Kashmiri, the protagonist in the sequel, to take on the tyrannical forces happened in real life as Kamal announced his entry into Tamil politics on 21 February 2018 with the Makkal Needhi

Maiyam (MNM), a new political party. The reel and the real stories were now running parallel.

Uttama Villain

Trying to locate *Uttama Villain* is certainly going to be the most difficult task. After the *Vishwaroopam* debacle, Kamal was hell-bent on pulling all punches and providing a fitting answer to all the humiliations he had undergone under the ruling government. He drew energy from his mentors, his film buddies and fans. For a start, he chose to reinterpret a film—*Uthama Puthiran* (1958)—that had brought his idol, Sivaji Ganesan, into the limelight. Kamal must have seen this film as a four-year-old in 1958 and been entranced by the make-up, double roles, split screens, songs and dances, as well as the world of the great Alexandre Dumas, whose famous novel *The Man in the Iron Mask* (third part of *The Vicomte of Bragelonne*) provided the basis for the film. Kamal, Sivaji Ganesan and Dumas ... what a combination! Anything that the ethereal spirit of this trio could conjure was bound to be successful.

On taking a closer look at *Uttama Villain*, one can clearly see Kamal deploying a strategy where he believes that the best way forward is to expose himself by balancing his enormous talent with his eccentricities, his reputation as a complex screenwriter with the complexes that he suffers as a 'reluctant' actor, and the great responsibility he has to shoulder as the renowned 'exemplary' Tamil filmmaker with typical audiences that forever want him to declare who are the good guys and who are the bad ones.

Analysing *Uttama Villain*, which translates as 'The Good Villain' from the Dumasian angle, is therefore also about exploring an oxymoron—does the hero sometimes wear the mask of a villain? Can a good character deliberately choose to play his own evil twin? So, were director Ramesh Aravind, music director Gibran and cameraman Shamdat ready to meet all the challenges laid down by Kamal and the producers?

To engage with such a narrative, screenwriter Kamal starts out by telling the story of a successful film star, aptly named Manoranjan (entertainment) played by him. This star is married to Varalakshmi (Urvashi, his co-star in many other films) and is the son-in-law of an equally successful producer, Poornachandra Rao (played by Kamal's Telugu cinema mentor, K. Viswanath). At the pinnacle of his success, two skeletons roll out of the closet. He discovers that he has a daughter born out of wedlock with another woman with whom he was in a relationship before his marriage and who is now dead, and that inside his body lurks a malignant cancer that will kill him shortly.

The hero's world is blown apart and he goes to seek advice from his first mentor, aptly called Margadarshi (he who shows the right path, played by K. Balachander). In real life, Kamal had found out that his guru was not in the best of health and so wanted him to co-star in this film as his possible swan song. In an almost documentary-style conversation, Margadarshi suggests that cinema's future path can be best guided by one's own social folklore and its stylistics. For it is only in folklore that the borders between morals and pragmatism are blurred to accommodate the vicissitudes of existential reality, where common sense dominates over legalese and where the sacred and the profane enjoy equal space.

The successful star Manoranjan commences the production of a film within this film, based on the folk/Puranic story of how Vishnu takes on the avatar of Narasimha, half-man and half-lion, to eliminate a cruel king called Hiranyakashyapa who was torturing a young devotee called Prahlad. From here the film goes on a roller-coaster ride intertwining with developments in Manoranjan's life—a young psychoanalyst, Dr Arpana (Andrea Jeremiah) who comes to counsel him; his co-star in the film, Karpagavalli (Pooja Kumar), who develops a soft corner for him; his children despising him for his vagrancies; the neurosurgeon who keeps warning him about his failing health; and his mentor egging him on to complete the film.

The stylistics of Dumas's *The Man in the Iron Mask* dominate the form of this film. Kamal decided to incorporate the traditional Keralite masked folk-dance style called Theiyam into his role. With some splendid make-up and costumes, the narration woven into the background score and songs composed by music director Ghibran, leaves the viewer spellbound. While the film ends with the hero dying of brain cancer and his mentor Margadarshi completing his final film, in reality, it was the opposite. K. Balachander did not live long enough to see the completed version of this film. He passed away on 23 December 2014, bringing an end to an amazing innings in Indian cinema. His son Bala Kailasam, a brilliant documentary filmmaker and TV producer, had also passed away a few months earlier in August 2014.

The film was released in May 2015, the month that schools are shut and when Southern audiences migrate to air-conditioned theatres to seek respite from the heat. Somehow, the expected crowds eluded Kamal once more. Yet again, audiences were unable to navigate through the choppy waters of his complex thought waves. When I met him a few weeks later, he commented, 'I wish I had more time and resources to do a more detailed job with the large amount of computer graphics involved in the folklore cinema portions. Almost eighteen months in the making, I never anticipated that the cost of these special effects would shoot up so high and, unable to wait, the producers too threw in the towel.'

Looking back, in 1958 when Sivaji Ganesan completed his *Uthama Puthiran*, all the special effects were done in camera and audiences were capable of accepting it. But today's audiences are well informed with most of Hollywood's computer graphic spectacles and they are in no mood to settle for less!

The saga of the bahuroopi's masquerade, which started in 1960 with a five-year-old Kamal appearing as a child actor playing the role of an orphan, has indeed been a breathtaking journey. A reluctant actor who appeared in over 260 films was a combination of narrator, performer, critique and an objective witness to his own ups and downs, his own foibles and virtues and his own critics and fans. At one level, he seems to belong to a very long lineage of bahuroopis or street mendicants who would go from door to door telling stories, some very old and stale and some very raw and new. They were willing to do anything and everything to keep themselves alive between their poorly paid performances. Their dreams were more important than their reality. Fortunately, Kamal was steered by some friendly mentors and massive numbers of fans who made him enjoy what must have been a very lonely, frustrating and rough journey.

22

INTO THE REALM OF THE SPECTACLE: *VIKRAM 2, INDIAN 2* AND BEYOND

On 24 February 2022, Russia invaded its neighbouring country Ukraine to 'reclaim' the land and coastline on the Black Sea that used to belong to them in the erstwhile Soviet times. A few months later, on 3 June, an expensive multi-starrer titled *Vikram 2* with Kamal in the lead, directed by Lokesh Kanagaraj, was released. This film went on to become a blockbuster hit, the likes of which was never witnessed before in Kamal's film history.

While there is no direct connection between the two events, one factor in the narrative stands out, namely, the modus operandi. A big chunk of the Russian force is commanded by a privately operated apparatchik called 'Wagner', or a team of blindly devoted snipers who use their authoritarian discretionary powers at will to fulfil their goal of 'providing security' to the host nation. On ground, the real Russian army is also fighting the war at an 'official' level. In *Vikram 2*, Karna aka Vikram (Kamal) commands a sleeper cell force hidden within the Indian government's security system sets his own strategy to bring down a narcotic manufacturing unit incognito. In the film, we also witness a parallel independent police unit openly igniting a string of destructive and disruptive attacks on the drug mafia under the command of Amar (Fahaad Faasil). They are fighting the same

234 KAMAL HAASAN: A CINEMATIC JOURNEY

war, triggering huge amounts of expensive pyrotechnics and performing complex action scenes, resulting in the death of hundreds of menials.

Without getting into the 'good' and 'bad' of such deployment, what is this 'Wagner' syndrome all about? Is it announcing the fact that the elected welfare democratic countries must henceforth engage and collaborate with independent capability-driven invisible enterprises to serve the people? *Vikram 2* begins with Karna being blown up by a grenade and declared dead. Kamal is consequently not part of the first 70 minutes of the film. Midway he makes his entry like a ghostly character (having stage-managed his own killing in the opening) and takes over the mantle from Amar to execute his side of the action. The second half is about the final destruction and mayhem with some comic relief introduced in the way Kamal protects his phono-phobic grandson from the loud noise generated by the villains. (As if Anirudh's background music was not loud enough!)

Looking back, we see that the disruptive or chaotic entertainment that is served in *Vikram 2* has historically been associated with counter-cultural movements. In Tamil cinema, such a movement began around the turn of the millennium, with a series of films directed by Bala—*Sethu* (1999), *Nandha* (2001), *Pithamagan* (2003). Many more directors joined him to portray a dystopic vision of Tamil society where the dominant emotion was 'disgust'. Although people collectively experience a sense of fear combined with frustration, mainstream films don't see this, since heroes either fight back or succumb to wounds. But when neither happens, we feel the emotion of disgust. How does Kamal's film deal with it? Romantic dramas or parental/ fraternal sentiments have long become part of the old cinema culture. These movements challenge established norms, formulas and authorities, but they do not occupy the position of sanctioned 'state' authority. Instead, they often operate at the margins of mainstream culture, with a hero, a villain and a joker participating in formulaic scenes of excessive violence, explosives, gunfire and massacres. Watching *Vikram 2*, one is almost tempted to ask what happened to the Kamal who had sworn by Mahatma Gandhi and his appeal for non-violence, wanting to abolish the death penalty and striving to provide an equitable space for women on-screen by acting in and producing the films which we have discussed so far.

Let us pause a moment to locate Kamal in his journey through Tamil cinema. In 2013, he took on the ambitious two-part project titled *Vishwaroopam I* where he played Wisam Ahmed Kashmiri, an Indian military agent delegated to eliminate a senior ISIS leader to protect the sovereignty of a world at severe risk of survival. Cut. Before he decided to don the greasepaint for *Vikram 2* in 2021, Kamal did an amazing film called *Papanasam* (Vanquishing One's Sins; 2015), directed by Jiju Joseph, where he played an ordinary satellite cable TV agent named Suyambulingam, who accidentally gets involved in a murder and tries to save himself and his family from the fallout. This film was a phenomenal box-office hit, asserting Kamal's capability to channelize a good script into a more superior form of cinema through his convincing performance. While *Papanasam* (a remake of the Malayalam hit *Drishyam*), was a delicate Hitchcockian family thriller, *Vishwaroopam* attempted to give Indian cinema a very nuanced Rambo/James Bond-like experience in a global ecosystem.

After Papanasam, Kamal headed out to finish an old commitment, *Vishwaroopam 2* in which Wisam tries to balance the guilty emotions of a good military man having to sort out interpersonal issues in the forces with the need to enter the chambers of a cruel ISIS tyrant/ leader and eliminate him and his global associates. This film, though, turned out to be a box-office disaster. Surely this would have put Kamal in a quandary. Would the market allow for another actor-dominated film like *Papanasam* to become a success? Or should it be a film dedicated to sheer action-domination, the current market favourite genre?

Kamal chose the latter. With his penchant for experimentation, the time had also come for him to enter a new arena with a more global formula, namely the big-budget super-action drama. Kamal reopened *Vikram*, an older franchise of his company, by announcing the production of *Vikram 2* in 2021 to navigate the spectacle of excess, such as in the fantastic sci-fi world virtually propelled by Marvel Studios' 'Cinematic

Universe', which dominates theatres and OTT platforms across the world with multi-star casts, lavish sets, extensive use of computer graphics, loud music and thrilling action sequences.

In the context of cultural products such as films or commodities, Slavoj Žižek uses the concept of 'surplus enjoyment' to explain the global appeal of disturbing, shocking or excessive content. The trend set by Hollywood's Marvel Cinematic Universe or the DC Universe, drawing inspiration from real-world espionage, covert operations and national security concerns, puts us on the edge of a fictional 'reality show'. The use of characters like Batman, Spider-Man or Iron Man, affiliated with secret organizations or underworld forces, taps into the intrigue and complexity associated with these themes to convince their viewers that this fiction is in fact 'the reality'.

The villain in *Vikram 2*, Sandhanam, is a clownish Joker-like character played by Vijay Sethupathi. The Joker in the DC Universe is often considered Batman's antithesis. While Batman is driven by a desire for justice, the Joker operates without a clear motive, only wanting to spread chaos. The Joker's existence serves to highlight and challenge Batman's own principles and beliefs. In *Vikram 2* Sandhanam, introduced like a hulk, plays a narcotic drug manufacturer, producing cocaine on a 'massive scale', who supposedly has the power of destroying not only India but the whole world. The story remains silent on the veracity of such high-volume drug business in 'real' India. And we have all accepted that clarifying such information is not necessary at all. Fake news has become reality.

The masquerade or secrecy surrounding such 'mythological' characters and organizations ends up serving as a narrative tool to explore the themes of power, responsibility and accountability. In *Vikram 2*, a local drug lord's daughter's marriage scene shows Sandhanam waiting to attack while cooks sing out cookery ads and visitors dance to popular music. In such a bizarre intersection masked men (headed by Kamal, also in a mask) enter on motorcycles, wipe out Sandhanam's men and even end up kidnapping the drug lord. The portrayal of unregistered or 'secret' national security forces can be interpreted as a commentary on real-world concerns related to government secrecy, classified operations and the lack of transparency. But does it resolve the balance between national security imperatives and the public's right to know in any tangible manner? No. The narrative thus mimics the opacity of existing news media, mostly packed with opinions and even fake news.

Like in Marvel and DC movies, all forms of 'ground logic' get hijacked to give way to a new-age spectacular circus. Žižek discusses the idea that surplus enjoyment involves a certain kind of cathartic release, where the excess disrupts and breaks through the normal order of things. In the context of music nowadays, particularly live performances, we see the intense and immersive experience of rock and metal concerts, accompanied by giant LED screens and powerful surround-sound speakers, as a form of modern consumerist catharsis.

Superhero narratives have a long history of reflecting and commenting on contemporary social and political issues. The portrayal of secret national security forces may resonate with concerns about the expansion of government surveillance, but the use of covert military operations and the implications of unchecked power in the real world provide a new level of credibility for modern-day governments. I am sure that Kamal is aware of such dangerous intersections and implications in real-day politics, where he is a committed player, and therefore the structuring of logic and reasoning into a film like this becomes important.

One can clearly see this in the insertion of a scene with Vikram's chosen members where he delivers a five-minute-long sermon about his rationale for doing whatever is being staged in the film. The setting is a dim basement packed with all kinds of ammunition. Vikram's team members are feeling unsure about the plan and he replies, 'So, you think I am doing all this to take revenge for my son's murder? My son died to give us a drug-free society. Should we not respect his sacrifice? This drug will soon take us back to the law of the jungle, namely, to multiply and procreate with no awareness of who your mother, sister or daughter is. You all came to me because of an ideology. Whoever we have killed is not murder, but a statement to clean the crap out of our society. And a masked face is necessary nowadays to carry out even a good deed. I am an agent and known for my secrecy. I have a success track record which I cannot reveal to the world because I am an honest militant. And our society should know that is the legacy we want to leave behind and for that Sandhanam must be killed. One man's terrorism is another man's revolution. The freedom song of yesteryears has become our national anthem today. Rebel is not a curse word, but a virtue. Sorry boys, I am lecturing. We are warriors of tomorrow but now, grow up, guys!'

The Preamble to our Constitution assures for all citizens 'justice, social, economic and political' and a *rejection of violence* as a means to achieve justice. With this 'statement' in the film, is Kamal propagating the need for violence as a contingent measure when law and order go out of hand? Or is he announcing the new 'Wagnerian' narrative as the norm?

Acknowledging this monologue in the film as a 'lecture' is in fact Kamal's statement to his audience. Most of the lines spoken here are in the English language, subtitled in Tamil. Watching so much English spoken here and in many other Tamil films today is a clear indication of the 'surplus enjoyment' provided. Finally, the tone and delivery of Vikram's speech here is a tribute to the legendary Sivaji Ganesan, Kamal's idol. Registering such a memory also portrays Kamal's disposition to the well-proven narrative, namely, the need to clearly register the hero as a 'positive' person with no ambiguity at all which, strangely, is clearly not the narrative of the Hollywood superhero films.

After the huge success of *Vikram 2*, Kamal is wrapping up the final portions of another sequel, *Indian 2*, directed by Shankar. Soon after this he will enter the set of a Telugu film, *Kalki 2898 AD*, directed by Nag Ashwin; and by early 2025 he will team up with Mani Ratnam to do a film called *Thug Life*. The very titles of all these films indicate spectacular scenes and gigantic budgets for our screen icon Kamal Haasan.

Kamal has surfed and navigated a lot of tidal waves, manoeuvring the peaks and troughs, combining rare intelligence and commonly available intuitions to overcome unimaginable crises all his life. There is no looking back at the past, for his only motto has been 'Tomorrow belongs to us'!

AFTERWORD

Singeetam Srinivasa Rao

When I hear people say that the Singeetam–Kamal partnership is one of the best director–actor collaborations in film history, I am elated. The secret behind it, I think, is our innate capacity to laugh at ourselves, to make jokes about ourselves. This inimitable synchronicity of our wavelengths makes even a smidgen of ego disappear.

It all started after a screening of my Tamil film *Dikkatra Parvathi* (1974) when Kamal came up to shake hands with me and then left without a word. I thought he did not like the film. I did not know of the future partnering plans raging in his mind at the time. Our next encounter was at the Filmfare Awards in Bombay, where I had come to receive the Best Director award for *Dikkatra Parvathi* and Kamal to receive the Best Actor award for a Malayalam film. He approached me and, holding my hand firmly, said, 'We have to make films together.' That marked the beginning of our collaboration.

We set out to make a serious, film-festival-worthy film, but ended up making a full-length double-role comedy in Telugu—a commercial film titled *Sommokadidhi Sokokadidhi* (1979). It was a huge hit. In that movie, Kamal played an absent-minded doctor. Before shooting started, I had suggested that he think of a person from real life whom he could imitate for a near-perfect characterization. Kamal nodded and, when the cameras rolled, he walked with an odd, swinging gait, was indecisive and talked in half-sentences, switching topics abruptly. It was a character brilliantly portrayed. Only at the end of the day's shoot, when I asked him about the inspirational source, did I realize he had wholeheartedly followed my advice—he was imitating me!

One day, Kamal called and asked me to direct what would be his hundredth film as an actor. I was both honoured and delighted by the challenge. The film, called *Raaja Paarvai* (1981) in Tamil and *Amavasya Chandrudu* in Telugu, had him playing a blind violinist. Without any instructions from my side, he wanted to perfect the bow-and-finger movement of violin-playing. So, he engaged a violin tutor and practised for four months. That was the dedication of Kamal Haasan.

More than the success of his films, Kamal's passion, commitment and artistry are the qualities that make him unique, especially in a community of very 'ordinary' standards. He is constantly in the pursuit of perfection; every time he makes a film, he wants it to be better than his previous one.

After our next release, *Apoorva Sagodharargal* (1989; *Appu Raja* in Hindi), everybody was full of praise for Kamal for portraying a dwarf with the available technical resources at the time. Dr Rajkumar, the doyen of the Karnataka film industry, made a valuable comment—'The technical aspects and the efforts are praiseworthy, no doubt. But me being convinced that Kamal Haasan was really a dwarf was what astonished me.'

All shots of the dwarf took longer than usual to film. Sometimes we only managed a couple of shots with Kamal before lunch break. Despite knowing the schedule, all the other actors reported at 9 a.m., whether they needed to or not. This was their way of showing appreciation for Kamal's efforts. It was their tribute to him.

Kamal Haasan's portrayal of a character is impeccable. There is no superficiality in him. For our next venture, *Michael Madana Kama Rajan* (1990), I was blessed with a highly talented ensemble cast accompanying him. So, there wasn't a doubt about how the scenes would work out. But as a director, I realized that the biggest challenge confronting me was the ending, when four identical Kamals had to appear on screen. Any confusion in viewers' minds would be a disaster for the film. I planned out the shots carefully on storyboards to eliminate any confusion. But when the time to shoot came around, the exercise proved to be so simple, thanks to Kamal's understanding of the storyboarding and the peculiar portrayal of each character.

Kamal always believes that nothing comes easily. He works hard and expects all others to do the same. This does not always go down well within the industry. Some find him unreasonable. Kamal will suddenly ask for a storyboard. 'We are so used to shooting while the story is still developing; where will we go for a storyboard?' lament producers.

On one occasion he had to shoot a song for four days. Kamal asked for two days of rehearsal time with the heroine and choreographer. The producer had his inhibitions: 'Kamal sir is a highly talented dancer, why does he need a rehearsal?' Helpless, he instructed the production manager to get the heroine's and choreographer's dates for the rehearsals. The production manager came back with a half-smile on his face and reported that both parties were away shooting in foreign locations and would only land on the morning of the shoot. After his arrival, Kamal thought about it and said that they should use those four days to rehearse and when they would have the new available dates, they could jump straight into the shoot and execute the movements they would have already learnt.

In an industry accustomed to on-the-spot action, creation and delivery, there is probably reason for people to call Kamal Haasan unreasonable. For the public at large, Kamal is a star. For the people who have worked with him, he is also a hard worker.

Once I met Kamal at a waterfall location near Kochi, Kerala, where he was shooting with director K. Balachander. They were filming Kamal jumping down from a tree. The close-up shots were all taken using the actor. For the long shot, Kamal's dupe, a stunt actor, was to jump from a tree. The ground was eliminated from the shot. Out of the frame, four stunt people were holding a net for the dupe to fall on, but they were not strong enough. To my surprise, I saw Kamal Haasan rush to join in, holding the net with all his strength to keep the double safe.

I was always on the same page as Kamal when it came to crediting workers. During the shoot of *Raaja Paarvai,* he came up with a brilliant idea for the credit roll. 'All the credits can appear in order of seniority, irrespective of designation or rank,' he suggested. I approved of this. The technician titles came rolling. Being the oldest, my name came first and was followed by other technicians. Then came the list of actors. The first actor's name was L.V. Prasadji—he was the senior-most, of course. Next came Kantha Rao, followed by Kamal Haasan. Later, it was found out that Kamal, having entered the film industry earlier as a child artiste, was higher in seniority. So, his rank went up to number two and Kantha Rao came down to three!

In life as well as in films, Kamal has had successes and failures. But he never let either one get to him. The sense of humour with which he looks at the world gives him the required detached equanimity. For him, conviction is always more important than calculation. A calculative person would not have agreed to do a film like *Pushpak* (1987). Despite many people warning me that a silent film with no songs and dialogues would not perform well, Kamal had full faith in the script and made this venture workable. When I went to receive the National Award for the film, Kamal was also there to receive the National Award for Best Actor for a different film. While we participated in the mock rehearsal for the ceremony, he spontaneously hugged the officer who was standing in for the President of India. And when he was told that he couldn't hug the actual President, he said, 'I know, but I wanted to satisfy myself this way. I hope you don't mind!'

Anybody can write a biography, but only a few deserve to be the subject of a study of this kind. Kamal Haasan is certainly one among them. It was extremely gratifying when I learned that such a valuable filmographic study was being written by K. Hariharan, an acclaimed film academician with a deep knowledge of world cinema. I have been watching him closely, especially after 2004 when he became the founder-director of the LV Prasad Film & TV Academy near my house in Vallasarwakkam, Chennai. In Hariharan's hand this book is sure to reach the quality it requires. This book is sure to occupy a place in history as a classic.

KAMAL HAASAN'S FILMOGRAPHY

Year	Film	Director	Remarks
1960	*Kalathur Kannamma*	A. Bhimsingh	Child artist
1962	*Parthal Pasi Theerum*	A. Bhimsingh	Child artist
1962	*Paadha Kaanikkai*	K. Shankar	Child artist
1962	*Kannum Karalum*	K.S. Sethumadhavan	
1963	*Vanambadi*	G.R. Nathan	
1963	*Anandha Jodhi*	V.N. Reddy, A.S.A. Sami	
1970	*Maanavan*	M.A.Thirumugam	Uncredited
1971	*Annai Velankanni*	K. Thankappan	Uncredited
1972	*Prathikaram*	Kumar	Uncredited
1972	*Kurathi Magan*	K.S. Gopalakrishnan	
1973	*Arangetram*	K. Balachander	
1973	*Sollathaan Ninaikkiren*	K. Balachander	
1974	*Paruva Kaalam*	Jos A.N. Fernando	
1974	*Gumasthavin Magal*	A.P. Nagarajan	
1974	*Naan Avanillai*	K. Balachander	
1974	*Kanyakumari*	K.S. Sethumadhavan	
1974	*Anbu Thangai*	S.P. Muthuraman	Uncredited
1974	*Vishnu Vijayam*	N. Sankaran Nair	
1974	*Aval Oru Thodar Kathai*	K. Balachander	
1974	*Panathukkaga*	M.S. Senthil Kumar	
1975	*Cinema Paithiyam*	Muktha V. Srinivasan	
1975	*Pattampoochi*	A.S. Pragasam	
1975	*Aayirathil Oruthi*	Avinasi Mani	
1975	*Then Sindhudhe Vaanam*	Ra. Sankaran	
1975	*Melnaattu Marumagal*	A.P. Nagarajan	
1975	*Thangathile Vairam*	K. Sornam	
1975	*Pattikkaattu Raja*	K. Shanmugam	

Year	Film	Director	Remarks
1975	*Njan Ninne Premikkunnu*	K.S. Gopalakrishnan	
1975	*Maalai Sooda Vaa*	C.V. Rajendran	
1975	*Apoorva Raagangal*	K. Balachander	
1975	*Thiruvonam*	Sreekumaran Thampi	
1975	*Mattoru Seetha*	P. Bhaskaran	
1975	*Raasaleela*	N. Sankaran Nair	
1975	*Andharangam*	Muktha V. Srinivasan	
1976	*Agni Pushpam*	Jeassy, P.N.Sundaram	
1976	*Appooppan*	P. Bhaskaran	
1976	*Samasya*	K. Thankappan	
1976	*Manmadha Leelai*	K. Balachander	
1976	*Anthuleni Katha*	K. Balachander	Cameo
1976	*Swimming Pool*	Sasikumar	
1976	*Aruthu*	K.S.L. Swamy	
1976	*Satyam*	S.A. Kannan	
1976	*Oru Oodhappu Kan Simittugiradhu*	S.P. Muthuraman	
1976	*Unarchigal*	R.C. Sakthi	
1976	*Kuttavum Shikshayum*	M. Masthan	
1976	*Kumara Vijayam*	A. Jagannathan	
1976	*Idhaya Malar*	Gemini Ganesan. Thamaraimanalan	
1976	*Ponni*	Thoppil Bhasi	
1976	*Nee Ente Lahari*	P.G. Vishwambharan	
1976	*Moondru Mudichu*	K. Balachander	
1976	*Mogam Muppadhu Varusham*	S.P. Muthuraman	
1976	*Lalitha*	Valampuri Somanathan	
1977	*Uyarnthavargal*	T.N. Balu	
1977	*Siva Thandavum*	N. Sankaran Nair	

Year	Film	Director	Remarks
1977	Aasheervaadam	I.V. Sasi	
1977	Avargal	K. Balachander	
1977	Madhura Swapanam	M. Krishnan Nair	
1977	Aaina	K. Balachander	Uncredited
1977	Sreedevi	N. Sankaran Nair	
1977	Unnai Suttrum Ulagam	G. Subramaniam	
1977	Kabita	Bharat Shumsher Jung Bahadur Rana	
1977	Ashtamangalyam	P. Gopikumar	
1977	Nirakudam	A. Bhimsingh	
1977	Ormakal Marikkumo	K.S. Sethumadhavan	
1977	16 Vayathinile	Bharathiraja	
1977	Aadu Puli Attam	S.P. Muthuraman	
1977	Aanandham Paramaanandham	I.V. Sasi	
1977	Naam Pirandha Mann	A. Vincent	
1977	Kokila	Balu Mahendra	
1977	Satyavan Savithri	P.G. Vishwambharan	
1977	Aadhya Paadam	Adoor Bhasi	
1978	Madanolsavam	N. Sankaran Nair	
1978	Kaathirunna Nimisham	Baby	
1978	Anumodhanam	I.V. Sasi	
1978	Avalude Ravukal	I.V. Sasi	Guest appearance
1978	Nizhal Nijamagiradhu	K. Balachander	
1978	Aval Viswasthayayirunnu	Jeassy	Guest appearance
1978	Maro Charitra	K. Balachander	
1978	Ilamai Oonjal Aadukirathu	C.V. Sridhar	

Year	Film	Director	Remarks
1978	*Amara Prema*	Rama Rao Tatineni	
1978	*Sattam En Kaiyil*	T.N. Balu	
1978	*Padakuthira*	P.G. Vasudevan, P.G. Vishwambharan	Guest appearance
1978	*Vayasu Pilichindi*	C.V. Sridhar	
1978	*Vayanadan Thamban*	A. Vincent	
1978	*Sakka Podu Podu Raja*	S.P. Muthuraman	Guest appearance
1978	*Sigappu Rojakkal*	Bharathiraja	
1978	*Manidharil Ithanai Nirangala*	R.C. Sakthi	
1978	*Aval Appadithan*	C. Rudraiah	
1978	*Thappida Thala/Thappu Thalangal*	K. Balachander	Guest appearance
1978	*Yaetta*	I.V. Sasi	
1979	*Sommokadidi Sokokadidi*	Singeetam Srinivasa Rao	
1979	*Sigappukkal Mookkuthi*	Valampuri Somanathan	
1979	*Neeya?*	Durai	
1979	*Allauddinum Albhutha Vilakkum/Allaudinaum Arputha Vilakkum*	I.V. Sasi	
1979	*Thaayillamal Naan Illai*	R. Thyagaraajan	
1979	*Ninaithale Inikkum/ Andamaina Anubhavam*	K. Balachander	
1979	*Idi Katha Kaadu*	K. Balachander	
1979	*Kalyanaraman*	G.N. Rangarajan	
1979	*Nool Veli/Guppedu Manasu*	K. Balachander	Guest appearance
1979	*Mangala Vaathiyam*	K. Shankar	
1979	*Neela Malargal*	R. Krishnan, S. Panju	

Year	Film	Director	Remarks
1979	*Azhiyatha Kolangal*	Balu Mahendra	Cameo
1979	*Pasi*	Durai	Guest appearance
1980	*Ullasa Paravaigal*	C.V. Rajendran	
1980	*Natchathiram*	Dasari Narayana Rao	Guest appearance
1980	*Guru*	I.V. Sasi	
1980	*Varumayin Niram Sivappu*	K. Balachander	
1980	*Maria My Darling*	Durai	
1980	*Saranam Ayyappa*	Dasarathan	
1981	*Aakali Rajyam*	K. Balachander	
1981	*Meendum Kokila*	G.N. Rangarajan	
1981	*Ram Lakshman*	R. Thyagaraajan	
1981	*Raja Paarvai/Amavasya Chandrudu*	Singeetam Srinivasa Rao	
1981	*Thillu Mullu*	K. Balachander	
1981	*Kadal Meengal*	G.N. Rangarajan	
1981	*Ek Duuje Ke Liye*	K. Balachander	
1981	*Savaal*	R. Krishnamurthy	
1981	*Sankarlal*	T.N. Balu	
1981	*Tik Tik Tik*	Bharathiraja	
1981	*Ellam Inba Mayyam*	G.N. Rangarajan	
1982	*Vazhvey Maayam*	R. Krishnamurthy	
1982	*Andagaadu*	Pendyala Venkata Rama Rao	
1982	*Anthiveyilile Ponnu*	Radhakrishnan	
1982	*Neethi Devan Mayakkam*	Bapu	Guest appearance
1982	*Moondram Pirai*	Balu Mahendra	

Year	Film	Director	Remarks
1982	*Maattuvin Chattangale*	K.G. Rajasekharan	Uncredited
1982	*Simla Special*	Muktha V. Srinivasan	
1982	*Sanam Teri Kasam*	Narendra Bedi	
1982	*Sakalakala Vallavan*	S.P. Muthuraman	
1982	*Ezham Rathri*	Kalanilayam Krishna Kumar	Guest appearance
1982	*Rani Theni*	G. N. Rangarajan	Guest appearance
1982	*Yeh To Kamaal Ho Gaya*	Rama Rao Tatineni	
1982	*Pagadai Panirendu*	Dhamodharan N.	
1982	*Agni Sakshi*	K. Balachander	
1983	*Zara Si Zindagi*	K. Balachander	
1983	*Uruvangal Maralam*	S.V. Ramanan	Guest appearance
1983	*Sattam*	K. Vijayan	
1983	*Sagara Sangamam*	K. Viswanath	
1983	*Sadma*	Balu Mahendra	
1983	*Poikkal Kudhirai*	K. Balachander	Guest appearance
1983	*Benkiyalli Aralida Hoovu*	K. Balachander	Guest appearance
1983	*Thoongathey Thambi Thoongathey*	S.P. Muthuraman	
1984	*Yeh Desh*	Rama Rao Tatineni	
1984	*Ek Nai Paheli*	K. Balachander	
1984	*Yaadgar*	Dasari Narayana Rao	
1984	*Raaj Tilak*	Rajkumar Kohli	
1984	*Enakkul Oruvan*	S.P. Muthuraman	
1984	*Karishmaa*	I.V. Sasi	
1985	*Oru Kaidhiyin Diary*	Bharathiraja	

Year	Film	Director	Remarks
1985	*Kaakki Sattai*	Rajasekar	
1985	*Andha Oru Nimidam*	Major Sundarrajan	
1985	*Uyarndha Ullam*	S.P. Muthuraman	
1985	*Saagar*	Ramesh Sippy	
1985	*Geraftaar*	Prayag Raj	
1985	*Mangamma Sabatham*	K. Vijayan	
1985	*Japanil Kalyanaraman*	S.P. Muthuraman	
1985	*Dekha Pyar Tumhara*	Virendra Sharma	
1986	*Swathi Muthyam*	K. Viswanath	
1986	*Naanum Oru Thozhilali*	C.V. Sridhar	
1986	*Vikram*	Rajasekar	
1986	*Manakanakku*	G.N. Rangarajan, R.C. Sakthi	Guest appearance
1986	*Oka Radha Iddaru Krishnulu*	A. Kodandarami Reddy	
1986	*Punnagai Mannan*	K. Balachander	
1987	*Kadhal Parisu*	A. Jagannathan	
1987	*Vrutham*	I.V. Sasi	
1987	*Kadamai Kanniyam Kattupaadu*	Santhana Bharathi	Guest appearance
1987	*Per Sollum Pillai*	S.P. Muthuraman	
1987	*Nayakan*	Mani Ratnam	
1987	*Pushpaka Vimana*	Singeetam Srinivasa Rao	
1988	*Sathyaa*	Suresh Krishna	
1988	*Daisy*	Prathap Pothen	
1988	*Soora Samhaaram*	Chitra Lakshmanan	
1988	*Unnal Mudiyum Thambi*	K. Balachander	
1989	*Apoorva Sagodharargal*	Singeetam Srinivasa Rao	
1989	*Chanakyan*	Rajeev Kumar	
1989	*Vetri Vizha*	Prathap Pothen	

Year	Film	Director	Remarks
1989	*Indrudu Chandrudu*	Suresh Krishna	
1990	*Michael Madana Kama Rajan*	Singeetam Srinivasa Rao	
1991	*Gunaa*	Santhana Bharathi	
1992	*Singaravelan*	R.V. Udhaya Kumar	
1992	*Thevar Magan*	Bharathan	
1993	*Maharasan*	G.N. Rangarajan	
1993	*Kalaignan*	G.B. Vijay	
1994	*Mahanadhi*	Santhana Bharathi	
1994	*Magalir Mattum*	Singeetam Srinivasa Rao	Cameo
1994	*Nammavar*	K.S. Sethumadhavan	
1995	*Sathi Leelavathi*	Balu Mahendra	
1995	*Subha Sankalpam*	K. Viswanath	
1995	*Kuruthipunal*	P.C. Sreeram	
1995	*Drohi*	P. C. Sreeram	
1996	*Indian*	S. Shankar	
1996	*Avvai Shanmugi*	K.S. Ravikumar	
1997	*Chachi 420*	Kamal Haasan	
1998	*Kaathala Kaathala*	Singeetam Srinivasa Rao	
2000	*Hey Ram*	Kamal Haasan	
2000	*Thenali*	K.S. Ravikumar	
2001	*Aalavandhan/Abhay*	Suresh Krishna	
2001	*Paarthale Paravasam*	K. Balachander	Guest appearance
2002	*Pammal K. Sambandam*	Mouli	
2002	*Panchatanthiram*	K.S. Ravikumar	
2003	*Anbe Sivam*	Sundar C.	
2003	*Nala Damayanthi*	Mouli	Guest appearance
2004	*Virumaandi*	Kamal Haasan	

Year	Film	Director	Remarks
2004	*Vasool Raja MBBS*	Sarann	
2005	*Mumbai Xpress*	Singeetam Srinivasa Rao, Dinesh Shailendra	
2005	*Rama Shama Bhama*	Ramesh Aravind	
2006	*Vettaiyaadu Vilaiyaadu*	Gautham Vasudev Menon	
2008	*Dasavathaaram*	K.S. Ravikumar	
2009	*Unnaipol Oruvan*	Chakri Toleti	
2009	*Eenadu*	Chakri Toleti	
2010	*Four Friends*	Saji Surendran	Guest appearance
2010	*Manmadan Ambu*	K.S. Ravikumar, Rajesh M. Selva	
2013	*Vishwaroopam*	Kamal Haasan	
2015	*Uttama Villain*	Ramesh Aravind	
2015	*Papanasam*	Jeethu Joseph	
2015	*Thoongaa Vanam*	Rajesh M. Selva	
2015	*Cheekati Rajyam*	Rajesh M Selva	
2016	*Meen Kuzhambum Mann Paanaiyum*	Amudeshver, Manickam Baskaran	Cameo
2018	*Vishwaroopam 2*	Kamal Haasan	
2022	*Vikram 2*	Lokesh Kanagaraj	
2024	*Kalki 2898 AD*	Nag Ashwin	
2024	*Indian 2*	S. Shankar	
TBA	*Thug Life*	Mani Ratnam	

ACKNOWLEDGEMENTS

To start with, I must record my sincere gratitude to Kamal Haasan who let me look at his works with a completely open mind. He constantly urged me to think critically and reach out to modern readers with new perspectives. This is truly 'our' book. The journey with Kamal has been a definitive turning point in my understanding of Indian cinema as a whole.

The idea for the book came about in mid-2012 when Kanishka Gupta called me to work on it, and the journey would not have been possible without the help of many people, directly or indirectly. My opening thanks must go to the late Prof. Satish Bahadur at the Film and Television Institute of India, who introduced me to the art of film analysis. In the same campus I met my first gurus, the late Mani Kaul and Kumar Shahani, who enabled me to see latent and abstract patterns in cinema. My sincere thanks to Prof. David Ludden, who appreciated the way I approached Indian cinema aesthetics and helped me commence my academic journey at the South Asia Studies Department at the University of Pennsylvania, where I also received valuable insights from Profs David Nelson, Babu Suthar, Guy Welbon, Richard Cohen and Michael Meister. I cannot forget Prof. Shekhar Deshpande at Arcadia University, Prof. Meta Mazaj at the University of Pennsylvania and Prof. Pete Martin at Miami University for their valuable encouragement and emotional support.

Back home I must acknowledge the perceptions offered by Kamal's sister Nalini; brothers Chandrahasan and Charuhasan; filmmakers Singeetam Srinivasa Rao, Santhana Bharati and S.P. Muthuraman; and screenwriters Madan, Era Murugan and E. John. Thanks to conversations with A.R. Venkatachalapathy, S. Ramakrishnan, Swarnavel Pillai, Arunmozhi and Baradwaj Rangan, the book acquired new dimensions. My gratitude to the encouragement provided by Ramesh Prasad, Hugh and Colleen Gantzer, and Rohit Khattar. I could not have done all this without the loving support of my children, Anjali and Vivek, along with the continuous critical appreciation from my dear wife, Rama. How I wish my parents and my in-laws who supported me in all my filmmaking ventures were around to see my first book ready for release! Finally, I must thank Kanishka Gupta, my agent, and Udayan Mitra and Amrita Mukerji at HarperCollins, especially for her patient readings and suggestions to improve the narrative flow.

NOTES

2. Working with K. Balachander

1. *Outlook*, 12 December 2016
2. *Outlook*, 12 December 2016
3. Diehl, Anita, *Periyar*, BI Publications, 1978
4. *The Week*, 25 December 2016

3. *Manmadha Leelai*: An Exploration of Sexuality

1. White, Patricia, *Feminism and Film*, Oxford: Oxford University Press, 1998
2. Source: https://faculty.gcsu.edu/custom-website/mary-magoulick/popculture.htm
3. Fromm, 'Social Thought and Research', {1932a} 1970, p. 149

4. *16 Vayathinile*: The End of a Utopian Dream

1. Source: https://www.youtube.com/watch?v=q_S7Gt54wFM

5. *Varumayin Nirum Sivappu*: An Exercise in Non-Narrative Cinema

1. Keay, J. (2014), *Midnight's Descendants: South Asia from Partition to the Present Day*, Basic Books, New York.

2. Brody, R. (2008), *Everything Is Cinema: The Working Life of Jean-Luc Godard*, Metropolitan Books, New York.

6. *Raja Paarvai* and *Ek Duuje Ke Liye*: Two Milestones from the Early 1980s

1. Kawin, Bruce, *How Movies Work*, California: University of California Press, 1987, p. 74

7. *Sakalakala Vallavan* and *Enakul Oruvan*: Ventures into Popular Cinema

1. http://www.arvindguptatoys.com/arvindgupta/hegemony-nandy.pdf
2. http://archive.unu.edu/unupress/unupbooks/uu05se/uu05se07.htm

9. *Nayakan* and *Oru Kaidhiyin Diary*: Examinations of Modern India

1. https://www.thehindu.com/features/magazine/kamal-too-didnt-expect-much-from-the-film/article4053951.ece
2. Nandy, Ashis, *An Ambiguous Journey to the City: The Village and Other Odd Ruins of the Self in the Indian Imagination*, New Delhi: Oxford University Press, 2001

10. *Swathi Muthyam*: Pearls of Tragedy

1. https://www.americanpearl.com/historyoyster.html
2. Source: https://www.psychologytoday.com/us/blog/in-flux/201508/10-ways-rituals-help-us-celebrate-our-lives
3. https://www.press.jhu.edu/news/blog/modernism-and-opera

11. *Pushpak*: A Comedy Par Excellence

1. https://www.rogerebert.com/reviews/great-movie-playtime-1967
2. https://www.criterion.com/current/posts/3338-jacques-tati-historian

13. *Gunaa*: A Study of Androgyny

1. https://www.filmcompanion.in/sab-john-interview-with-baradwaj-rangan-Gunaa/

14. Twins, Quadruplets and Kamal's Passion for Chaplin

1. Nelson, T.G.A, *Comedy: an introduction to comedy* in literature, drama, and cinema, Oxford: Oxford University Press, 2012, p. 48.
2. Ibid., page 124
3. A term I have borrowed from North, Michael, *Machine-age Comedy*, Oxford: Oxford University Press, 2009
4. Ibid.
5. Ibid.: page 197
6. Ibid.: page 56

15. *Thevar Magan*: Coming Home

1. https://www.hindustantimes.com/south/temple-festival-in-tn-shelved-for-4th-year-in-a-row-over-dalits-taking-part/story-X5y5dwcBZlcObzjap1GCGN.html
2. Kothari, Rajni *Politics in India*, Boston: Little, Brown & Co., 1970.
3. Ibid.

16. The Spartacus Trilogy: *Mahanadhi, Kuruthipunal, Indian*

1. PTI, 'Free India's first terrorist was a Hindu, his name is Nathuram Godse: Kamal Haasan', The Hindu, 13 May 2019. https://www.thehindu.com/news/national/tamil-nadu/free-indias-first-terrorist-was-hindu-his-name-was-godse-says-kamal-haasan/article27114060.ece
2. Campbell, Joseph, *The Hero With A Thousand Faces, (The Collected Works of Joseph Campbell)*, third edition, New York: Perseus Books, 2012.

18. *Aalavandhan*: An Encounter with the Fantastic

1. Todorov, Tzvetan (1975), *The Fantastic: A Structural Approach to a Literary Genre*, Cornell University Press, Ithaca; page 25.

2. https://indianexpress.com/article/entertainment/tamil/when-quentin-
tarantino-was-inspired-by-kamal-haasan-5901680/#:~:text=In%20a%20
chat%20with%20director,animated%20sequence%20in%20Kill%20
Bill.&text=Kashyap%20earlier%20told%20Mid%2Dday,Ramchandran%20
first%20told%20me%20this.

3. https://www.indiatoday.in/magazine/cover-story/story/19960531-taken-
by-storm-753136-1996-05-31

4. https://shodhganga.inflibnet.ac.in/bitstream/10603/190224/10/10%20
chapter%204.pdf

5. The Natya Shastra is ascribed to Sage Bharata and was supposedly written
between 400 and 700 CE

19. *Anbe Sivam*: Walking the Road of Compassion

1. Debray, Régis, *Media Manifestos: On the Technological Transmission of Cultural
Form*, New York: Verso, 1976.

20. *Virumandi*: A Whodunnit Saga of Caste Politics

1. https://www.indiatoday.in/magazine/indiascope/story/20030707-kamal-
haasan-latest-venture-sandiyar-runs-into-trouble-792450-2003-07-07

21. The Masquerade Trilogy: *Dasavatharam, Vishwaroopam* and *Uttama Villain*

1. https://www.indiatoday.in/india/west/story/vishwaroopam-kamal-haasan-
tamil-nadu-government-152977-2013-01-31

ABOUT THE AUTHOR

Graduating in direction from the Film and Television Institute of India (1976), K. Hariharan has made nine feature films and over 350 short and documentary films. His works have won national awards and been selected at international festivals too. As a writer-critic, he has contributed to a variety of books and journals on media and cinema.

HarperCollins *Publishers* India

At HarperCollins India, we believe in telling the best stories and finding the widest readership for our books in every format possible. We started publishing in 1992; a great deal has changed since then, but what has remained constant is the passion with which our authors write their books, the love with which readers receive them, and the sheer joy and excitement that we as publishers feel in being a part of the publishing process.

Over the years, we've had the pleasure of publishing some of the finest writing from the subcontinent and around the world, including several award-winning titles and some of the biggest bestsellers in India's publishing history. But nothing has meant more to us than the fact that millions of people have read the books we published, and that somewhere, a book of ours might have made a difference.

As we look to the future, we go back to that one word— a word which has been a driving force for us all these years.

Read.

Harper
Collins

HARPER
FICTION

HARPER
NON-FICTION

HARPER
BUSINESS

HarperCollins
Children'sBooks

HARPER
DESIGN

Harper
Sport

HARPER
PERENNIAL

HARPER
VANTAGE

हार्पर
हिन्दी